My Dear Jamal

(Morocco Bound)

Joyce Edling

My Dear Jamal
(Morocco Bound)

by

Joyce Edling

NEW MILLENNIUM
292 Kennington Road, London SE11 4LD.

Copyright © 1996 Joyce Edling

Printed and bound by
Morgan Technical Books Ltd. Wotton under Edge, Glos.
Issued by New Millennium*
ISBN 1 85845 084 5
*An imprint of The Professional Authors' & Publishers' Association

Dedicated to all the *Ilal Amam* group
convicted in the 1977 Casablanca trials.

CONTENTS

LIST OF ILLUSTRATIONS

Page

x

FOREWORD

Jamal Benomar was arrested and jailed in Morocco in 1976. He was beaten, he was subjected to appalling torture, he was found guilty of crimes he did not commit after an unfair trial and sentenced to ten years in prison. Why? Because he advocated change in Moroccan society. The movement of which he was a member, *Ilal Amam*, used peaceful means to promote these changes but even this was outlawed.

Joyce Edling had joined her local Amnesty International group and was involved in writing letters on behalf of Prisoners of Conscience like Jamal. Little did she know then just where it was going to lead.

For this is an adventure story and a love story sensitively told, but it is also the story of the grave injustices dealt out to those who dare oppose an oppressive regime.

There are still many thousands of innocent people languishing in prisons around the world like Jamal was. They need support from the outside world. Amnesty International is still running its campaigns on their behalf. Join us and help us to help them. You will be part of Amnesty International's one million plus supporters working to uphold human rights standards. We cannot guarantee that you will have an adventure like Joyce did, but you can assist people like Jamal.

David Bull
Director
Amnesty International (UK)

This account shows a side of Morocco which is not often presented to the public. I am aware that some of the events described may seem so implausible that they will not be believed. I wish to make it clear, however, that *every single fact recounted here is true* and I relate it exactly as it either happened or was told to me. Some names have occasionally been altered to avoid the possibility of unpleasant repercussions to the persons concerned; I have indicated where this happens in the text.

My main reason for wishing to share this story with a wider audience is to show the remarkable unassailability of the human spirit as well as the power of each individual to get involved - however marginally - in counteracting brutality and the abuse of power. If this book encourages even a few people to join an Amnesty group, then it will have been worth the effort. There are also rewards, especially in terms of one's own personal development and awareness.

There have been many changes in the lives of both Jamal and myself since this book was written but these do not, in my view, detract from the authenticity of the profound feelings that grew between us during that important stage in our human experiences.

What has not changed is the corrupt regime of King Hassan, against which Jamal fought, and continued suffering of all those like him who dare to question it. Daily repression lives on, not only in Morocco but in many other places in the world where greed for power paralyses compassion for fellow humans.

All the letters in the book were written in French and the translation of them here is my own.

Finally, I would like to make an acknowledgement to my dear friend, the writer Niema Ash. Without her encouragement and positive energy this manuscript would have remained in a cupboard and without her constructive criticism, I fear the script would have been infinitely poorer. I would also like to thank my editor Linda Lloyd for her dedicated work and her great interest.

Chapter 1

That night was etched on his memory forever. I was to hear the whole gruesome account of it later.

It was an hour before midnight on 19 January 1976 in the flat in Rabat, Morocco, which Jamal, a 19-year-old Sociology student, shared with five other students and his older brother. He had that day come from his home town Tetuan, in the North, and he lay on the bed reflecting upon the subject of the new flat he would be moving into the following day. As fate would have it, the agent in charge of the property had not wished to give him the key until the next day. Jamal had desperately wanted to get hold of the key that day, but did not wish to insist too much for fear of arousing suspicion. Well, he told himself, trying to dispel his fears, one day won't make that much difference. As it happened, it made all the difference in the world.

The sense of urgency to leave the flat which Jamal had felt, was linked with the arrest of a colleague from Tetuan, who knew his whereabouts in Rabat. The organisation they both belonged to was *Ilal Amam*, a radical movement trying to promote a society very different from the corrupt dictatorship of King Hassan. Although it was a strictly non-violent movement which confined its activities to holding meetings and peaceful demonstrations and leafleting work-places, the Moroccan authorities did not tolerate opposition, so it was outlawed. Its members - those who hadn't already been arrested - were all now operating underground. There were rumours that some members had been taken to that most brutal of places, the detention centre feared above all others: Derb Moulay Cherif.

Suddenly an explosion seemed to shake the flat, and through a crack in the door of his room, Jamal could see the hallway fill up with about a dozen armed policemen. They had come for him. He rushed to the window. No, out of the question. The place looked

1

as if it were under siege - police vehicles and armed guards everywhere and the whole area cordoned off. All this show of power just to collect a slightly-built 19 year old student who had never handled a firearm in his life.

As the police burst into his room, Jamal's first emotion was anger directed towards the thin, sour-faced estate agent who could so easily have given him the key to safety.

"Are you Jamal Benomar?"

Jamal hesitated but saw it would be useless to deny it, especially given the terrified expressions on the faces of the other dumbfounded students, who had appeared at the sound of the commotion and now stood clustered together in the doorway. Apart from his brother, these students knew little about him except for the one currently vital piece of information: his name.

As he acquiesced, he was handcuffed and kicked into a corner. The police searched the place, pouncing triumphantly on leaflets, and confiscating Jamal's Sociology literature, which was later to be produced as proof of his subversive activities.

"We've arrested all the other members, you are the last one," they told Jamal. "Your organisation is as dead and impotent as you will be by the time we have finished with you."

Jamal was led out to a car, filled with police, which left the area at great speed. He felt strangely calm now that the situation for which he had been psychologically prepared for so long, had materialised. Watched intensely by the travelling 'companions', his handcuffed hand managed to fish out a packet of cigarettes from his pocket and he asked the police ironically if they would like one. There was an astonished silence.

Then a senior officer said: "You bastard. Do you think you are going to a party or something? Well, we won't disappoint you, will we?" All the police laughed. Jamal was immediately blindfolded and the kickings and beatings started there in the car and didn't stop until they reached the police station in Rabat.

At Rabat, the interrogation began at once, led by the infamous

Mr. Kholti. Names and addresses were demanded, but Jamal refused to speak. They tore off his clothes and strung him up naked on to an iron bar straddled between two desks, ready to begin 'falaka'. Many willing hands were there to assist in the operation. As one group of police forced Jamal's head back into a bucket of excrement, another group whipped the soles of his feet, and those with nothing else to do amused themselves by savagely beating and kicking Jamal's slender body.

More police appeared on the scene to join in with savage delight, and bottles of whisky were produced and consumed amidst general merriment. Cigarettes were handed round, smoked and then stubbed out on different parts of Jamal's body. As the beatings and whippings became more and more frenzied, he was asked: "Well, are you enjoying the party?" and "Why don't you invite all your friends, we'd love to meet them" and "Do you want to go home?" all of which produced much mirth among the police.

This first torture continued all night long. Jamal was told: "If you find yourself suffocating and you want to save your life, hold up a finger." This he did many times but then refused to speak each time until in the end, the police ignored the finger and only pulled him out of the bucket when he lost consciousness, upon which he was immediately brought round and then subjected to a further session. How much can the human body take? Could it really be any worse than this in Derb Moulay Cherif?

At dawn, Jamal was rolled up in a blanket and taken to a dungeon. A cell door opened and Jamal, in the blanket, was projected at some distance and height into the middle of the cell, where he landed heavily on top of a huddled heap of sleeping prisoners. The cell door closed with a resounding bang.

So ended the first few hours of a nightmare and so began a series of events which were to have the most profound consequences on the lives of both Jamal and myself.

4

Chapter 2

At the time of Jamal's arrest, I was quite unaware of the appalling tragedies of conscience-bound individuals in Morocco. My reality and priorities were worlds apart.

I was born in Kent and brought up in Cambridge. My parents were keen for me to have a musical career, so from an early age I learnt the piano and violin, which I subsequently studied at the Royal College of Music, gaining an ARCM diploma.

Up to then, there had been two very important people in my life. One was my violin teacher, Anne Macnaghten. I adored her. She was a progressive and assertive woman in her 50s, whose musicality shone out of her, but more than that, she understood instinctively the vulnerability of children, how the rights and needs of youth were often ignored. It was not difficult to love her. She had the most beautiful smile, which she would employ in a special way, if she felt I was being unreasonable. This had a greater effect on me than any amount of lecturing or scolding. My main aim in life was to be like her. She shook a lot of my hitherto unquestioned notions on accepting the status quo of society (nurtured over the years by the Cambridge environment, plus a conservative father) but never in an overtly didactic way. She caused me to start thinking about the lot of the underprivileged. This was not something entirely strange to our family, as my mother was a nursing sister in a psychiatric hospital and therefore had sympathy with those in distress. However, my views were different. I was more interested in an ideal world where, instead of broken people being patched up, there existed a social structure which minimised the numbers of those broken in the first place.

Where Anne had started, someone else took over. At the young age of 14, I met Axel from Sweden. To put it in a romantic way, we met in Brahms' Second Symphony. Axel was studying English in Cambridge for 3 months and was an excellent cellist. He joined the local amateur orchestra at the same time as I did, and we were 'just good friends'. When he returned to Sweden, we corresponded for three years. Our love built up during the correspondence, to explode when we met again in France, three years later. I was 20, Axel 24 when we got married and I moved to Stockholm. Axel was a remarkable man with a strong sense of social justice and equality and I had great love and respect for him, which is why his views had such an impact on me.

Axel was a lawyer and we moved town a few times in Sweden. I had given up any thought of music as a career. I felt passionately about music and wanted to enjoy it, not feel it was a chore necessitating the long daily grind of rehearsals and practice, to be perhaps at best a third-rate player in the back desks of a large orchestra, presided over by a stick-wielding dictator. All my life, I have had an ambivalent relationship with Authority. I hated it, kicked against it like a small child, yet mostly felt forced to accept it, with the ensuing resentment building up. There was no way I wanted such a relationship with music, which I felt should be my oxygen, not my oppressor.

So I kept music as my hobby, playing in groups and orchestras with Axel, and I studied for a degree in Modern Languages and Psychology at Gothenburg University, adding to my degree a diploma in Pedagogy at Stockholm University. I then got a job teaching English as a mother-tongue to immigrant children. We bought a large detached house in the suburbs of Stockholm with its own inbuilt sauna bath and a pleasant forest-type garden.

I remember when we bought this house in 1976, I felt distinctly miserable and had an odd feeling of aversion to it. The day we moved in, I cried nearly all night long for no particular reason. At the time, I put it down to my grief at the recent death of a friend, yet somehow the grief seemed to be attached to the house. Perhaps, with hindsight, it was some sort of premonition that my cosy stable life, symbolised by the sturdy brick structure of the four walls, was soon to be shattered.

Chapter 3

The shaping of Jamal's character and ideas did, as I was to discover much later, bear little resemblance to mine. He came from an average-sized family by Moroccan standards, with five brothers and sisters. If my thoughts at the age of 14 centred around music and captivating Nordic cellists, his took a distinctly different direction.

Jamal's father was a kindly soul, always willing to help others, especially those in distress, and would often - to the exasperation of his entire family - give away a good part of the meagre wages he received as a factory worker, to someone he felt sorry for. Jamal's mother, Fatima Lamrani, as I was also to discover later, was a strong dominating and manipulative woman. Whenever she felt she was not getting her way, she would dissolve into tears, which would prompt her caring husband to capitulate. On the other end of the scale, she was a tough disciplinarian, beating misdemeanours out of her children with a leather belt. They were in awe of her.

I can only speculate on why Jamal left his Moroccan home at the young age of 14, something almost unheard of for someone in his culture. I believe that he, like me, always had an ambivalent relationship with Authority. Parental authority is usually the first to be encountered but whereas I clung to the protection of the family home, preferring to submit - however unwillingly - to an authoritarian upbringing rather than face the perils of the unknown, Jamal was more courageous. At 14, he left home to look for a job.

His first attempts to fulfil this longing were memorable. He had heard of a French company which owned a chain of luxury tourist establishments and had found out that one of the directors would be recruiting workers the next day. He went there at seven in the morning. The recruiting session was to take place on a large expanse of open ground. As Jamal approached, he could see hundreds upon hundreds of other unemployed people waiting. It was pouring with rain and there was no shelter, nothing to do except wait along with the vast crowd of doleful-looking men, mostly youngish, in their 30s, all desperate for a job, getting wetter and wetter until in the end it didn't matter any more, you melted into the rain, became part of it.

They all waited in this way from seven in the morning. Nothing happened until 5.30 in the afternoon, when a big black car drew up and a fat, impeccably-dressed Frenchman got out, smoking a large cigar and carrying a cane. Then a van drew up and a number of guards alighted, protectively encircling the Director. The latter looked disdainfully at the sodden amorphous straggle of young hopefuls, as if they were a plague of rats and he had been given 24 hours to rid the country of their presence.

Jamal tried to catch a glimpse of what was going on through the amassed bodies of his competitors. It wasn't easy to see. He was small for his age and by far the youngest person there. Conscious this would go against him, he had secretly borrowed his father's clot es to make him look older. Most likely, however, the clothes inevitably too big for him made him look even smaller. He no doubt cut a comic figure standing there in the rain, trying to peer above and around the others.

The voice of the aspiring Pied Piper rang out through the crowd. "I will need about 20 strong, healthy and hard-working men. Is there anyone here with a work certificate?"

About three contenders eagerly pushed their way forward, clutching the precious documents. They were ushered in the direction of a small hut. The next question, laden with irony, was: "Who is here through a *coup de piston*?" (A "piston" is an influential friend.)

One person came forward, proudly waving a letter from the Chief of Police. He was taken on straightaway. Another had a letter from a judge and a third knew the Governor of the town. All three were shown to the hut, which had inevitably by now become a sort of Muslim version of St. Peter's Gate. Then came the excluding of the others. The Director began the process by approaching one young, dark-skinned, worried-looking man, waving his cane and saying: "You have a most unpleasant face. You can leave." The man drew back and obediently removed himself. "And you," he said to the man standing beside him. The second man slunk off through the crowd. This method of de-ratting the community was evidently one which worked. The Director walked on for a few yards and stopped in front of a man listlessly smoking a cigarette. He said: "What do you think you are doing, showing such disrespect? Clear off and take all these people with you!" He shook his cane at a group of about thirty men standing in the vicinity. No one moved. The de-ratting technique was evidently not without flaws, but the Director reeked of power and success, in that order. He clicked his fingers and five guards rushed forward and started pushing and kicking the group of men whose lack of employment potential was apparently linked to their choice of neighbour.

Another group looked 'too wet for work' and yet another weren't standing properly. The guards were quick and efficient. As whole groups of dejected people were pushed or kicked out of the compound, the remaining would-be workers did not know whether to feel relief at not being so far excluded, or anxiety in case the axe should fall on them next.

Jamal was in a slightly different position. He was worried when he saw the Director examining the hands of each contender, dismissing those whose smooth hands bore witness to lack of heavy work; but by this time he felt he could use his advantage in being small. Each time the Director approached a group of people near him which looked as if they were heading for the chop, Jamal managed to sneak off unseen to stand with another group. When finally about twenty men had been picked out and the others had dispersed, he slipped unnoticed in among the men in the hut. These latter were being given directions one by one when suddenly the Director spotted Jamal standing there, almost literally swimming in the soaked remains of his father's best suit, with his head held high but his young virgin hands thrust firmly in his pockets, hidden from sight.

"What the hell are you doing here?" he was asked.

"What do you think?" answered Jamal, "Like everyone else, I've come for a job."

"A job?" expostulated the Director, as if he had just been asked to sign away the company profits to the homeless, "What job would the likes of *you* possibly be capable of?"

"I can do everything and I've got lots of experience," came the confident reply, "and what I don't know, I will learn in no time at all. You will take me on and then you will see."

The Director looked in astonishment at this defiant little fellow in the over-sized clothes. He was silent for a few minutes, tapping his cane on the ground as if to gather inspiration from the movement. Then he said: "All right, I'm going to take you on. And don't think it's for all this vast amount of work experience which you must have gained two years ago changing your own nappy. It's for your sheer nerve."

So Jamal got his first job without ever having to undergo the hand test. It was a tough job in a hotel, involving a lot of lifting and shifting heavy loads, serving, waiting and being general dogsbody, eight in the morning until midnight, day after day, seven days a week. His accommodation was a small room shared with thirteen other people. There wasn't much time or energy left over for reading, although Jamal did what he could. Being an avid reader since the age of twelve, he had learnt about the political situation in the Middle East, the cultural revolution in China, and about Indo-China. He had been particularly interested in the student uprisings in Europe in the late '60s. His hunger for books was almost an obsession. He borrowed them from libraries, from school, from friends. They were the only presents he ever wanted. A certain degree of militancy was in his blood, through his grandfather, Sadek Lamrani, who had been a well-known nationalist leader during the Rif wars of the 1920's.

There were constant disputes with management in this first job. The food was a typical source of grievance. The workers were given only the hashed-up leftover food from the previous day's tourists. Jamal worked there for a few months without complaining too much. Then one day, when the food seemed to have reached a new all-time low, he stood up and said to the other workers: "It's disgusting! It's not food. We won't eat it. We can't eat it." Everyone was in agreement and someone sent for the hotel Manager. He was a podgy little man, expensively dressed. There was little doubt which food his podginess could be attributed to. The workers had asked many times to get decent food, but all previous requests had been ignored. It was time to go on the offensive. Jamal said:

"We've had enough of this manure you call food. We can't eat it, which means that we are starving while being expected to work all hours of the day and night."

The Manager was somewhat taken aback. He peered into the saucepan and said: "It looks all right to me. It is certainly better than anything you would get from your families." There were loud protests at this. Jamal looked at him with contempt. "You wouldn't even feed this to your dog."

The Manager was not used to giving in. He picked up a spoon and fished out of the saucepan some of the glutinous debris floating around in the rancid grey liquid. He put the spoon in his mouth. To do his palate justice, he did turn a bit pale, but bravely went on chewing to prove his point. "There you see, it's delicious. You're just trying to make trouble."

Jamal was so furious, he picked up the saucepan and tipped out the entire contents on the floor. "Your dog would never touch muck like this but the rats - if they're really desperate and the sewers are already empty - may come and clear it up."

There were loud cheers from the others. The Manager, humiliated, turned on his heel and left. An hour later, the Head of Personnel summoned Jamal to his office. "Please will you leave immediately. Give me back your keys."

Jamal told him: "I'm being sacked for asking to be treated like a human being. We work like slaves here. We can't even enjoy ourselves in the few hours we do have free, as the owners have privatised the beaches and forbid us - we, the Moroccans in our own country - to use them. This is apartheid every bit as bad as in South Africa. You are Belgian, are you not?"

The man nodded.

Jamal went on, warming to his theme: "Imagine that the Germans invaded your country, were thrown out but then returned, welcomed by your leaders, to erect luxury hotels for themselves and foreign tourists while refusing to allow you to use your own beaches. How would that make you feel?"

The Head of Personnel shrugged his shoulders. "I don't make the rules. My job is to see that they are implemented. My orders are to make sure you are off the premises within the hour, failing which I will call the police."

The whole system was sewn up. The heads of police were regular visitors at the hotel and were given unlimited free drinks in the most convivial of atmospheres. In return, the unspoken arrangement was that they would 'deal' with any 'trouble-makers'. Jamal knew it was no good staying on to plead his case or to use any sort of legal procedure. He left. Almost immediately, he got a job in another hotel. Here, conditions were still terrible but the hours were slightly better: from 8 a.m. until 7 p.m. This gave him the chance to do a lot more reading and also to study other school subjects, as he was aiming to take his Baccalaureat (the equivalent of 'A' levels). It was also the scene of his first political activity of any note. He, with other like-minded people, started a Union for all the hotel workers in the region of Tetuan.

His first 'job interview' had left its mark. The 14-year-old had been moved by the scene of hundreds of willing and capable men prepared to wait a whole day in the rain for the slightest chance of a job, only to suffer the indignity of being dismissed with such contempt. And for the few who did - by hook or by crook - make it past St. Peter, what was their great reward, their prize? The Kingdom of Heaven awaiting them was an insecure job in appalling conditions, working inhumanly long hours for starvation wages. The biggest irony of it all for Jamal was that they were working for French masters, the French who had colonised most of the country between 1912 and 1956, stripped it of its assets, broken up the traditional lifestyle of the people and forced the indigenous population into what almost amounted to slave labour. Now, 15 years after the end of colonial rule, here were those same people begging their former adversaries for work and often having to endure being spat at into the bargain. Was this really the best that independence could achieve? Had anything changed?

The Union initiative was successful. The demands of the workers, although quite revolutionary compared to what they were getting, were modest for the 70s: an 8-hour day, 1 day off a week, equality of pay for men and women, recognition of the Union and an increase in wages. When these demands were not met, the hotel workers went on strike. It caused complete chaos in the lucrative business of luxury hotels. After a week, with the workers as determined as ever, management had no option other than to back down. All the workers demands were met.

Jamal felt the need to widen this experience. At the end of 1972, when he was 15, he joined what was then a radical socialist student organisation called *Ilal Amam*, the aims of which were to promote a more just and democratic society. The activities were numerous and included production of a Newsletter, infiltrating and leafleting factories and similar work-places, organising peaceful demonstrations, holding meetings, pushing for social and educational reform and so on. The organisation was banned by the authorities and had to operate underground.

In late 1974, Jamal got himself a job as night porter at a hotel, which meant he could study all night long, sleep for a few hours, then devote himself to political activity for the rest of the day. In 1975, he passed the Baccalaureat with such high marks that he got a scholarship to study at Rabat University. He enrolled as a student of Political Science and managed to combine his studies with political activities and casual work at hotels and factories.

His involvement became all absorbing. Jamal threw himself into it with great determination and energy. His desire for reform was overwhelming. The need existed everywhere, he knew this not only from his own experiences, but also from what he saw as he looked around him. The fact that so many other young students were demonstrating similar energy and commitment at such great risk to themselves, was not only encouraging, it was also proof of how desperate the situation had become. The following (translated from the French) is an extract from Jamal's diary of that time:

10 March 1975.

Day started at 5 a.m. to leaflet workers at textile factory. (Leaflet usual one about lack of Trade Union rights). Was particularly interested in this factory as it was here workers were sacked for trying to set up Union.

No informers appeared to be around. Was at first disappointed when some workers declined to take leaflets but then remembered that many couldn't read or write. Spoke to them instead. They showed interest and seemed touched that someone not working with them should take the trouble to turn up at this hour to support them.

11a.m. Appointment with K. Again, worry when he was late. As usual, only 7-8 minutes but I impressed on him the seriousness of not observing the rule of strict punctuality. While waiting for him, all sorts of reasons for his possible lateness went through my head, none of them too pleasant. Perhaps he'd been taken to Derb Moulay Cherif, was being tortured, or perhaps police would be dragging him there to expose me, perhaps he'd left the town and gone underground to escape imminent arrest. I also imagined him naked and tortured but

14

defiant! Then he appeared. What a relief! But bad news - more arrests, new networks completely disbanded by security forces. I experience now a deep sense of survival - wonder how long it can last. When will it be my turn? No, never, they won't catch me and even if they do, I won't say a word, whatever they do to me.

Went to library to study, then to work. Must do something about work. Staff dispirited over new working regime. Apathy must not be allowed to reign. We will organise and overcome!

Chapter 4

November 1976. It was almost a year after Jamal's arrest and he was still languishing in Casablanca prison. There seemed little hope of a trial. The terrible year he had gone through kept coming back to him in flashes. He vowed to himself that if ever he were to see daylight again, his first priority would be to expose the appalling horrors which he and many others had been through and were still going through. He told himself that the only way even to attempt to stop this from happening again was to let the world know. Prevention by exposure. But would anyone believe his remarkable story? Who could begin to imagine that a simple human being could survive such events? In his mind, he saw himself being interviewed. His 'interviewer' (whom he even named 'Little Ben') came alive for him in the solitude of his cell, became the friend to whom he could tell everything. It was also a way for him to go through all that had happened so far, to remember it and to try and come to terms with it. What follows is a faithful account of Jamal's cathartic conversations with 'Little Ben'.

"How was it the police found you, Jamal?"

"This is a painful episode for me. My nearest colleague in the organisation was a man we can call Youssef, a trusted friend. We worked together with another man we will call Mahmoud. We knew quite a lot about each other, always a dangerous thing when working in an underground organisation.

"One day, Mahmoud was arrested. He was the only one with a key to the house (in Youssef's name) where the literature of the organisation was kept. Under pressure, he divulged the address of the house. Youssef panicked when he heard of the arrest and insisted that I go with him to break into the house and remove all the incriminating literature. I refused, saying that it would be to walk straight into trouble. We therefore parted company. I left for Rabat, and Youssef went to the house just outside Tetuan. As I

17

had predicted, the police had lost no time. There was indeed a reception committee waiting for Youssef there, but he managed to escape from them and went straight to Rabat.

"The police didn't give up that easily. They went to Youssef's father, a kindly man who was seriously ill, and tried to pressurise him. They also approached a well-known relative of his.

"Now Youssef had a vulnerable spot. He had a girlfriend in Tetuan to whom he was very attached. He realised now he could never return to Tetuan without being picked up immediately by the police. He felt miserable and depressed as he envisaged a girlfriendless future existence living in hiding, constantly in fear of being discovered. His famous relative had also tried to persuade him to give himself up, saying it was only a matter of time anyway before he would be caught, but if he gave himself up voluntarily the police had promised that they would, after an initial questioning, set him free; all they needed was information. It was the classic bait and Youssef - his motivation dispelling any rational judgement - swallowed every bite. He went to the police and told them everything - apparently a more cooperative assistant would have been hard to find. I found this out a long time afterwards.

"He divulged names and whereabouts of all the senior members he knew in the organisation. It was remarkable how he managed to direct them to my flat. A strict rule was that when colleagues went to other colleagues' homes, they were blindfolded to prevent disclosure of the address. Youssef had been blindfolded. Yet now he was able to retrace his journey there, this time with the police. When one sense is removed, the others sharpen. His powers of smell and hearing, particularly keen when blindfolded, now assisted while directing the police there. He recalled hearing a tailor on this corner, smelling a greengrocer's on that, sensing a taxi-rank here, feeling a market there, and so on until the goal was reached. That was how the police found me."

"Was Youssef actually arrested and was he with you in the prison?"

"I'm coming to that later. On the day of my arrest, I was tortured until the early hours, then thrown on to a heap of other prisoners: 9 of us crammed together in a space about as big as a garden shed. I can still hear and smell that place. There was a hole in the ground to perform our bodily functions. No privacy, of course. Every 2-3 minutes, a jet of water would cascade into the hole. Beaten up and exhausted as I was, and with my body crying out for sleep, still I was unable to sleep there. It was damp and the smell of urine and faeces was overpowering. The worst, however, was this waterjet, almost like a time-machine. If it had been a constant process, I would have assimilated it, but it was the sudden rushing on and then the equally sudden turning off which was so unnerving. It made me feel very on edge."

"Who else was in your cell?"

"One was a common-law prisoner[1] (whom I later found out was an informer) and 5 were students, nice and sympathetic. They told me their story. These were 5 friends always together in a group. One day, the police somehow found a letter one had written, an ordinary friendly letter between students but containing criticism of the government. These students were non-political; the letter voiced a complaint about some policy which affected the student adversely. The police arrested the whole group and brought them here 2 months ago. You can see how jumpy the regime was. Another man was slouching on the ground in a sort of depressed stupor. He wouldn't speak to anyone, even though we tried. His hideously swollen legs told their own sorry tale. The other man was in his 30s and had a remarkable story. He had been working in Libya at a time when relations with Morocco were exceptionally bad. One day, the Libyans arrested him, accusing him of spying for Morocco. In vain the poor man protested his innocence. He was just an impoverished worker, labouring in Libya to send money to his destitute family. He was tortured in the most horrendous way - he showed us the scars on his body, it was a gruesome sight - and he also went through mock executions. In the end, he was released

1. One accused under the criminal code.

and put on the plane for Morocco. When he got to the airport, he went straight to the police to describe his ordeal. To his great amazement and distress, he was arrested while the police 'made their investigations'. No treatment for his most awful torture, no opportunity to contact his family, nothing. Imagine being tortured for no reason in another country, then the relief of coming 'home' only to find that instead of the sympathy and help you so desperately need, you are just met with brutality - this time from your own people."

"Were you given any food or drink in your cell?"

"No. One of the students had managed to come by a few crusts which he shared with us. We drank water from the toilet jets in cupped hands."

"What was your next contact with the police?"

"About 5 hours or so after arriving in the cell, 2 police officers came for me. They blindfolded and handcuffed me, so I knew something serious would happen. They told me to walk up the stairs. My feet were so swollen and bruised from the torture that I couldn't walk, so I was pushed and dragged. My feet had never let me down before but then they could never dream of receiving such punishment, either. I felt physically and mentally exhausted, very apprehensive and in great pain. I was taken to the office of some obviously high-ranking official (I could see this through cracks in the blindfold.) The office seemed spacious and comfortable with carpeted floors. The official behind the desk said to the police:

'Did you get everything out of him?'

'No. He's being very stubborn'.

'So go and show him what we can do. We have a good record in giving suitable treatment to stubborn people'.

They all laughed and I was dragged off."

"Did you try and resist at all?"

"No, it would have been no use. I was taken down to another room, stripped and made to lie down naked on the cold stone floor. I could hear what sounded like a bucket being slammed down beside me, right by my head. I heard and smelt one of the police peeing in the bucket. Then he turned his body-jet away from the direction of the bucket and straight on to me! The humiliation, the degradation of having someone pee on you, I just can't describe it. It's not just the physical discomfort, it's the feeling that you have lost the last vestiges of your human dignity. In a way, this was the worst torture I suffered. I felt lower than an animal. It was as if I had lost my identity.

"The torture then continued, the main method being the 'falaka', also known as 'le roti', because you are in the position of a trussed chicken. The pain was indescribable, so was the worry - how much of this can the body take without being permanently paralysed?"

"Did the police give any indication as to why they were torturing you?"

"They wanted information. They kept saying: 'Give us your contacts. Give us your contacts.' I kept saying 'I don't know what you are talking about. I don't have contacts.' Almost like a game, but at this stage, no-one could read the other's hand. I couldn't know how much they knew and the police couldn't be certain if I were telling the truth. This was frightening. I was determined not to talk, and they were obviously going to continue the torture until I had spoken so it was a sort of stalemate. The police had many resources at their disposal. I only had the one body and mind."

"Did you ever give them any information about your colleagues?"

"No, never. At the time, the police already had many prisoners who were helping them and I was one of the last to be arrested."

"What kept you going?"

"Two things. One of them was that I kept telling myself either I am a true activist or a coward. The word activist definitely has a nicer ring to it! The other thing was my firm conviction that I was fighting a just cause: to try and abolish the tyranny of King Hassan.

21

Another important thought was that others outside would continue the struggle."

"What was in your mind at this time?"

"One slight comfort was that, unbearable though my situation was, at least I did not appear to be going to the dreaded Derb Moulay Cherif. Another thought was of appointments I'd made with some important members of the organisation, so I was trying to concentrate on not giving away this information. In addition, in view of the literature the police had found which I'd denied all knowledge of, I was worried that suspicion could fall on the others in my flat. The worry was relentless. The second torture lasted about 4 hours. Afterwards, I couldn't get up at all. It was as if my whole body had gone on strike. I was numb with pain but at the same time, I was triumphant as they hadn't made me talk.

"The next day, there was exactly the same procedure of torture. I wondered idly if the body can build up an immunity to torture. Many times I screamed out, as much with the injustice of all this degrading cruelty as with the pain itself. Then the next day, after about 2 hours, the police suddenly stopped the torture. They removed my blindfold. I was wary of the change. I didn't dare believe that the end of the nightmare was in sight, but my hopes were raised.

"Then the door opened and to my surprise, the police led in Youssef. My gut reaction was one of pleasure to see a familiar face amidst all this horror. The thought went through my mind - perhaps they are going to put us together. How comforting! He felt like my brother. I was so delighted to see him. However, I soon knew that something was wrong. Youssef wouldn't look me in the eye. The police prodded him. He cleared his throat, fell silent, then cleared his throat again. He was obviously very moved. He looked at his feet, looked at the ceiling and then back at his feet again. The policeman became impatient. He loomed over Youssef and dug him in the ribs. 'Go on, tell him'.

"Youssef said: 'Come on, Jamal. It's no use. The police know everything. They know you organised that big meeting in Rabat, that you produced those leaflets, they know our contacts. You might just as well come clean and you'll be let off, too.' He then started divulging highly incriminating facts, exposing not only me but also some of the leading members of the organisation.

"Oh, the dismay! The disillusionment! Could this be my friend Youssef? Here was I, limbs distorted, black and blue, intense pain throbbing all the way around my body, sick, exhausted, crying, sobbing with agony and enduring all this because of refusing to give away the name of Youssef and many others he had just denounced and this now all for nothing. My sense of shock and anger equalled the deep sense of betrayal. It then struck me that perhaps it was Youssef's fault that I was here at all! The anger I felt, frustrated by my impotence! I scarcely knew how to contain myself.

"I denied everything. Then the police tried a further trick. They led me into another room. Before my eyes, I saw - and even more strongly smelt - Mahmoud, eating a whole chicken hungrily, licking his lips. I realised immediately that the reason for this confrontation was double-edged. Firstly, I was kept starving, so the sight and smell of the chicken was intolerable. But more importantly, the aim of the police was to demoralise me, show my former colleagues now collaborating. It certainly did have a demoralising effect - how would you ever be able to trust again when those you had faith in had turned informer, and as I was to discover later, the selfish wish of one man to see his girlfriend had resulted in the detention and torture of myself and many others? I felt I hated humans at that point - they weren't worth the struggle. But I fought against this feeling of despair because that was playing into the very hands of the police.

"I was brought back to Youssef. I continued to deny everything. Then an amazing thing happened. As Youssef was talking, he faltered and I felt one of the police starting to doubt him. As I hadn't broken down under torture (so many others had) perhaps I had nothing to tell and all their efforts were in vain. They would never be any wiser. Then the seemingly doubting policeman stood up. With a swift stroke, he hit Youssef across the face and said 'You're not making all this up, are you?' Youssef was silent. The policeman persisted. 'Are you telling us lies?' Youssef looked completely broken, crushed, on the verge of a breakdown. I've never seen such a picture of dejection. In spite of everything, as a basic human reaction, I actually felt sorry for him.

"He opened his mouth and shut it again. I stared at him, willing him to try and somehow undo the damage he had done. I felt quite desperate - it could be that my whole life and most certainly my near future depended on him. There was a heavy silence. Then the scream of someone being tortured cracked through the stillness like a burst of lightning. The pressure on Youssef was intense, I could almost feel the vibrations. Then he raised his head slightly and said: 'It was all lies.' He put his head in his hands and started sobbing loudly and uncontrollably.

"My God, the relief I felt! I wanted to go and comfort him, hug him and shout and dance. The wounds and bruises on my body - this body which only minutes earlier was throbbing, racked with violent pain - were as if suddenly swept away and my body was reborn. The police said, 'Take him away' and I was taken back to my cell, my heart dancing."

"Were you set free at once?"

"No. For four wonderful blissful days, there was no daily round of torture. Once I was taken to see the high-ranking official. The whole atmosphere had changed. The police, instead of dragging me up the steps, half-lifted me, almost apologetically. I was beginning to feel human again. The official was chatty, even giving me a chair to sit on, like an equal. I was half expecting him to offer me a cup of mint tea! He asked a few questions, testing me, questions such as what was the difference between Marxism, Communism and Socialism. I deemed it best to play the ignorant. I said, 'Well, there isn't any difference, is there? Marx was a

Communist and a Socialist, wasn't he?' He said, 'You know, for a Political Science student, your knowledge isn't that great'. I smiled at him apologetically. Perhaps it was not such a good idea to be so ignorant, after all. Then he said: 'The level of University students is pretty low these days'. I smiled at him again, half nodding.

"I left his office with elated spirits. All that night, my head was filled with eager anticipation. I was definitely going to be released. How I cherished my freedom, now that I had been without it under such appalling conditions! What a lot I would have to tell the organisation now that I'd had a glimpse from the inside. I would boast a bit and say, 'Well, they tortured me and tried to lock me up but they were no match for me'. I would contact the foreign press to tell them what was going on. My experience had only strengthened my resolve to continue the struggle. Oh, and I would have a long hot bath and get all my wounds seen to. I was going to be released, going to be free! I pictured all the food I was going to eat, massive helpings of all of it. I was just getting through my third couscous when my dreams were abruptly shattered. Two policemen threw open my cell door and dragged me out by my hair. They hit me, kicked me, stamped on me.

"'You bastard!' they were shouting, 'You lying bastard! You son of a whore! We'll kill you!' They dragged me up the steps, beating, punching and kicking me. I was taken to the high-ranking official. No chairs or polite conversation this time. He looked at me with anger and contempt. 'You bloody liar!' he shouted. 'All this time you've been wanted by the police in Tangiers!' He threw something across his desk. It was a photo of me headed 'Jamal Benomar. Subversive element'. Underneath it was what seemed to be a description of me.

"I was taken away and tortured mercilessly. This time it was sheer savage sadistic torture, not designed to extract information - no questions were asked - but simply to get revenge. They used a torture method known as the 'aeroplane' in which the body is faced downwards with hands and feet above in such a way that the spine is curved. Then a big heavy person sits on the spine. I can hardly bear to talk about it, the pain is excruciating - you feel as if your back is going to break, to crack into two pieces. Can you imagine what it feels like to be cracked into two, like a dry bone? After about two hours, I was dragged back to my cell and thrown in there, feeling more dead than alive. My body had been stretched to its limits. I was hungry, thirsty, and suffering the most terrible physical agony, but even more than that, I was completely demoralised. Freedom had been so close, just within my grasp. The next morning, two police officers from Tangiers came to fetch me. I was taken the long six hour journey there by coach, my hands handcuffed behind my back but with a coat thrown over so as not to attract attention, and one policeman on each side of me digging a pistol in my ribs. I didn't dare speculate on what horrors lay ahead of me in Tangiers."

Chapter 5

I was having a comfortable life in Stockholm. It was a protected existence. Stockholm is a very beautiful city, calm, serene, frostily inaccessible in the winter, mellow-eyed in the summer, the "Venice of the North" without the crowds but without the cosiness. Sweden seemed such a remote place, almost like one of the far edges of earth or even more, an appendix to earth rather than part of it. From this perspective, I began to peer down at what was happening in the rest of the world. It was no beautiful picture. The 70s was a new high-tech era in the field of repression, the latest technique achieving remarkable success: that of disappearances. The plight of disappeared persons was highlighted in the Swedish press by the case of Dagmar Hagelin, the teenage daughter of a Swedish official stationed in Argentina. She had gone to visit a friend in Buenos Aires, a friend who, unbeknown to her, was being watched by the police. As she knocked on the door, there was some sort of shoot-out; she has never been seen since. What was happening to thousands of other innocent citizens in Argentina was subsequently also given prominence in the Swedish press. One story which particularly touched me was the fate of an Argentinian bookshop owner. The police had turned up one day at his bookshop, looking for some apparently subversive character who they knew used to go there frequently. By the end of the day, he had not shown up, whereupon the police - unwilling to leave without some evidence of their eagerly anticipated haul - seized the astonished owner of the shop and his equally astonished wife and children. The entire family disappeared without trace.

Another case which haunted me was that of the Chilean poet and singer Victor Jara, accused of contaminating his fellow countrymen with criticisms of the Chilean regime. What the military junta did to him must almost send shudders down the back of the most hardened torturer: they cut out his tongue.

I began to feel very disturbed by the thought of these horrors, started to have nightmares about them. One night, I woke up screaming. Axel put his arms around me, calmed me down. "What were you dreaming about, Joyce dear?"

"The police," I sobbed, "they had just taken you and they had come back to get me."

"No, there's no-one there."

I lay for a while, exhausted, shaking, reflecting on my dream.

"Axel, I feel I should be doing something. I can have a nightmare and be woken up and comforted. It's all so easy. What about those whose waking hours give them no relief from their nightmare? What are we doing about these people, we who live in peace and comfort?"

"What do you want to do?"

"I don't know, I don't know," I groaned, turning my face into the pillow. What could I do? I felt so small. The stark contrast between tongue-cutting Chilean officials and my own everyday life was overwhelming. The sense of frustration at my powerlessness was almost intolerable. How could I, with my limited resources, change the minds and hearts of self-appointed despots or whole governments in such far-flung places as Chile, the Soviet Union, South Africa, Turkey? And yet how could I go on enjoying my comfortable life with a clear conscience while fellow human beings, who probably shared similar aspirations in life to my own, were being systematically tortured, killed, driven mad or held indefinitely in secret detention?

"Axel, my life lacks direction."

"What do you mean?"

"There's no challenge. I get up in the morning, drive off to work in my comfortable car, teach some reasonably interested and motivated children, then drive back again to my nice warm house. I have a good salary, long holidays. But there's no challenge, nothing for me to pit my wits against. Am I ungrateful?"

"Possibly." Axel grinned.

28

"Can't we do something different?" I pleaded. Axel looked as if he knew what was coming. "Can't we go to England, just for a year? I really feel I want to experience living in England as an adult. I was only a child when I left my country."

Axel drew me closer to him. "Look, Joyce, I know you miss England, but I don't know what to do about it. I have my job here, we have built up our lives in this country."

"But just for a year. You could take a sabbatical, get a student grant, I could work, we could save up."

"We'll see."

This did not inspire me with much hope. Our conversations on this topic usually ended in the same way, 'We'll see' becoming synonymous with 'Present crisis calmed. Respite until next time'.

A few days later we were invited to a party. I had the beginnings of a cold and had decided not to go as I didn't feel very sociable. However in the end, the promises of Thomas' good food made me change my mind and we went to his beautiful flat on Strandvägen overlooking the harbour and the seduction of a life beyond the Stockholm shore. It was at this party that I met Britta Boden, and started to talk to her. Britta was the secretary of a local Amnesty International group. I had always been vaguely interested in Amnesty, without knowing all that much about it. I asked Britta to tell me about the organisation.

"Amnesty's main work is for the release of prisoners of conscience," she told me. "The working definition of prisoners of conscience is that they should have neither used nor advocated violence, but be imprisoned solely on account of their beliefs, the non-violent expression of their convictions, their race, sex, colour or religion, their adherence to a Trade Union or other organisation. Amnesty also opposes detention without trial, the death penalty, torture or any other inhuman and degrading treatment. The headquarters of Amnesty is the International Secretariat in London, where all the research takes place. Then there are national sections in many countries, such as the Swedish section here. These sections set up groups of people interested in working for the organisation on a purely voluntary basis."

"Where does the money for the administration and research come from?" I asked. "It must be quite costly to run. Is it funded by governments?"

"No," said Britta, "Amnesty won't take money from governments as we have to be seen to be strictly impartial. We would have our wings severely clipped if we started taking money from governments we wanted to criticise and the richer regimes would be in a stronger position to buy our silence. No, the organisation is funded entirely by its members. Each group gets together its own money - it could be by donations both inside and outside the group, fund-raising efforts, street collections or whatever is the most practical for the group. Each group has to give a large amount of money, also, to the National sections which help fund the central organisation."

"Is all that really enough to meet the huge expense of running such an organisation?" I asked incredulously.

"Oh yes, you'd be surprised at how many people feel very strongly committed to such a cause and, as such, are willing to make sacrifices in both time and money."

"How does the group work?"

"Each group 'adopts' three political prisoners or prisoners of conscience, ideally one from the East, one from the West and one from the Third World, to ensure neutrality - a very important basis for Amnesty's work. In our group, there are about ten active members and about forty passive ones, the latter not taking part in the group's work but supporting Amnesty's aims and sending donations. Of the active members, some correspond with one of the adopted prisoners and/or write letters to Heads of State, Ambassadors, Ministers etc., some organise fund-raising events such as raffles or jumble sales, some liaise with the press; one person endeavours to increase the membership, another is responsible for compiling a very basic Newsletter containing details of the work of the group and the prisoners, intended to encourage passive members' interest; another carries out simple but very essential tasks, such as stuffing envelopes, mailing etc. You see, there's room for all sorts at Amnesty."

I was impressed by this and by what I already knew about Amnesty, for two reasons. One was the idea that people from a whole range of backgrounds, educational levels and skills (or lack of them) could meet together in a common cause, each one able to contribute something, however modest. I was also fascinated by another concept. On the one side, there was the sheer scale, the enormity of the atrocities carried out in the name of God or Allah or the people or duty or whatever, which appeared as a general annihilistic drive towards the extermination or silencing of whole movements, organisations, communities. The other side was Amnesty's method of actively working on individual cases but such a huge number of them, and with such widespread and far-reaching effects. Repressive regimes were targeting whole groups of people, even entire populations and working downwards to individuals, whereas Amnesty was starting at the bottom with the individual and working upwards to encompass and focus on the mass repression.

I had a fairly hazy notion about world politics. I was aware of the attractions and drawbacks of the two dominating ideologies - capitalism and forms of socialism - and had a vague knowledge of different sorts of repression machinery used to enforce these ideologies. I was seemingly a passive observer. Although deep inside me, I could feel the most intense outrage at individual acts of cruelty, I had never experienced or even thought about experiencing different ways of channelling these strong feelings into any type of constructive action. I had little self-confidence, which made it all the easier to remain passive - even if I *could* do anything, who would listen to me? I didn't accept misplaced and misused authority but I never dared raise my voice too loudly against it, either.

I told Britta that I was interested in Amnesty, and we

exchanged telephone numbers. I never fail to be amazed at the tiny insignificant events and choices, which can determine the whole of one's future. This chance meeting with a woman at a party, which I nearly missed anyway, was to lead to the most dramatic and radical changes in my life.

Chapter 6

During his interviews with 'Little Ben' (in his cell) Jamal would relive his experiences which had started with his arrest in Rabat and treatment at the hands of the police there, and had led to his transfer to Tangiers police station.

There, the police had been waiting for him, swearing because of the trouble he had caused them. There were three interrogators: the big boss, a sneaky sort of man who appeared to have a lot of hate inside him. Then there were two extraordinary men: one terribly fat and the other terribly thin, just like Laurel and Hardy. 'Laurel' was aggressive and stupid; 'Hardy' was frightening because of his incredible memory and sharp intelligence. Something suddenly happened which took Jamal quite by surprise. He was standing up, being questioned about some member of the organisation, when with no warning at all, he felt a searing pain on his neck which sent him spinning. The pain and the shock were so sudden and intense that he didn't for a moment actually know what had hit him. After that moment of utter surprise, however, he understood: the sneaky policeman had *kicked his neck*! It was an exercise in martial arts. Then he was taken to a cell, deep underground.

Here he found about twenty-five other political prisoners, all handcuffed and blindfolded and lying on the floor, rather like a battle-ground after the battle. Jamal was still handcuffed from the journey and the police had blindfolded him again. He tried to feel what his new 'home' was like. There was an all-penetrating smell of urine (he was to discover that toilet visits were infrequent, so needs were often performed on the spot). The cell was terribly cold, as if they had been put into a deep freeze. He was wearing the clothes he had been arrested in: a pair of jeans, a T-shirt and a thin jacket. It was really freezing, he had never been so cold in his life, nor even imagined what it could be like to be so cold. But at least he knew that Tangiers police station, for all its horrors, was better than Derb Moulay Cherif Detention Centre.

The prisoners were not allowed to talk to each other but when the guard on watch disappeared every now and then for a short while, they took the opportunity for a quick whisper.

Jamal managed to peer from under his blindfold and identify two people: one of them whispered that it would be better for them 'not to know' each other and Jamal agreed. The other one was Mahmoud, the police collaborator. Jamal tried in spite of the circumstances to sleep but his anxiety kept him awake. He was never free of this anxiety. It followed him everywhere like a nervous friend. He was anxious about the organisation, anxious that most of the members could have been rounded up and that it would therefore be the end of the movement, this movement they had invested so much in, at such great risk and now at such great cost. He was anxious that he might, in spite of himself, give something away under torture. He was anxious about his family, who didn't know where he was. He was anxious for his life: he felt he was too young to die. He was anxious about the next minute, the next week, the next year. He felt he was floating in a sort of half-life, that he didn't have control any more.

The next morning, he was taken up many steps to the office and his blindfold was removed. The sneaky man was sitting on a comfortable chair, high up, flanked by 'Laurel' and 'Hardy'. They made him sit on a small wooden stool quite a way below them. Sneaky started histrionically to pour out delicious-smelling mint tea and smoke a cigarette. After a while, he said: "We know your ideology, it created the Vietnam war and the civil war in Lebanon and you want to create another one here!"

Jamal replied, "Look, I am a pacifist, I don't know what you are talking about."

Sneaky brought his fist down on the desk and raised his voice. "Oh no? However peaceful you may say your views are, opposition is opposition. It creates hatred against the one you are opposed to and this hatred develops into civil war, as in Vietnam and Lebanon. So you have no right to oppose. Opposition is destabilisation." Oh, he was a real fascist, this man. Jamal told him he found it difficult to follow his logic. He was threatened with court-martial if he didn't collaborate.

Jamal was taken down to another room where he was stripped and made to lie naked on the cold flagstones, handcuffed and blindfolded. The *falaka* torture began. The pain was unbearable. He screamed and screamed but wouldn't say a thing. Every so often, he lost consciousness, to be dragged across to a tap of freezing cold water and revived so that the session could continue. It lasted about five hours altogether. His torturers kept firing questions at him and coming up with the most remarkable allegations such as: "You were arranging for a shipment of arms to come from China, from the Soviet Union."

Jamal was physically and mentally burnt out by the time he was thrown back into his cell. It was freezing cold, his feet were swollen, throbbing, bleeding, his back completely disjointed, his head felt as if about to be severed. He was sore and wounded and yet had this inner comfort that he had not disclosed anything! This feeling of having at least beaten them on this was to provide him with a lot of strength and moral courage in the days and weeks to come.

The police asked him regularly about his part in *Ilal Amam*. He admitted that he had links with it, but minimised his role, saying he had run a couple of errands for them once and agreed with their aims and didn't see why he should be imprisoned and tortured for this when the Moroccan constitution allows freedom of speech.

In the beginning, he was tortured every day, but then as the police either began to believe him or else saw that he wasn't going to talk anyway, they temporarily lost interest. However, if a new story was brought to their attention and there were conflicting versions of it, Jamal would be sent for and tortured again. This was almost the worst, the anxiety of hearing the footsteps in the corridor, to listen on tenterhooks, wondering if they were going to stop outside his cell, and then when the door opened whether he was going to be the one sent for today. Also, his cell was next to the torture chamber so he could hear the agonised screams from the latest victim, coming in a constant torrent, ripping into the dank moroseness of his environment.

Part of the torture was leading him past Mahmoud and other collaborators tucking in to appetising-looking and smelling meals. Jamal and his co-prisoners were allocated half a loaf of bread every day and a bucket of water was kept in the middle of the cell for them to grope their way to and drink from. The food was thrown into the cell as if it were pig-food going into the trough. In fact, the whole eating and drinking ceremony was reminiscent of the pig farm. Not only were they kept half-starving, but when you are handcuffed and blindfolded, table manners are not a first priority.

The actual torture sessions became more spasmodic. In a way, Jamal was lucky to have been caught much later on than a lot of the others. In the beginning, when the police had very few leads and were desperate for information, those people they did get hold of were tortured practically night and day. Then, following the death from torture of Abdellatif Zeroual in late 1974, they had to ease up slightly. After all, apart from the scandal, there's not much information you can extract from a dead man...

"Did the police go on believing you were only small fry in the organisation, Jamal?"

"That was an interesting point. One of the biggest ironies was when I was tortured for information about a man called Rachid, a fairly important member of the organisation in Rabat. The irony lay in the fact that I was Rachid, but the police hadn't realised it, they knew me by my real name, not my name in the organisation. If they had found out the truth, not only would the torture have increased to force me to divulge the sort of highly incriminating material which someone in a more senior position in the organisation would be in possession of, but also, if ever we were to be brought to trial, Jamal would be infinitely less vulnerable than Rachid. Laurel asked me constantly about Rachid.

"'You must know him. He is tallish, slim, fair-skinned, walks with his feet turned out.'

'Have you got a photo of him?'

'No.' (That was a relief, anyway)

'He usually wears a checked jacket, in fact rather similar to the one you are wearing now,' whereupon, to my great consternation, Laurel fingered my jacket. However, he didn't appear to make the connection.

'No,' I said innocently, 'never heard of him.'

"I was delighted that I had managed to fool them."

"Were you in Tangiers Prison for long?"

"From January to May - four long months. This was the pattern of my life there. I was handcuffed and blindfolded all the time. My domicile was this cramped cell I shared with about 25 people. My bed was the freezing stone floor. My companions were not allowed to communicate with me nor I with them, under threat of torture. My daily nourishment was a stale piece of bread and some dirty water. My clothes were the jeans, T-shirt and jacket I had been arrested in, all by now quite disgusting. Of course, there was no change of clothing. Fleas were in abundance, they were multiplying with relish all over my body which was racked with pain and made all the more unbearable by the itching. Relief from both was almost impossible because of the handcuffs.

"After a while, 21 of the prisoners were removed. I felt sure they had been released and, although of course sorry (not to say worried) not to be among their number, I was really happy for them as I could see that some of them were verging on madness. However, I learnt later that they had just been moved to Casablanca Prison.

"A few weeks later, the police came for the rest of us. Our handcuffs and blindfolds were tightened and we were put into a van. One of the most awful parts of the whole of this nightmare was never, ever knowing what was going to happen. We were being moved. Were we being released? Were we going to be executed? Were we going to another prison? Fear struck my heart that we might be going to Derb Moulay Cherif, the notorious concentration camp, without even the daylight and fresh air. People have died from torture there, previously strong and healthy people have been turned into raving lunatics or manic depressives. Derb Moulay Cherif drew the same response from those who knew of it as Auschwitz. It was a terrifying prospect.

"The journey took 8-9 hours. We stopped twice on the way for the driver and crew to refresh themselves. Of course, there was nothing for us, starving though we were. We were being fed by our anxiety.

"The van eventually stopped for the last time. The sound of the opening and clanking shut of an iron gate of some size plus the barking of dogs, indicated to me that we had reached our destination. It was not going to be release, in any event. The van doors opened and we were pushed out, exhausted and staggering. To get our first glimpse of Derb Moulay Cherif."

Chapter 7

I had finished classes early and had decided to treat myself to a long walk in the surrounding forest. It was late Spring/early Summer of 1976 and Sweden was at its best. The pale sun, not yet having quite come to grips with the fact that Winter was over, was shining tentatively through the tall dignified pine-trees. The birch trees were all freshly clothed in their new Spring attire: this was how I loved them best, while they still had their delicate virgin demeanour. Underneath my feet was a mossy carpet which crackled as I walked. I took some deep breaths, to get myself re-acquainted with the delicious smell of pine, hoping to encourage the earthy fragrance to enter my body.

I walked to the lake and sat on a rock, gazing into the clear water. Here was peace, perfect peace. Sweden was a beautiful country. It had treated me well. So what was the reason, I wondered, for my obsession with leaving it whenever I could, to go back to England?

Even the long summer holidays - nearly 3 months - which I invariably spent in England, were not enough to quench my insatiable thirst for my native country. Yet I would never, Heaven forbid, think of myself as being nationalistic. I abhor nationalism, which can lead to fanaticism, that superior mentality - quite frightening, especially with the Nazi regime still within living memory.

So what is that special about Britain? It's overcrowded, polluted, the weather is appalling, the Green Belt slowly disappearing, it's full of litter and being taken over by football hooligans and aggressive pop music totally alien to me. Yet I longed for it. Whereas many of my Swedish friends were saying: "I'd love to go and live in another country," my British friends in the UK were saying: "I don't know how you could live in another country." What drew me to Britain so forcefully? Was it that the British really knew how to enjoy themselves while in Sweden I sometimes felt it was almost sinful to let your hair down? Was it my sister's accounts of hair-raising adventures and fun in the orchestra she toured with, which I compared with my sedate existence as school-teacher? Was it the greater sense of informality in communication with others, as typified by the British pub? Was it the British humour? Humour has always been important to me and I found a certain lack of it in Sweden, with a few notable exceptions. Was it just that I needed to be where my roots were? Or was it simply that I was an active person feeling a singular lack of challenge in my life? Perhaps it was a combination of all of these things and others. Whatever it was, the overall feeling was a powerful one, although difficult to tell which was stronger, the 'push' or the 'pull' factor.

I couldn't find a solution to this as I sat there by the lake, drinking in the peaceful surroundings. I was not at peace, that was for sure. Perhaps I never would be, although I do not perceive myself to be one of life's discontented. I had a strange feeling that there was this passion inside me somewhere waiting to explode but which was being heavily subdued by outside forces.

The sun went in, and the sudden chill reminded me that it was still some time before summer was here. As I walked home, I pondered on what I could do to try and bring some meaning into my life, ranging from the ordinary such as changing my job, becoming politically active, joining local campaigns, to the more radical and patently unattainable, such as that world trip alone with my violin; adopting thirty children of different nationalities to live together along socialist principles; going to carry out some research on an unknown tribe somewhere in a remote African country. Everyone has dreams, some more modest and attainable than others.

Some time after these reflections, I bumped into Britta Boden again, the woman involved with Amnesty International.

"You never rang me up," she admonished me lightly "We could do with you in our Amnesty group. How about it?"

"Could I come and meet you and see how you work?" I

offered.

"Of course. We'll be meeting again in about three weeks' time, so do come along, won't you?" She gave me the details and on the appointed date, on a cold and dark November evening, I turned up at my first Amnesty meeting. It was held in a narrow room dominated by a long table where about ten people of mixed age and sex were sitting. It was a well-organised well-structured meeting with an agenda for the most part adhered to.

It started off with an account from Eva (who I understood had just taken over the job of bookkeeper for the group) about the donations received from passive group members in response to a plea in a Newsletter, circulated sporadically. There was some merriment when it was pointed out to Eva - who had never done book-keeping in her life before - that one does not use Tippex in the accounts book! It was all very good-humoured, and Eva laughed at the mistake as much as anyone. This was the very best way of learning a new skill.

Next on the agenda was a request for 'Urgent Action' by Amnesty. The group received such requests about once a month, typically about someone who had just disappeared, or someone who it was feared was being tortured to death, or someone about to be executed. These 'urgent actions' were sent to many people in different countries and it was the job of the group then to write to the relevant authorities expressing concern. It meant that the authorities would be getting thousands of letters from all over the world, focusing on the fate of a single individual. So within the space of 48 hours, thousands of telegrams and telexes would be pouring on to the oppressors' desks. The current case was a man from Chile called Jaime Valdas, a 26-year-old married law student and leader of a student union before the military coup in 1973. He was physically handicapped, with polio in both legs. He had been arrested in Santiago fifteen days previously, since when he had 'disappeared'. Group members were urged to write to some named authorities expressing concern that the arrest had not been acknowledged (as is required by Chilean law) and requesting information about his place of detention and the charges brought against him. The group was further requested to encourage other organisations and/or professional individuals to send appeals and to give the case maximum publicity. All the ten members at the meeting agreed to write to the authorities and to ask at least one friend to do likewise.

Then came the most exciting part of the agenda. The group had just received its first letter from the Rhodesian prisoner it had been allocated. The letter was held up for all to see by Erik, a tall thin Swede in his thirties, who had been the one responsible for writing to the prisoner, and it was then read out by him to a spellbound audience. It was written by a youngish man, arrested on some trumped-up charge for the non-violent expression of his beliefs and then put into detention to languish without trial. A picture emerged of an intelligent, warm and caring person, much less worried about himself and the horrors he had endured than about his wife and three children who, deprived of the only breadwinner in the family, had been left destitute. Full details of the names of his family and an address where they could be reached were included in the letter. An immediate decision was taken by the group to send a fairly substantial sum of money to the family and also to organise hiring a lawyer, which the group would finance, to attempt at the very least to get him a trial. People in the group who had children of the same age promised to send clothes and toys for the prisoner's children, while others promised to get together a parcel of toilet articles, books, writing materials, clothes etc. to send to the prisoner himself. As they were discussing the details, the logo of Amnesty sprang to my mind: a lit candle emerging from barbed wire. This, then, was really the beginning of the light even if it was still only a flicker, and it was we simple modest human beings, with all our limitations, who were providing that light, that ray of hope in the darkness. It was we who were responsible for making sure that the candle didn't stop burning until it had melted away the barbed wire. It was uplifting.

The other prisoner of the group was then discussed. There had never up to this point been any contact with the prisoner from Taiwan, it was a very closed country, difficult to work on. The group was waiting to be allocated a third prisoner.

The tasks to be carried out before the next meeting were then circulated. These included replying to the prisoner's letter, writing more letters to the Rhodesian authorities, plans to send along a delegation to the Rhodesian Embassy, renewed attempts to get in touch with the prisoner from Taiwan, plans to get cards printed with the names and details of the prisoners to be given to all our friends to send off, and the compiling of the next Newsletter. There was a final discussion about fund-raising, whether through a jumble sale, a raffle, a sponsored walk, appeal to rich friends and relatives with a conscience, or a combination of all these things, and the meeting came to an end.

There and then I joined the group. Little did I suspect the dire effect this seemingly harmless action was to have on my life.

Chapter 8

I could not possibly have been aware of it then but it was on a certain day in May 1976 when Jamal passed through the desolate gates of Derb Moulay Cherif.

Together with three other prisoners, he was taken to what seemed to be a big hall and made to face the wall. It went through his mind that this could be a mock or even real execution. His blood froze and his hands clenched as he stood there with the other three, steeling himself for a shot. Then he heard a voice from behind: 'You will have to shave their heads.' He was pushed down on the floor, still facing the wall, and his blindfold was ripped off. His head was forced down. Then his hair was - impossible to be called 'cut' - rather scythed off with a pair of blunted shears. He had a beard (access to shaving material not being distinctly noticeable during secret detention) and this was now wrenched off with the same shears. It was excruciatingly painful and there was blood everywhere. He was told "You should forget your name. From now on, you are just a number, number 58."

They were blindfolded again and taken to a small cell, where they were ordered to lie down on the floor. All movement was strictly forbidden. Toilet visits were permitted three times every 24 hours in an open toilet with the guard making a countdown in front of them. It was humiliating and conducive to a state of permanent constipation. The whole scenario was designed to give each prisoner the status of a small child: a child with no real feeling of own identity, whose toilet visits are public, who is given food at the will of others and who has to obey unquestioningly.

Jamal's cell was small, cramped and humid. There was no door, but a guard with a large whip sat permanently at the entrance. For four days they were not allowed to sleep. Every time it looked as if someone was in danger of doing so, the guard would get up and start kicking, beating and abusing him. One guard was

45

particularly vicious, taking a delight in being so. Jamal once caught a glimpse of his face. It was the most hideous face he had ever seen. Happiness had certainly never spent the night within its features. The owner of the face seemed obsessed with preventing the prisoners from ever seeing it. He would say: "Your blindfold is too loose. Tighten it!" Jamal would tighten it the best he could with handcuffed hands. "More!" the guard would shout. Jamal would try to obey. "No, much, much more!" he would scream.

A favourite trick of his was to say that the prisoners had been talking when they hadn't. "You've been talking and you're going to be punished for it!" How could they deny it? Again, the helpless child being punished for being naughty. He would then beat them and strike them with his whip.

The same guard would turn toilet visits into humiliating drama. "Toilet, please," Jamal would say. There would be a long silence, then the guard would retort, "So why don't you get up then?" Jamal would get up and start to move in the direction of the primitive latrines. The guard would suddenly shout: "Stop! What the hell do you think you are doing? Where are you walking to? Do you think this is some sort of park or something?" Jamal would get beaten up. The toilet visit would get forgotten.

Once he took Jamal by himself to a small room. He ordered him to stand on one leg. It should be remembered that Jamal's legs were swollen, sore and wounded after the falaka torture and his back had never recovered, either, so it can be appreciated what a difficult task this was. He stood there until he collapsed. Then the guard beat him up for not holding out longer and made him do it again, over and over again.

At first, Jamal screamed with pain from the whippings but then he noticed that the more sound he made, the more perverse pleasure the guard took in it, it was a sort of orgasm for him. Oh, they really knew how to choose their guards in this living hell. One day, Jamal decided to try and exercise supreme self-control by not uttering a sound when he was beaten up. He managed. The guard beat him harder. Jamal held out. The guard grew desperate and beat him with all his might. Not a sound. Then suddenly he stopped. Jamal was never beaten again after that.

Strangely enough, there were some light moments to punctuate the horror and break the monotony. One such event was when a prisoner suddenly started talking of food in his sleep. "Apples!" he was saying, "Yum yum! Bananas mmmmm! Oranges, oh Mon Dieu!" Jamal was dying to laugh, it was such a contrast to their grim reality. However, the grim reality soon intruded. They were all beaten up because this prisoner had broken the silence rule - a rule evidently to be adhered to even while sleeping.

The other event was when the police went, as the prisoners found out later, to arrest a member of the organisation but he was not at home. Instead, a friend of his was there, who was drunk. The police - no doubt hating to return empty-handed - took him to Derb Moulay Cherif, blindfolded and handcuffed him and threw him on to the prisoners. Still drunk and, his condition lacking the inhibitions governing the rest of the inhabitants, he started protesting vehemently against such treatment, which livened things up somewhat in the depressed atmosphere before his unexpected arrival. What must it have felt like to hear this: on the one hand, compassion for an innocent person brought along to this underground cave 'in error', as it were; and on the other hand, the comic relief provided by his drunken outpourings, shattering the deathly hush of this living morgue. When the outpourings became too vociferous, he was beaten up by the guards and left unconscious. The next morning, in what would have been the cool clear light of dawn in a slightly better world, the man - by now sober if severely bruised - awoke to find himself blindfolded and handcuffed in secret detention. He wondered aloud in astonishment what had happened to him and what sort of punishment was being meted out to him simply for having had too much to drink. He was then released - the incident probably transformed him into a teetotaller.

Another more serious case was that of the Saharan Otmani,

47

whose disappearance was investigated by Amnesty International. He was forced to recount - in front of his half-starving colleagues - the food he would like to be eating. After he had finished his list of rabbit with almonds, chicken couscous and fish tagine, he was told by the police 'and here is your dessert' which was a massive beating-up. He was not seen since.

Jamal - along with his colleagues - was taken away and tortured whenever the police made some fresh discovery and wanted information. In fact the whole of the prisoners existence there was one long torture.

For several reasons, Derb Moulay Cherif was the worst experience of all for the prisoners. For one thing, the psychological aspect: all who went there got the feeling that Derb Moulay Cherif was the end of the road and that you had been brought here to die a hideous death. Then the whole atmosphere - words cannot describe vividly enough a true picture of the horror. It was austere, silent, like a mortuary. The only feeling in existence seemed to be cold calculated cruelty. There was a complete prohibition on talking or any form of communication. Life did not appear to be guaranteed here and you could be broken down to such an extent that in the end, you'd want to die, be begging for it even. Jamal thought it was a place from which he would never be released. Here were these sadistic hate-ridden people who were prepared, for political, ideological and - who knows? - personal reasons, to kill you or watch you slowly die with great satisfaction.

The whole system at Derb Moulay Cherif was much stricter than anything Jamal had known before. In Tangiers, the guards weren't so bloodthirsty, he could even sense a flicker of sympathy emanating from one or two of them, which put the prisoners' plight into some sort of human perspective. Also, the guards in Tangiers sometimes disappeared from their posts for short periods and even when they were there, they stood outside the cell door which meant that the prisoners could whisper to each other, loosen their blindfolds and sometimes even giggle a little just to release a bit of the tension.

In Derb Moulay Cherif, there was always a guard sitting right on top of them, and their blindfolds and handcuffs were tight to the point of strangulation, which not only hurt but also restricted their movements to a much greater extent.

But for Jamal, the most devastating of all was the slow and painful realisation that the police had really done a good job in rounding up nearly all the members of the organisation. He had refused to believe this at first, and had thought they were lying when they said so, but then during torture, he was confronted with first one and then other top members of the organisation, most of them divulging everything about the secret life of the organisation. All that he had tried to hide from his interrogators had by now been told in detail by others. On one occasion, two senior members of *Ilal Amam* were brought into the interrogation room with him. In the beginning, he did not know they were in the same room, as he was blindfolded. His interrogators first asked if he knew them. Up to then, he had thought they were carrying on the work of the organisation outside, which had been a comforting reflection. So he said he didn't know them. What a shock when one of his interrogators suddenly removed his blindfold and he saw them there in front of him: these two leaders whom he had admired so much and even tried to protect by not giving any information which could lead to their arrest. Here they were in front of him, both appeared broken men and they started to give all the missing information about Jamal and his activities as he stood there, forced to listen. What a devastating blow. So it had all been in vain. How could Jamal ever come to terms with this unbearable reality? IT HAD ALL BEEN IN VAIN. The time, the skills, the efforts, the training, the arrests, the torture, the detention, the worry, the sacrifice. Oh, the waste! It was too awful to think of. This is what turned Derb Moulay Cherif into a real mortuary for Jamal: *the death of their hopes*.

Chapter 9

I had been working as a teacher of mother-tongue English to immigrant children for a couple of years now. My classes consisted of small groups from seven to 16-year-olds. As well as giving English classes, I also coached them in their general lessons so that their lack of knowledge of Swedish would not impede their progress in the school curriculum.

The work itself was not unrewarding and was quite varied, as my pupils came from a wide range of backgrounds and countries: India, Africa, the USA, Australia and Canada as well as the United Kingdom. Some of the children were delightful. I especially remember Claes, a gruff little 10-year-old. I returned a piece of previously corrected work one day which was still faulty. "Claes *dear*," I said sarcastically, "you've got it wrong again."

Claes snatched the book away, read the offending piece through, then looked up and scowled at me. "No, I have *not*," he retorted, "and don't you call me 'dear'!"

I enjoyed an informal contact with the children, sitting on their desks, all of us on first name terms, forming the basis for mutual respect - as one responsible human being with needs and feelings relating to another. I tried to be less their teacher than their friend and I learned a lot about their problems and fears, which helped towards understanding what my aims were. This was made easier by the small groups I was teaching. If nothing else, my training in Pedagogy had taught me that you get the best out of people by treating them as equals and being honest with them about your feelings, while recognising and respecting theirs. It had also taught me that teaching is less about stuffing children with a lot of facts to be regurgitated at exam time and more about helping them get in tune with their own feelings and aspirations and to articulate these: that is, to help them develop as human beings. In any case, these were my ideals, which didn't mean I always attained them.

One of my failures was with a 14-year-old girl who reminded me a bit of myself at that age: rebellious and disruptive, and she even looked a bit as I had as a teenager. When she went too far - as she often did, whether on purpose or not - my means of punishment were rather limited, consisting of a cold and resigned attitude in communicating with her, keeping her behind after school, and also exerting my power over her when giving the dreaded end-of-term marks. My methods of dealing with her went against all my beliefs about teaching. I never attempted a discussion of her evident problems and fears: it was out-and-out war between us right from the start. I don't know why this particular girl had such an effect on me. Perhaps I identified too strongly with her; perhaps I was afraid that by talking to her, I would find out too much about myself, a prospect I recoiled from. I wasn't ready at that stage in my life to confront my inner child. It was a more familiar approach to punish her, thus punishing myself.

I seemed to be stuck with this teaching job, or perhaps I stuck with it because it provided me with the possibility of long holidays in England. Even at the time, this seemed to me a basically flawed situation: to stay in a job only because it afforded the opportunity of temporary escape. It was doomed to disaster. One thing I disliked was the big turnover of pupils who tended to come from very mobile families. So as soon as you got to know someone, s/he moved on, often without warning. Also, the English-speaking population was not concentrated in one area, which meant I had to travel from school to school. This gave me a feeling of isolation, accentuating my alienation from Sweden: I didn't 'belong' anywhere. No-one really missed me if I were away, I never got to know the other staff members properly, I was just a figure who came and went in each school. "Oh yes, here's Joyce. It must be Thursday." Any person who has been a peripatetic teacher will, I am sure, know what I mean and how I felt.

I had a reasonable amount of spare time, some of which I spent on musical activities. I had also been to the Amnesty group a few more times. Then one day, Britta rang me up, quite excited. "Joyce, can you speak French?"

"Yes."

"What a relief, you are the only one in the group who can. We've just been allocated a new prisoner from Morocco. His name is Jamal Benomar. All the correspondence has to be in French. Would you like to be his case-worker?"

She did not have to ask me twice. I had always felt how exciting it would be to have my own case to work on, almost like having someone's fate put into your hands, an awe-inspiring task, yet an infinitely challenging one. I put the phone down, feeling elated. Now where was Morocco? I got out the encyclopaedia. Ah yes, there it was across the sea from Spain, that narrow stretch of water was the only thing separating it from Europe, and two Spanish enclaves - Ceuta and Melilla - on the Northern coast of Morocco only served to emphasise the proximity. The North of Morocco was all coast, as was the West. In the East, it was bordered by Algeria and in the South, there was the Saharan Desert. Wasn't there some sort of war with the Saharans? There was no reference to any war in the encyclopaedia but then it had been published several years ago. I learned from it that Morocco had received its independence after more than forty years of colonisation by France and to a lesser extent Spain, and that King Hassan 11 had been made Head of State in 1961, four years after independence and that he had ruled ever since. There was also a slight hint that his reign was one of the old-style absolute monarchies.

I went to the next Amnesty meeting knowing a little more than before. I was given the Moroccan prisoner's case-sheet to study. From the scant details there, I learned that he had been born in Nador in Northern Morocco twenty years earlier. He was a member of a group of radical socialists called *Ilal Amam*, an organisation which had neither used nor advocated violence, which is why they fitted into the Amnesty mandate: its members had been rounded up solely for their political beliefs. One of the beliefs (and,

I was to learn later, the most damaging one) was that the Saharan people, now that they were no longer colonised by Spain, should be allowed to choose (through a referendum) whether to belong to Morocco (or to Mauritania, which at that time was also laying claim to the territory) or whether to be independent. It seemed a harmless enough belief for me.

There was no photo on the case-sheet and I tried to form a picture in my own mind of the fervent 20-year-old who had, it was alleged, been imprisoned and tortured solely for his beliefs. We had been instructed by Amnesty to write directly to the prisoner in French as if he were an old friend. On no account were we to mention Amnesty.

As soon as I got back from the meeting, I tried to write my first letter to Jamal. "My dear Jamal." My pen stopped. Whatever should I say? I stared at the blank sheet of paper in front of me. How can I write to someone I have so little knowledge about? My dear Jamal, mon cher Jamal. What do you say to someone in prison? You can't talk about your last great holiday or the price of beer. I read the case-sheet several times, hoping for inspiration. Moroccan, third world country. A radical socialist. OK, so nothing about my bourgeois lifestyle. The problems of two car families and fitted kitchens were not for the revolution, I felt. An Arab. Hmmm... probably someone with fixed ideas about the place of women in society, so nothing more than a few discreet allusions as to my position on feminist issues. How easy for the stereotypes to abound and reproduce in the absence of any clue about Jamal's personality.

Should I be formal or chatty? Whatever I told him about myself would surely make him depressed, when he compared my freedom to his miserable experience behind bars. So I shouldn't sound too bright and happy, but on the other hand, I wanted to cheer him up. It is, I was beginning to discover, difficult to write a letter to someone you don't know, especially given his situation and especially given that you are supposed to be his friend. Nor did I want to include anything which might annoy the authorities or arouse their suspicion. I began to feel almost like a spy.

I made many attempts at this first letter, so important to me. In the end, I settled for a short, non-informative letter. After all, my anguish was probably wasted. I didn't know if he would ever receive it.

19 May 1977
My Dear Jamal

I wonder how you are, what you are doing at this very moment. I am trying to picture you in my mind. I don't know if there is a smile on your face, but I would like to do what I can to put one there.

I would love to hear from you, share your thoughts and feelings and learn a little about your life. I won't write any more for the moment. I just want you to know I am thinking about you.
Joyce

I posted the letter to the prison address we were given and waited in eager anticipation for a reply. In the meantime, I studied the case-notes very thoroughly. Jamal had been sent for trial in Casablanca in February 1977. Amnesty and other human rights lawyers had been present at the hearing, which had apparently been a mockery of justice. I had read about it in the French newspaper *Le Monde*, had heard Amnesty's comments about it and got to know more details later.

Chapter 10

If I had but known, around this very time and many hundreds of miles away, Jamal was going through the trial ordeal in his mind and what had gone before it.

While he was in Derb Moulay Cherif, despite being blindfolded and handcuffed in secret detention for eight months, Jamal managed to keep track of time. It felt very important to him. He knew when night turned into day as the guards changed, and also he picked up pieces of their conversation with each other. To keep track of the days of the week, he set himself the following exercise: on Saturdays, he went to the theatre, that is to say he relived a whole play he had seen, in the minutest detail, as if he were seeing it again there and then. On Sundays, he 'read' a book. Monday night was movie night and so on.

Jamal was aware of his situation changing in August. Torture suddenly stopped, the prisoners' food rations increased and improved in quality, they had the luxury of taking one weekly shower - a cold one - and they were given their own clothes. They were obviously supposed to look as if they had just spent a few weeks at a holiday camp. Two weeks later, they were transferred to an ordinary prison. It must have felt strange for them coming out of that detention centre. Their faces had become very swollen through bad diet, no fresh air or exercise, their limbs so stiff, through lack of use and from the torture, that they could hardly walk, and with the blindfold suddenly removed after such a long time, even the weakest light seemed dazzling. But at least they had the hope that things were getting better - they couldn't, anyway, get much worse.

The order of Jamal's periods of detention was as follows: he was arrested in January 1976 in Rabat and kept there for a few days. Then he was taken to Tangiers where he was kept in secret detention until May 1976, when he was transported to Derb Moulay Cherif in Casablanca. He was incarcerated there until

September 1976, when he was transferred to an ordinary prison, also in Casablanca. Shortly after this he was brought before an examining judge (*juge d'instruction*) at the Criminal Court.

It was the job of this judge to question each of the 242 prisoners individually. He was a white-haired, bureaucratic-looking man in his fifties, who seemed less interested in finding out about any criminal activity than in examining Jamal's opinions. The dialogue went roughly like this:

Judge - "What are your views about the Western Sahara?"

Jamal - "It is none of my business whether the Saharans wish to become independent or to become Moroccan. What does concern me though, in principle, is that they should be given the right to choose on this important issue."

Judge - "Choose? What do you mean?"

Jamal - "I am in favour of a referendum organised by the United Nations, in which the Saharan people would have the right to express their own desires for their future. If they choose Morocco, then it will be on the basis of a democratic vote and should therefore be respected. But so far, they haven't even been consulted."

Judge - "Why did you do all this, create opposition and criticise the rulers of our wonderful country, belong to an unauthorised organisation, try and set up Unions and so on?"

Jamal - "When I was 14 years old, I worked an 18 hour day under terrible conditions and for miserable wages. This gave me a strong desire to fight for change. Morocco is corrupt, we want democracy. As to what I have 'done', it is that I have exercised my constitutional right to freedom of expression. I have not taken part in any criminal activity, no violence, nothing: no-one has even accused me of this."

Judge - "I don't understand you. Morocco is a lovely country, we have all the rights we could wish for, everyone is very happy here, we have a wonderful King, everything is fine. Why are you acting against our beloved ruler? Are you a Marxist?"

Jamal - "Is your definition of a Marxist someone who denounces social injustice, someone who would like to see change in a regime based on inequality?"

(The judge remained impassive).

Jamal - "Because in that case, most Moroccans are Marxists, even though they have never heard of Marx."

Judge - "Then you must be against the holy creed of Islam?"

Jamal - "I am certainly against the way it is used in this country by the King and his followers to exploit people's beliefs and fear of Allah to ensure continuity of their own dominance and oppression."

The judge looked resigned. He knew the whole thing was a futile exercise. Nothing he could do or write would make any difference to the future of these prisoners: this had already been decided by the very person he was defending. Jamal wondered what he actually *felt*, this judge. He was an educated man, obviously intelligent and, given the career he had chosen, one who must have some sense of justice. He must have known that the picture he had painted of Morocco, of a wonderful country where everyone went around in a permanent state of bliss, was false. Didn't he see the extreme poverty and complete lack of justice around him? Or had he been so conditioned to his role that his perception had become blurred?

This was the pre-trial. The trial itself, as I read about it in the French newspapers, and heard later in fine detail, was dramatic. The prisoners had to stage a hunger-strike in order to get a trial at all. This was at first ignored, but then events turned in favour of the prisoners. During the strike, the King had paid a state visit to France, where there had been a lot of publicity about the prisoners' situation.

Wherever the King went, he found many people -especially journalists - asking uncomfortable questions about them. Keeping 242 opponents of the regime first in secret detention and then in jail without trial, was somewhat incommensurate with the image His Majesty preferred to promote during his trips abroad: that of a democratic country with an impeccable legal system, worthy of partnership in the European Community. The Governor of Casablanca, along with the Minister of Justice, were hastily dispatched to the prison to negotiate with the group of prisoners striking on behalf of the 242 detainees. The immediate release of 103 of the prisoners plus a trial within a month were promised if the hunger-strikers called off their strike. It was a deal.

The trial started on 3 January 1977, 6 days before the first anniversary of Jamal's arrest. Every morning, a cavalcade of 10 van-loads of prisoners accompanied by 10 van-loads of police and at least a dozen motorbikes, screeched their way from the prison to the court, tyres and motors roaring and sirens wailing. The courtroom itself - a building about the size of a small concert-hall - swarmed with security guards holding cocked machine-guns. Present were also many policemen, both with and without uniform. It came as a shock to Jamal to see among these latter the faces of those who had tortured him.

Journalists were forbidden but foreign lawyers were let in. Families of the prisoners were allowed in theory; in practice, however, they were so hassled by police and security guards that many of them could not face attending. They knew, anyway, it would be a complete farce of a trial. Jamal's family had a friend in government who, before the trial had even begun, had told them that Jamal was one of the 'lucky' ones. He was 'only' going to get ten years.

The trial started with the prosecution reading out the names of the accused and the charges against them, before the judge and the six assistant judges. The charges ranged from that of setting up unauthorised organisations, to conspiracy, to threatening the internal security of the state. It took 2 whole hours just to present the names and charges.

Then began the long laborious task of questioning the accused one by one. Each person was asked his or her (there were 3 women among the accused) name and profession. A typical questioning went as follows:

Judge - "Are you a member of a subversive organisation? Answer yes or no."

Prisoner - "If you call subversive activity campaigning for democratic freedoms and better living conditions, then I could well be."

Judge - "Respond with yes or no!"

Prisoner - "I used my constitutional right to express my opposition to the current regime in a non-violent way."

Judge - "HAVE YOU UNDERSTOOD? Are you a member of a subversive organisation? You either are or you aren't. Yes or no!"

Prisoner - "I want this court to know that I have been kept in secret detention for a year, where I have been brutally tortured and ..."

Judge - "Silence! This is a Court of Law, not a political conference. You will answer the questions I put to you by responding yes or no! Now, were you arrested because of your adherence to a subversive organisation?"

Prisoner - "You should know the real *reasons for my arrest. They are ..."*

Judge - 'Take him down!'

One prisoner, Mustafa Waham, who had been driven insane by torture, was called upon to answer the charges against him. It hardly needed an expert to see that he was in no state to be questioned. When the defence lawyers protested, saying that he should be referred for medical treatment, the judge turned to the prisoner and said: "Are you mad?"

"No," answered the prisoner.

The judge turned back to the defence lawyers. "There, you see there's no problem", and continued to question the poor insane man mercilessly. As the judge put his questions, the prisoner's response was to sing, to speak of his love for football, and to recount a visit to the cinema in great detail.

The trial became a trial of the regime. The prisoners swung it to put despotism, oppression and human rights' violations on trial. Many prisoners took every opportunity to describe their terrible torture, baring parts of their abused bodies to the entire courtroom. The judge did, of course, try and put a stop to this but the united power of these young committed people, who saw this as their only chance of exposing the savagery of the treatment they had received, was overwhelming. Their vibrancy permeated every corner of the courtroom; it was as if the sheer force of their combined energy could burst the walls and force the roof off. The greatest show of energy had yet to come, however.

After a harrowing day of questioning and following a particularly callous observation made by the judge, one of the prisoners called out: "Fascist!"

There was a stunned silence. The police started, the guards stood up straight, the lawyers spun round, the entire attention of the public gallery was focused on the accused. The judge turned purple. "Who said that?"

The whole group of 139 prisoners jumped to their feet. "Fascist, fascist, fascist!"

The cries rocked the court. The lawyers panicked, the security guards leapt to attention, clicking and shaking their machine-guns, and the seven judges and prosecution got up and left the courtroom.

Almost as if on cue, the prisoners broke out into song and the courtroom became transformed into an arena of defiant enthusiasm. The revolutionary songs were given full throttle and soon the impromptu male voice choir was joined by a whole

62

orchestra of women in the public gallery who punctuated each line of the songs with high-pitched war cries. It was a moving spectacle and Jamal saw a guard standing near him actually begin to cry over his gun, the gun which a few moments earlier had been pointed at him so aggressively.

After about twenty minutes, the judges and prosecution returned. The judge held up a piece of paper and read:

"Following the incidents which we have witnessed in this courtroom, we have decided to punish all the accused with two years imprisonment, as well as the imposition of a fine of 5000 dirhams."

The judge sat down and the other judges and the prosecution looked well satisfied with themselves and the statement. The Chief of Police rose to his feet and approached a group of prisoners. "Well, we've had the *hors d'oeuvre*. Now let us continue with the main part of the trial."

The judge, remaining seated, peered over his desk at the accused and said: "Prisoners will not in future follow court proceedings but will be kept in the cells below the courtroom and brought up one by one, as and when they are needed."

The defence lawyers protested at this gross violation of the Moroccan legal system, but to no avail. The response of the prisoners to this turn of events was to stage a hunger-strike which lasted for 19 days. Their lawyers were then blamed for this and the Ministry of Information issued a press release stating that they had incited the prisoners to go on hunger-strike.

These brave lawyers actually had an unenviable task, and the violations of their rights as lawyers were many and frequent. They were not allowed access to their clients during the course of the trial and they were often ridiculed by the judge. On one occasion, one of them asked a prisoner: "Were you tortured while under arrest?"

Before he could answer, the judge's voice rang out. "That is a preposterous and highly provocative question. There is no such thing as torture in this country." He went on in a threatening tone: "Once this trial is over, you can be sure there will be a new one, where all you lawyers will be prosecuted."

He turned to the prosecution: "These lawyers are defending the prisoners because they share the same political views."

In the murmurings that followed, a mixture of indignation, incredulity and resignation could be felt emanating from the ranks of the defence. Then a senior lawyer stood up. "May it please this court to know that:

1) All lawyers have been sworn in.

2) We are part of the legal system and the whole court set-up.

3) Lawyers defend people regardless of their alleged crimes.

A defence lawyer is therefore not defending a view or justifying a crime, but is ensuring the right of each individual to a fair and balanced trial."

The defence had asked for medical examinations of some of the worst tortured prisoners and had also requested that the prisoners' statements to the police be disregarded as they were extracted under duress and most prisoners had been forced to sign them while blindfolded.

A strong wave of repression hit the lawyers. They were threatened and intimidated, had their phones tapped and some were put under house-arrest. Of the ones who remained, there were frequent threats to dismiss them from court. It all served to underline the farcical nature of the court proceedings.

The prisoners, still on hunger-strike, decided not to co-operate any longer with the trial, and as each one was called for questioning, he or she gave a statement. Jamal said the following: "I was arbitrarily arrested, put into secret detention for eight months and tortured, and I have since had some very heavy charges levelled against me. I deny them all, and from the way in which the court case has been conducted, it appears that my rights of defence have been removed. As I am not given the chance to explain myself, I do not wish to play your game any more. I would further add that

I am on hunger-strike in protest against this travesty of a trial."

The sentences which, as previously mentioned, were all pre-determined before the trial had even opened, were as follows:

Five of the accused got life sentences, twenty-one got 30 years, forty-four received 20, forty-five got 10 years, sixteen were sentenced to 5, and the rest got 5 years suspended. Thirty-nine of the accused, who had managed to escape arrest, all got life in absentia. All the prisoners were given the *hors d'oeuvre* sentence of two extra years on top of their original sentences. *Not a single one of the accused was acquitted.*

Chapter 11

It was a month after I had sent Jamal his first letter and I had not received a reply. I sent off another letter in similar vein. Again, no answer.

I started to write to him about once a month but I still didn't hear from him. I thought perhaps he had not been given the letters, and I imagined a massive dustbin placed either outside the prison or at the Interior Ministry, where all letters written to or about political prisoners were dropped. It also occurred to me that perhaps he did receive the letters but was unable to send a reply. It was a little discouraging to have all these letters met with total silence, yet I still felt highly motivated to continue writing, being convinced that somehow, a letter was going to get through in the end and I would receive a reply. I also began to feel a sense of loyalty towards this unknown individual who had met with such an awful fate merely for trying to express his opinions, a right which I took completely for granted, and I felt a bond with him which compelled me to go on writing. *There was no way I could let him down.*

I would write short, non-controversial type letters, just asking how he was, lamenting the fact that I hadn't heard from him recently, asking if there was anything I could do for him and saying that I was thinking of him. I also made sure that my name and address figured prominently on the letter. I never mentioned Amnesty - we were told that Morocco was very sensitive to Amnesty pressure - I was merely writing to a friend.

I was also writing - using the name and address of another group member - to the Moroccan Ambassador, Interior Minister, Minister of Justice, Prison Director and King Hassan himself. These letters were sent in Amnesty's name. They were meticulously polite letters - if edged with a certain irony - showing a respect which, with my knowledge of the repressive Moroccan regime, I certainly did not feel. I wrote to the King expressing my concern at how the existence of prisoners of conscience was tarnishing the reputation of so great a country. I explained that we would do our bit trying to restore the shattered faith in Morocco, but hinted that His Majesty would also have to pull his finger out, as we needed all the help we could get. My letters remained unanswered. I had marginally greater success with the Moroccan Ambassador to the Scandinavian countries who, after my third letter, sent back the standard reply that there were no political prisoners in the Kingdom of Morocco. The prisoner I had mentioned had committed an offence and, as in any country, those who violated the law could expect to be punished. I became so taken up with the fate of this unknown Moroccan that I joined an Amnesty co-ordination group specialising on Morocco, acting as a link between Amnesty's International Secretariat in London (where all the research takes place) and the groups in Scandinavia with adopted Moroccan prisoners.

Working on Morocco was an eye-opener for me. Before I got involved, I knew virtually nothing about the country except for a few stereotypes. Insofar as I had thought of it at all, I imagined it as some sort of liberal democracy set in Exotica. Tangiers conjured up visions of belly-dancing in crowded taverns; Casablanca symbolised *La Dolce Vita* as immortalised by Humphrey Bogart; Meknes and Fez breathed of tradition and folklore: magical sounding names, all of them. The magic vanished along with my illusions as the veil was slowly lifted and I began to get a glimpse beyond the thousand and one nights facade. Tangiers became for me the town of one of the most savage police squads in the country, well-known for its sadistic torturing of not only political prisoners but their families as well; Casablanca became associated with the notorious secret detention centre, Derb Moulay Cherif, where political prisoners were kept for months on end, handcuffed, blindfolded, frozen stiff in an underground cave and periodically tortured. (It is also one of the many towns in Morocco where there is widespread child slave labour). Meknes became the place of the 100 detainees who were refused trial. The map of Morocco was changing rapidly before my very eyes.

I wrote to Jamal month after month. I knew little about him, I couldn't even be sure he existed. I heard nothing from him. I felt not so much discouraged as sad and worried that there was never a letter from Morocco in the mail. Since the trial, there seemed to be complete silence about Morocco, almost as if the trail had stopped there. How could I get in touch with Jamal? It occupied my mind a great deal. To keep up my hopes of a reply, I explored other avenues of contacting him: using different writing, typing, different size and colour envelopes, borrowing a name and address from a friend. I sent letters, greeting cards, picture postcards, registered letters, small parcels and even telegrams. I so desperately wanted him to know I existed and cared for him.

In the meantime, I had struck up a fairly close if ambivalent friendship with Simon, an Englishman whom I had first met at University in Gothenburg and who had now, like me, come to live in Stockholm. Simon was on the way to becoming a successful banker. He was a self-styled, self-assured pragmatist and not at all the sort of person I would have been interested in getting to know if we had met in England. We had nothing in common - I don't believe we shared a single value judgement. However, there was something so essentially English about him that it drew me to him. Perhaps also, I needed him as a sort of adversary.

Simon was a bit on the plump side, with carefully-groomed blond hair cut closely to his scalp. He had a round baby-like face half-hidden behind an enormous pair of circular frameless spectacles. He became a regular visitor to our household. He liked Axel; Axel tolerated him, understanding how important it was for me to have a piece of England around. Simon and I had many arguments which underlined our incompatibility. I spoke to him about Amnesty and the Moroccan prisoner. He was not too happy that someone else was taking up my time and sympathy. He voiced his scepticism. "Sounds like a waste of time if he's not getting the letters."

"He may well be getting them," I retorted on the defensive, "but perhaps he's not able to answer. For one thing, he may have no access to pen and paper. For another thing, I've heard of prisoners only being allowed to write one letter every six months. If this was the case, he would obviously want to write and reassure his family rather than waste his precious biannual letter on some unknown woman in Sweden."

I got up to draw the curtains. It was November and getting dark, even though it was not yet 3 o'clock in the afternoon. The enormous living-room with its parquet flooring and the fireplace we had had installed to be a bit more reminiscent of England, became silent. The pine-trees surrounding our redbrick house looked dignified and serene in the falling darkness.

"This Amnesty business," continued Simon, evidently wishing to make a point, "I knew an Amnesty woman who wrote to some guy in Venezuela. Never got a reply. In the end, she just packed it in. Found out later chappie had died in prison. Complete waste of time."

"That's the logic of the hangman," I said contemptuously. "What you're saying makes me all the more determined not to give up. Perhaps the prisoner wouldn't have died if your friend had continued writing, who knows? Each letter - whether the prisoner gets to see it or not - is proof to the authorities that the case is not unknown and that someone more than 2000 miles away cares enough to go on writing in spite of the lack of response." I looked at him sharply. "Surely you can see that you play straight into the hands of the authorities if they see their repressive tactics have a silencing effect on the outside world."

Simon sat stolidly in his chair, beer-glass in hand, his fairly ample frame exuding well-being. I desperately wanted to move him, wanted him to experience some of my passion. "My God, Simon, imagine being a forgotten prisoner of conscience! Can you think of many fates which are worse? Imagine trying to do your bit for humankind and then suffering torture and long-term

70

imprisonment for it, only to find that at the end of the day, not only have your efforts gone unnoticed and unappreciated, but no-one cares whether you live or die."

Simon tried to calm me down. He took my hand and said in a softer tone: "Joyce, you get far too het up about things which have nothing to do with you, things which you can't possibly influence. It's something I find very irritating about you. Once you get a bee in your bonnet, there's no stopping you. Why on earth you get so worked up just for one person, beats me. There are thousands upon thousands of - what's his name? - Jamals all over the world. All this time and energy spent on just one person, it's absurd. Even if you do get him freed, it's only one person..."

I snatched my hand away. "That's the last straw!" I cried passionately, scarcely aware that I was confirming his opinion of me. "*Only* one person! You are intolerable! If ever I was told that my efforts had saved just one single human being from torture and imprisonment, or even helped to do so, I'd be proud and happy and wouldn't feel that I had lived my life in vain!"

"Well, you'd never know, would you?" persisted Simon. "Chap gets banged up, chap gets released - how would you know it was *your* efforts which saved him?"

"I wouldn't," I replied, deliberately turning my gaze away from him and towards to the piano in the far corner of the room and Axel's cello and bow laid out on the floor. Then, turning back to Simon, I looked him full in the face and said stubbornly: "And I wouldn't care, either. I'm not looking for the Nobel Peace prize. For me, it's a matter of principle," I continued angrily and then, trying to provoke him, I added "But that is nothing you would understand."

"Oh, wouldn't I just," sneered Simon. "And what principles do you think you're talking about?"

Although I felt by this time that Amnesty would probably have to look elsewhere for future recruits, I nevertheless continued: "I believe that we each of us have it in us to get involved in the

71

injustice we see around us, even if only to stick one stamp a month on to a card demanding the release of a prisoner of conscience in the Soviet Union. It's not just that we can do this, I'd say we had a *duty* to, especially we who enjoy a comfortable life in a democratic country." I looked at Simon appealingly. "It's not even all that much time and effort. I could do much more." Simon remained impassive. I couldn't stop myself from adding: "And so could you, for that matter. Not that doing more would be so difficult in your case, mind you."

Now I had at last succeeded in making Simon irritated. He said testily: "Look, if I wanted to jump on my white charger and relieve my conscience by doing my bit for the world, I certainly wouldn't join Amnesty."

"Why not?"

"Well, for a start, Amnesty is against the death penalty."

"So what?"

"So how would you feel if your own mother was murdered, her murderer spent some time in jail and he was then freed?"

I stared at him. "Do you know, Simon, I can feel you appealing to my emotions rather than my reason, on an important intellectual issue. I must say, that's rich coming from you! You're always the first one to chastise me for my emotional reactions."

"You haven't answered my question."

"OK, well if you want my answer, here it is: I'm against the death penalty for *anyone*, and that would include - let me have it said now, please - even the person responsible for my own murder which, by the expression on your face, looks as if it's not going to be that far off."

Simon looked incredulous. "Bloody Hell, Joyce, you mean you would want a murderer let off virtually scot free?"

"Of course not. No convicted murderer gets off scot free. For one thing, they have to live with what they have done for the rest of their lives. They have their freedom taken away for many years at the very least and they are shunned by the rest of society."

"Yes, but..."

"Why would you want a murderer murdered, too? Not for pure revenge, surely, I would hope we had come farther than that?"

"No-o-o," said Simon a bit uncertainly. "It's a deterrent."

"It isn't!" I almost shouted at him. "Many murders are done on the spur of the moment from sheer uncontrollable rage or frustration. The person who kills is not deterred while in this frame of mind. Murderers killing in cold blood, usually for money, will reckon on not being found out. Therefore a death penalty won't deter them either."

"Well, I'm not so sure about that..." Simon began slowly.

Heartened by the slight doubt creeping into his voice, I carried on: "And what about the mistakes made? Innocent people hanged and the real murderer discovered later? This is one of the ugliest sides of the death penalty - it's irrevocable. Or let me use your reasoning: how would you feel if your own mother were executed for a murder which someone else later confessed to?"

"States have to show their abhorrence of murder," pursued Simon, refusing to be provoked by my last question. "They have to give the ultimate punishment for the worst of all crimes."

"No, Simon." I felt calmer now, more in control of the argument. "Murder is a horrific deed, I quite agree with you. It is the most appalling act to take away the life of someone. But it is just as appalling whether it is perpetrated by an individual, a group or the State. The State should set an example. When they kill, it is a premeditated act carried out in cold blood. How can State officials tell their citizens that such acts are unacceptable when they are carrying them out themselves?"

Axel came in at this point and entered into the discussion. He shared my views on this issue so Simon found himself outnumbered. I let the two of them carry on the argument, feeling gratified in hearing my own views endorsed and Simon's arguments becoming weakened even further by this second onslaught. Later on, when we were alone, Axel expressed mild surprise at my choice of such a friend whose ideas seemed so much at odds with my own, someone who really only came to life when the Annual trade figures were released or when Tottenham Hotspurs had given Everton their just desserts.

"It's one of life's mysteries," I grinned. "Simon is by no means stupid but I can set myself against what I consider to be his blinkered views, feeling my own views growing stronger as I do so. The discussion stagnates when you have no basic difference of views, there's no challenge. Actually, I think that is one thing I find difficult in this country. People tend to have the same views about things."

"Oh, come on," retorted Axel, "The gap between the views of someone in the Conservative Party and the Communist Party, which do, after all, share 7% of the vote, is pretty large."

"These are extremes," I replied. "Everybody I know reads the biggest newspaper *Dagens Nyheter* and one of the two daily evening papers, which although they are supposed to represent the views of different political parties, are in fact much of a muchness and their views are the ones I hear everywhere. I feel that in England, there is a much wider divergence of views among ordinary people, that there are many more eccentrics there and eccentricity is smiled at rather than frowned upon."

I was back again on my favourite theme about how much more interesting/stimulating/preferable my own country was than the one I happened to be living in. I was aware of how boring this topic must have become to Axel, and how powerless he felt to change the situation. I was also aware of how unfair such arguments were, especially considering the family I had married into. Axel's father and mother treated me like a daughter. We saw a lot of them, often at my instigation, because it was so pleasant being in their house. There was never a lack of stimulating discussion. I remember the long 'evening tea' sessions or the Sunday morning brunches we would share with some or occasionally all of Axel's siblings. Important topics were frequently discussed and each person's view was respected, even if not supported. I was impressed with how Axel and the others could shout down their mother or father, who would give as good as they got. They never shrank from criticism, indeed they welcomed it as being part of a lively and open communication system between the family members. As well as serious and informed discussion on a whole range of topics - nothing was taboo - there was also a lot of laughter and love in that household. And the radiance and confidence inspired by the parents was only too apparent in the warmth and stable personalities of their children.

Chapter 12

In stark contrast to these memories of happy family gatherings, Jamal was reflecting on other memories covering one of the most desperate periods of his prison existence. He was being questioned by his invisible interviewer, Little Ben, but it was a slow process because the scenes had been so painful that he often had to stop to recover.

"Where did you go after the trial, Jamal?"

"We were taken back to Casablanca Prison, where we were subjected to the most appalling conditions and treatment, locked up, three or four together in a cell made for one, for 24 hours a day. After about a month of this crowded monotonous existence, one of the prisoners was driven to protest, and he began banging on his cell door, shouting that he needed some fresh air and exercise. Some of the other prisoners followed suit, and soon the sound of banging reverberated around the entire quadrangle of cells. We all banged forcefully and elatedly, delighting in the solidarity but bracing ourselves for what would certainly happen soon. Sure enough, in next to no time, at least 30 guards appeared together with the Prison Director, a small, fat grey-haired man with gold-rimmed spectacles, accompanied by, of all things, a small white poodle looking highly incongruous in the austerity of the prison milieu. The prison cells, which formed a square around the prison yard, had small peepholes in each door so that what was happening in the yard was visible to each and every prisoner."

"What did you see?"

"It was no pretty sight. The guards barged into the cells, dragged out each prisoner individually, threw him (there were only men in this prison) into the centre of the yard and then set upon him. Each prisoner was kicked, beaten and whipped by all 30 guards at the same time, with the Director jumping up and down, shouting encouragement: 'More! Harder! Give it to him! Let the

77

bastard have it!' and the poodle joining in the excitement by straining at the lead and punctuating the performance with shrill yaps. There was a particularly awful moment when one prisoner was hurled head first at the stone wall. I will never forget the sound of that crack - I was sure that his head must have been shattered to pieces. As the guards drew nearer and nearer my cell, the four of us in there had a hurried whispered conference among ourselves about how we should react:

'We must cover our heads.'

'We must try not to fall on the floor, which would make it easier for them to beat us.'

'However much we are hurt, we will not utter a single sound.'

"After what seemed like an eternity, we were dragged out of our cells like the others and given a thorough beating. The guards appeared to be playing football, using each prisoner as the ball, which was then lobbied from one to the other around the circle of attackers, with a violent kick or punch propelling us to the other guards. The attacks continued until every prisoner was dazed and wounded. We were then dragged back into our cells and thrown together in a heap, hardly knowing whether we were dead or alive."

"Was this the end of the punishment?"

"We thought so at the time because a few days passed when nothing further happened to break the monotony of our existence. Then suddenly one day we were dragged out of our cells and taken to a sort of hall within the prison. There, each of us had his head completely shaved, we were all blindfolded and handcuffed and then taken out to the front of the prison, where we were loaded on to vans like cattle. Our destination this time was Kenitra Prison, the most feared prison in the country, the highest security prison, intended for the most hardened common-law prisoners serving more than 20 years. Upon arrival, we were strip-searched and then taken out into the prison yard to be confronted with one another. This was a terrible shock for us all. Imagine, we could barely recognise each other! Everyone looked so different, with shaved heads, pale faces, swollen limbs and bruised bodies. We were so dazed we could hardly summon up the courage to speak to one another."

"Why this confrontation?"

"It was to demoralise us, to show us who held the power, to show how all protests would be dealt with. We tried to adapt to our new situation and keep our spirits up to show that we were not affected by this abuse, but the conditions were appalling. We were kept isolated in our cells which were cold and dank. The food was unspeakable, and our only exercise was to be frog-marched around the prison-yard for about half-an-hour in complete silence. It was almost literally a dog's life: nothing to do except wait for the master to bestow food and walks upon us. Books, papers and magazines were strictly forbidden. There was no medical treatment despite the urgent need for it. We were now allowed visits from the family but these were confined to 15 minutes a week in terrible circumstances. There was only one possible response to this, the use of the only weapon we had at our disposal: a hunger-strike. This time, we were fully prepared to strike until death.

"The strike began on 8 December 1977. For the first three days, I felt very hungry. Then my body began to adapt to the new situation and started drawing from its reserves. The long period of waiting had begun. The cells had been stripped of everything except for a couple of blankets. All there was to do during each long day was to wait and wait and wait..."

"Did you have in mind what you were waiting for?"

"What were we waiting for? A softening of heart from Despot Hassan? Impossible. Death? Unthinkable. Pressure of public opinion? But what public opinion and where? There was not much to be expected coming from Morocco. Take the political parties, for instance. The whole of the political élite, which included the pro-monarchist as well as the Socialist and Communist parties, was completely unanimous in its support of the big contentious issue: compulsory annexation of the Western Sahara. (The position of myself and most of my colleagues was that Saharans should have a referendum to decide their own future.) The question of the Sahara was by far the most important political issue of the day. The main Socialist party (USFP) took a strong stand against the prisoners. Some USFP lawyers had actually agreed to defend us at the time, but then pressure from the leadership had caused most of them to withdraw."

"What about the Communist Party?"

"Oh, them! They went even further. It is interesting to note the background of their support for the annexation of the Sahara. During the struggle for liberation from French colonial rule which came to a head in the 1950s, the CP had actually been against independence from France. Their position then was that Moroccan workers should join forces with French socialist workers to create a united socialist France. This anti-nationalist stand, coming when it did, caused them a lot of trouble with ordinary Moroccan people longing for independence from the oppressive colonialists and they therefore lost a lot of support. So they were now anxious to prove what fervent nationalists they really were and by siding with the majority in favour of a Moroccan Sahara, here was their Heaven-sent opportunity. Not only did they denounce our position on the Western Sahara, but they also declared that we should be tried for high treason, a crime which carried the death penalty! So much for the caring Communists."

"The ordinary people, then?"

"They were much too repressed to dare consider speaking up in our favour. The only support we got, therefore, was from our own families, who made a brave attempt to confront and to demonstrate, often getting arrested in the process. Parents became particularly militant, especially the women. Take for instance the mother of Zaza, a life sentence prisoner who for some reason was singled out more than the others for brutal attacks. In response to the horrific treatment of her son, Zaza's mother found her political wings at the age of 80, when she joined vociferously in the protest actions, lobbying, bullying, demonstrating, rallying and campaigning.

These often elderly ladies were a constant source of discomfort to the police, a body of men who had not the slightest doubts or qualms when it came to meting out suitable treatment to these women's sons when they spoke out of turn. But what were they to do when an army of angry women past retirement age descended upon them, waving their arms together with a variety of missiles, shouting out their demands as well as what they would like to do with the police and the whole regime if they ever got their hands on them? Old women are treated with a lot of respect in Morocco and the police were at a complete loss as to what to do in the face of their threats and exhortations. They demonstrated, toured the offices of local newspapers, urging them to publicise the plight of their loved ones, and even occupied government buildings until the police arrived to remove them. The families suffered terribly all the time but never more so than during the hunger-strike when death was truly on the cards. Also, how could they sit down and enjoy a good healthy meal knowing that their sons or brothers were starving to death?"

"Tell me about the strike itself, Jamal."

"After the first few days I began to feel extremely tired, but sleep did not come easily. When I did manage to sleep, I had the most vivid dreams about sex. The dreams became a sort of substitute for my need of food, it was almost as if I were being fed from the dreams. It was December and very cold everywhere, but nowhere as much as in prison, where the cold penetrated our starving bodies mercilessly. During the day, we talked incessantly about what had become our favourite and sole topic: food. We were by this time allowed to talk to each other during the exercise period and all we could talk about was food. I often found myself to be the centre of attention, as I had worked in many a luxurious restaurant and knew a lot about a variety of dishes. One current favourite was an unusual dish called *omelette norvégienne*, and a typical conversation was the following:

'Jamal, tell us again how to make *omelette norvégienne*.'

'Well, you take a wafer and spread 2 dollops of ice-cream over it.'

'Only 2 dollops? What sort of ice-cream? Vanilla? Coffee? Strawberry? (Sigh) Chocolate?!'

'Any ice-cream. Then you cover it with meringue and put it in a hot oven very briefly so that the top sets but the bottom remains soft.'

'Do you serve it up like that?'

'No, you pour cognac or liqueur over it and then set light to it.'

"Every day, I would be asked with almost boring regularity to repeat some of the details. How do you make the meringue? How big is the wafer? What is the best ice-cream to use? What sort of cognac? What sort of liqueur? Describe the taste!"

"How did your body feel?"

"Well, on the tenth day of the hunger-strike, a slight dizziness set in, and exercising in the yard was already becoming a bit of a struggle. My head felt so light in contrast with my legs, which felt so heavy. My whole sense of equilibrium was vanishing."

"What was the authorities' response to the strike?"

"For about twenty whole days, it was met with complete silence. Then we were approached and told that if we would give up the strike, negotiations could start with us. Our response was that we would accept nothing less than a promise to meet our demands in full before there was any talk of stopping the strike. Our main demands were as follows:

Medical treatment.
Edible food.
Longer family visits.
Civilised visiting conditions.
The three women (plus another prisoner: Abraham Serfaty) who were still in Casablanca Prison to be moved to Kenitra Prison and the women to be allowed conjugal visits with

82

their husbands also in jail.

End of censorship of all books, magazines and newspapers.

The right to have a radio.

The right to take University exams from prison.

"What was the authorities response to your refusal to call off the strike?"

"They tried to force-feed us through the nose. The massive resistance to this from all the prisoners in spite of our weakened condition, was enough to make the authorities give up the idea. The battle continued. It was long and wearisome. I began to think obsessively about the amazing times when I had actually refused food, can you imagine! And those times when I had left food on my plate! What about when I had - unbelievably - even *disliked* certain foods and when I had - even harder to visualise - actually skipped a whole meal. What crimes these now appeared to be! Now as I lay in my tiny cell, exhausted and staring up at the ceiling, I felt as if I were in a living grave. A secret dread I had harboured in the past of being buried alive, enveloped me and the panic made me weaker than ever. It was a damp, cold grave, exactly as one could imagine. I felt death surrounding me - not an impassive cold finger of death but rather a Dark Heavy Boot grinding me down slowly and irrevocably. I felt oh so horribly alone. Was this what it would be like to die? Panic rose again. I didn't want to die, I wanted to live, I was 20 years old, I hadn't even seen life yet, I wanted to live, live, LIVE... It was deathly silent in the prison, a silence broken occasionally by the noise of rats, who were as much affected by the hunger-strike as we were ourselves. As there was nothing going down into the sewers, the rats - their aggression growing alongside their hunger - were coming up to the surface to look for food. They were also on hunger-strike, but theirs was not self-imposed. I felt that rats were at this stage almost to be envied - they had no dictates of conscience, they lived the most basic of lives in the sewers - not to everyone's taste, of course, but if you were a rat, you didn't know any better."

"What did you actually do? Did you sleep most of the time?"

"Some of the time, but by the 30th day of the strike, it was no longer possible, in spite of my enormous desire for sleep, especially when there was nothing else to do. On the 36th day, I collapsed. A male nurse was called (a particularly nasty character whom we had nicknamed *The Vet* as an allusion to the way in which he treated us) and he took me to the prison sanatorium. My blood pressure was by now at a dangerously low level and I was then taken to a local hospital in Kenitra, where there was already a sizeable number of the prisoners. There, I was put in a dormitory with 9 others, heavily guarded by the police. It was like a morgue. Of the 9 other prisoners, one never ever spoke or even moved and I actually wondered if he could be dead. Another had become mentally disturbed by seeing everything double, and two others kept vomiting all the time, but with nothing to bring up. On the 38th day, a policeman who had previously let it be known to us that, in spite of his profession, he was sympathetic to our cause and plight, came into the room and secretly gave me a piece of information: 'Saida Menebhi has died.' Oh, what a terrible shock! Saida, a young woman teacher, Saida with all her intelligence and commitment, Saida the wife of one of our colleagues. Even though we had, of course, reckoned on the possibility of a death, now that it had happened and had happened to Saida, it was too gruesome to think about. Everyone was stunned. Everyone felt completely helpless, despondent, demoralised.

"Now I saw Death approaching very clearly, it was no longer anonymous, it had a name and a shape and was tightening its hold on me, it was coming to get me! I was in great conflict. 'Am I going to meet it or retreat?' It became a personal challenge - my integrity versus my capitulation. The conflict deepened with the news of Saida's death, and the thoughts rushed to compete with each other:

84

Should we give up, before any more lives are lost?

No, they will have to act quickly now that Saida has died.

Saida's death will have been in vain if we give up now.

We can't stop after paying so high a price.

We've got to see that our suffering has not been for nothing.

"And so it continued. On the 42nd day, I completely lost the use of both legs. It was interesting to see how some parts of the body survived, while other parts collapsed. My eyes were badly affected, my limbs became quite useless, my chest was just painful. However, my mind remained lively - even energetic - and my sense of smell during starvation also remained strong. The functioning of my ears became much more acute, in direct contrast to that of my eyes. It was indeed my ears which sent the message to my still lively mind that, on the 45th day, things seemed to be happening. Cars drew up and many voices were all speaking at once. Lots of officials were pouring into the hospital, including the hated Prison Director. They came into the room where I lay, barely conscious. I saw them through a haze, a crowd of bodies all melted into one another, a conglomerate mass."

"You must have started to hope, at this stage."

"Oh, I can't describe the feeling! But I know the moment when I had the first glimmer of hope that our long ordeal might soon be over! This was when one of the prisoners, half-dying but apparently still with some fighting spirit left, shook a bony finger in the direction of the Prison Governor and croaked to the other officials: 'If you want to negotiate with us, you will first have to remove that... that animal.' To the amazement of everyone present, a senior official told the Governor to go, and he left the room. It seemed that they must be desperate. The officials lost no time. We were told: 'All your demands will be met, except that we will have to reconsider the right for you to have a radio and daily newspapers.' Oh, the relief, the utter relief, yet all we could do was to lie there like mummies, our bodies weighted down like lead but our souls soaring high."

"Did you stop the strike as soon as you heard this? You believed them?"

"Yes, the strike was stopped immediately. The weaning back on to food was a long and often painful process, especially for our stomachs, which couldn't accept anything after having adapted to nothing. I was surprised at how the seemingly tough and strong among us had been the first to crack up and were now the last to recover, while some of the small seedy ones appeared to have the greatest resistance. Right after the hunger-strike, we were given the drip, and then some sort of milk and later on some soup before going on to solid foods, just like babies."

"Were you sent back to prison immediately?"

"No, we remained in hospital for about 6 weeks. After that, when the authorities appeared to be dragging their feet in implementing their side of the bargain, we were forced to go on hunger-strike again, this time for 17 days. Then they finally gave in and conditions improved dramatically. So our fight had not been in vain, but the price had been devastatingly high and it was an experience I hoped never to have to repeat."

Chapter 13

For one-and-a-half years, I wrote regularly to Jamal. I knew practically nothing about him, I still couldn't even be sure that he existed. The scant details I had to work on included the fact that he was a student who had been arrested when he was 19 years old and was given a sentence of 12 years for allegedly plotting against the State. Up to now, I hadn't heard a thing from him. What an exciting change was about to happen!.

In the Spring of 1979, I attended an Amnesty meeting in Brussels. As usual, whenever I was away somewhere, I sent Jamal a postcard. This one, short and banal and written in pencil, read as follows:

"20-5-79

I am in Brussels at a conference for a few days. I've found some really nice people here, the hospitality is quite superb. I came by train from Stockholm with a friend. It took 24 hours. A small flat has been put at our disposal. Unfortunately, I will have to leave tomorrow to get back to work by Monday. I'm thinking of you –

Joyce. "

Jamal, as he wrote later, was in the prison yard when the card arrived. A little window from the administrator's office overlooked the yard and at 3 o'clock every day, this window was opened and the prison censor stood there, delivering the mail.

It was the highlight of the day for the prisoners. Between 2 and 3 o'clock, many of them would suddenly appear in the yard, pretending to be engrossed in some small task and completely uninterested in and oblivious of the window. The minute the first window-opening noise was heard, however, a massive crowd appeared as if from nowhere, clamouring for their post. Contact with the outside world took on completely different dimensions for these prisoners than for other people.

This was, in fact, Jamal's first contact with anyone outside Morocco since his arrest three-and-a-half years earlier. He sat down in the yard in the hot sunshine and read the contents over and over again, looking intently at the photo. It was of La Grande Place in Brussels lit up at night and showing all the promise of a night-life he could only dream about.

After a while, a friend who hadn't received any mail came over to share the card with him. They read it aloud to each other and speculated on the identity of 'Joyce'. The only Joyce these prisoners had ever heard of was James Joyce, therefore they assumed it must be from a man.

When Jamal had to return to his cell for the evening, he sensed that something new was about to happen. He had in the past been through the most dramatic events of his prison life with his imaginary friend, 'Little Ben'. Since he had last spoken to 'Ben' about the hunger-strike, there had been great improvements in the situation of the prisoners. They were now allowed out of their cells and into the prison yard from 9 in the morning until 6 in the evening. They were also allowed to mix freely with each other. The all-important family visits were now possible four times a week, morning and afternoon and in relaxed conditions. Medical treatment was provided. There were no longer any restrictions on reading material and prisoners were now permitted to take University exams from prison. The changes were quite dramatic. It was the hunger-strike which had been mainly responsible for this - the courage and determination of the prisoners had paid off - along with constant pressure from Amnesty. The price had been high but the prisoners and their families were now reaping the benefit. This did nothing to alter the fact that they had all been unjustly imprisoned, that here was the cream of Moroccan youth incarcerated in dank prison cells, that families had been split up and left fatherless and that physical and psychological torture wounds could not be healed by the occasional visit to hospital. But at least the day to day existence of the prisoners was now bearable.

In spite of the lessening isolation, Jamal still felt in need of confiding in a true friend, so now and then he turned to 'Little Ben' to share what was going on in his life.

"What's that you've got in your hand, Jamal?" Little Ben was curious.

"It's a card from someone called Joyce."

"Who is Joyce?"

"I don't know. At first, I thought it was a man but I have since tried to analyse the contents of the card and now I think it's a woman."

"What else has the analysis suggested to you?"

"The card is written in French and sent from Belgium but I don't think the writer is French or Belgian. Stockholm is mentioned but somehow, I'm not convinced that Joyce is Swedish, I don't know why. There is something about a meeting. My hunch is that this could be a meeting of Amnesty International and that the writer is a member of that organisation."

"You know about Amnesty?"

"Yes, I heard about it before my arrest. In fact, I contacted them when a close friend who was politically involved had disappeared. As I did so, the thought struck me that perhaps one day I might be needing help from them and that someone would do the same for me."

"What does it feel like to have received this message from an unknown person in a far-off country?"

"I feel elated! It shows me that I have not been forgotten, that someone out there knows about me and wants to express solidarity and make sure I will not be forgotten in the future. This is a very important day for me."

"Will you answer the letter?"

"Unfortunately, there's no address on this card. But I'm confident Joyce will write again giving an address and then I will answer immediately! I'll give her an address to send letters to, so they won't be soiled by the hand of the prison censor."

"How will you manage to do that when every outgoing letter is censored?"

"That is easy. I can get my letters smuggled out of prison in all sorts of ways, just as I can get letters smuggled into me here. The censor will remain in complete ignorance and Joyce and I will enjoy complete freedom of correspondence!"

A month or so after this, returning from holiday, I found a letter with a Moroccan stamp and postmark. It was a clean-looking airmail envelope with my name and address all spelt correctly, written in stylish handwriting. I had an intense feeling which made me quite dizzy with excitement that it had to do with Jamal, although I didn't for one minute imagine that it could actually be from him: I had been writing to him for so long now without ever getting a reply and there was nothing in the current state of events in Morocco to make me believe that he was in a position to be sending me a letter by ordinary post. Although I retained a small hope that it was some direct communication from him, to anticipate any disappointment I told myself it could be from a friend or his family. Even this, however, after such a long period of silence, would be wonderful. Wishing to savour this moment for as long as possible, while still almost dying with curiosity, I shook the envelope gently but it did not appear to contain anything other than paper. I stared at the address once more and then, with trembling hands, ripped open the envelope.

My heart leapt when I saw the signature at the bottom: "Jamal". It was a short and polite letter, thanking me for my interest and the little parcel I had sent containing some gifts along with my name and address. Jamal had also given me an address for my letters avoiding the prison censor to ensure that we could correspond *librement*. I read this fairly banal but oh! so exciting letter over and over again, trying to read into every word, every sentence what sort of person my correspondent was and under what sort of conditions the letter had been written and I fell into a kind of reverie. When I had recovered, I immediately seized a pen and paper, wrote him a letter back and rushed out to catch the post. A few weeks later, I received a reply from him, and thus the correspondence was underway. I asked him to send me a detailed account of what a day in prison was like for him which he did, giving me my first inkling of what it was really like to live in such a restricted environment.

"Prison Centrale de Kenitra   25-2-80
Dear friend

I was delighted to receive your letter recently, it helped me to get to know you a little better, especially reading of your opinions about a whole range of subjects (sport, the situation in Afghanistan...) I hope that you spent a good week's holiday in Finland. I have been thinking that it was very nice of you to tell me a little about these things, I know very well that you don't talk about your own life to just anyone!

"In this letter, I will try and describe a little about my life here in prison. We get up in the morning at 8 o'clock, awakened by the unbearable noise made by the guards opening the bars and locks of the cells. We leave our sleep to confront yet another day with its customary monotony.

"At 8.30. it's time for breakfast, composed solely of bread and boiling water. Before, we used to get a bitter sort of tea, which no-one could drink, so we asked if this could be replaced so that we could make something of our own. After this, we are allowed to go into the prison yard. Usually, we are in a hurry to get there - at least there we can breathe in a bit of fresh and natural air and forget the musty odours caused by the lack of ventilation in the cells.

"Our block consists of about a hundred single cells. It is the worst block, which is why it is known as 'the discipline block'. It was built in the 30s, during the French colonial rule,

being made specifically for the nationalists and those serving a sentence of hard labour. Now this has been inherited by the young, leftish 'militants'. In the prison, there is also a block for other political prisoners, the 'C' block. Here, you find 80 militants from the USFP, arrested during the bloody events of March 1973. It is easy to see that the social and intellectual life of our comrades in 'C' block is completely different from the atmosphere in our group. With us, the average age is between 25 and 28, most of us are students, teachers and engineers, whereas with them, the average age is much higher, most of them are more than 40, and they are mainly peasants who refused to accept a monarchy after independence in 1956.

"We can meet these prisoners only on public holidays. It's something I always look forward to - we can learn a lot from these people, especially from their invaluable political experience during the resistance, and after independence in the nationalist and progressive parties, even if many of them are illiterate. They are much simpler and less 'artificial' than my colleagues here, who are all 'intellectuals'.

"I should tell you that our group has started up 2 magazines: 'Le Gentil' which, as its name indicates, contains jokes and caricatures about different aspects of our life here in prison; the second one is called La Cour *(The Yard), of a more serious nature with literature, history, economy etc. I read it but I do not take part in it in any way. I prefer to write for a wider audience. I recently wrote an article of 20-odd pages, which took a good deal of time and effort. It was a criticism from an opposition point of view about political action in Morocco. I found it difficult to get published. It was impossible in this country because of censorship, but I am still awaiting a reply from an Arab magazine abroad, which I have approached. Obviously, neither the prison management nor most of my colleagues know about it. The walls, the bars and all sorts of repression I am subject to will never stop me from*

communicating with the outside world or publishing my ideas.

"In your last letter, you asked me several questions about my studies. Firstly, we do not work in any sort of group. We have no teachers or prisoners to help us, nor does anyone come from the outside. My studies are free-ranging and personal. I used to study independently in this way a long time before my arrest. Now, all my studies are concentrated on one subject only: economic, political and social changes in Morocco since the period of colonisation. I am also making a study of the labour movement in Morocco. This will take me about 2 years, then I will see what I shall do next. I get the material I need through notes taken by a student I know, who photocopies all the notes he has taken during the year and gives them to me with a few books at the end of the year. Even using these very limited means, I have always managed to pass my exams. Fortunately, the prison officials do not create any obstacles and they let us take the exams here, the same day that all the other students are sitting the same exam. These are the written exams. For the orals, we go to a prison in Rabat; it is the only time in the year when we have the possibility of meeting our teachers. In spite of all the circumstances, most prisoners pass their exams.

"It's 1 o'clock in the morning now, I will finish off my letter tomorrow. I forgot to mention that I am listening to music as I am writing you this letter. This must seem strange, seeing that we are not allowed to have radio or television. I will let you into one of my secrets: I have got a little radio here. I got it last summer, after a long long period of preparation. First of all, I had to find a way of getting it into the prison - this took nearly one-and-a-half years   - but the biggest problem was to find a safe hiding place for it (our cells are searched every now and then). In the end, I managed. Since then, my cell has been searched several times but the radio has never been discovered. I'm going to stop here for the moment, I can

hear Jacques Brel on the radio singing my favourite song: 'Of course we have had our storms, 20 years of love and what a mad love... Oh, my love, my sweet, my tender, my wonderful love, from the clear light of dawn to the end of the day, I still love you, you know, I love you...'

"You see how romantic the words are! And what lovely music. I'm jumping for joy! I haven't heard this song since my arrest more than 4 years ago. Now my eyes are closing of their own accord, Good night.

"26 February. I will continue to tell you about how I spend my day.

"In the prison yard, everyone goes into the sunshine to benefit from the rays for a little while. Our cells have never, in all their long life, ever seen the sun. There is not much to do there, we either read a book or start walking around chatting in groups of 5 or 6. Three times a week, we organise some sort of sport: football or volley-ball and some of us do some judo. I usually play football, it's quite fun but unfortunately, the area is much too small. Sometimes, I go and sit in a corner and read, I can concentrate better outside.

"At 11 o'clock, we have to go inside again. The cells are left open, but the door of the corridor is shut. Lunch is then served. It always consists of a ladleful of beans with a few carrots. It is quite inedible. We therefore have to wash it through with boiling water and redo it by our own means. We are not allowed any electricity or gas, so we have made some very primitive hotplates ourselves, using cooking-oil. It creates a lot of black smoke, but anyway, it works. We eat in groups of 4 to 6 people, taking it in turns to prepare the meal. The main things we eat are brought to us by our families.

"At 3 in the afternoon, we can go out into the yard again. It is during this time when mail is usually circulated from the window of the prison office overlooking the yard. Everyone waits impatiently for this window to be opened. When it does

open, a big crowd collects in a split second, everyone jostling to see if there is any post for them.

"At 5.30.p.m. it is roll-call and dinner is served. It usually consists of a couple of spoonfuls of rice or 3 or 4 potatoes boiled in a horrible sauce. We are also given 5 pieces of poor quality meat a week; half a tin of sardines every Sunday, and a packet of concentrated milk to make up to a litre, once every 4 days.

"At 6 o'clock, we are shut up again in our cells, where I listen to the news from the BBC or France-Inter. Then I absorb myself in my books. At 10 o'clock, I make tea, I listen to the news and then I carry on working until 1 in the morning. Since I have acquired my radio, I usually listen to a little music before sleeping. Generally, I put the sound down very low so as not to be heard, but tonight it is on rather high. This is because the guard who is on duty tonight is a very decent sort, we have been friendly for quite some time. He always turns a blind eye to anything forbidden and he has even helped me on a few occasions. For example, he gets me batteries for my radio. So you see that in this world of oppression, however depressing it may be, you can always find people on the inside, even the very machinery of that same oppression, who still have some human side and who can carry out acts of solidarity. They are rare, but you can always find them.

"I had a medical examination on the 28 January, as a consequence of which the doctor gave me a prescription. It is now the 26 February, and I have still not yet received the medicine from the prison officials, whose job it is to procure it. According to the doctor, I'm suffering from lack of vitamins caused by our 45-day hunger-strike.

"I'd be very happy to receive a photo of you, which would give me the impression of getting to know you better. Unfortunately, it is forbidden to be photographed here in prison, but when I enrolled at University, I had a chance to get

a photo taken. I'll send you a copy.

"Dear friend, I hope that our fraternal friendship will be even more reinforced by this correspondence. For me, every new friendship constitutes a victory, a great victory against the daily solitude and marginalisation imposed on me.

With all best wishes from Jamal."

Chapter 14

I read the letter many times. It told me quite a lot about the identity of the writer. The words and sentiments had a resounding ring of sincerity. This and subsequent letters depicted an observant, highly articulate and sensitive human being who had not been destroyed by the atrocities he had suffered - on the contrary, it seemed they had given him extra insight and heightened awareness of human related issues. He was a strong-willed person with an uncrushable spirit. He was also gentle and positive. He seemed to me one of the most complete human beings I had yet come across.

It was some time around this period that I had been in hospital for a surgical biopsy. It was a successful operation but one which left me feeling depressed. I was also off work for a couple of months, which gave me time for reflection. I was definitely unhappy with my life. I felt bored, miserable and resentful. This was all mixed with guilt, as I believed I had no right to feel this way. I was a spoilt child! I had a lovely house, cushy job, every material comfort, no financial worries, good friends and a husband who adored me. How dare I even give voice to this growing feeling of restlessness within me? I had suppressed it hoping that denial would make it disappear. However, this seemed instead to give it strength. Axel knew how I was feeling, although I hadn't liked to express it too much. It seemed unfair when he was so kind to me. Instead, I vented my spleen on Simon. In some ways, he was a receptive audience as my voice found echo in his feelings. He had come to Sweden because of family problems. He had felt himself to be a failure in England, so when he had fallen for a Swedish woman, he was delighted to leave. This relationship had subsequently broken down, but then he had embarked on a career in Sweden. His success in this career contrasted sharply with his failure in England, and had motivated him to stay.

In an odd way, we needed each other, Simon and I. We

needed to reassure each other that it wasn't us at fault, it was Sweden. This country, which had actually been kind to us both, became the villain of the piece. It prevented us from the pain of searching deeper inside ourselves for the root cause of our restlessness.

"Simon, I'm thinking of going back to England."

It was a cold winter's day in February. The snow was knee-high. The sun was shining, making interesting patterns in the white mass. We had been driving in my VW Beetle car for a game of badminton together, which we did once a week. On returning, the car had got stuck in a snow drift and we were making our way to the nearest box of sand. There had been a thaw recently and now suddenly a big freeze had hit the country with all the Arctic power it could muster. The traitor sun, symbol of warmth, only served to emphasize the bitter cold clawing its way into our bodies.

"Yes, it would be nice, wouldn't it?" he replied. We turned a corner to find another long road in front of us. No sign of any sand-box. We kept going. We weren't really dressed for an outdoor hike in the snow and our feet kept slipping in the treacherous ground beneath them. The tall pine-trees framing the road witnessed our difficult progress with cool detachment.

"No, I really am," I persisted. "I just can't go around feeling like this any more, with this longing to return to my roots and yet being forced to remain here."

Simon had heard this many times before. "Well, nothing's forcing you. This isn't a Communist state. You're a free individual, can come and go as you want."

I sighed. The ice was penetrating my nostrils and I felt as if my upper lip was divorcing itself from the rest of my mouth. "You know as well as I do that freedom is a relative concept. I agree with you that there is no repressive state machinery physically blocking my exit but there are other considerations."

"Such as?"

"I love Axel. I don't want to do anything to hurt him. We're in a good relationship."

Simon looked bored. "Doesn't sound that marvellous if you're longing to get out. Anyway, if he loved you as much as you reckon, he'd be doing something about your discomfort here."

This touched a raw point in me. I felt a bit angry with Axel that he never seemed to want to try and do anything concrete about our situation. There were several possibilities, I felt. However, I defended him.

"Simon, you know he can't do anything. He can't go and practise Swedish law in England."

"Where there's a will, there's a way." Simon always had an irritating platitude to cover every situation. "If you feel as strongly as all that, you can just up and go."

"Well, you feel just as strongly as I do against this country," I retorted, "So why don't you just up and go?"

"I will do, don't worry," said Simon darkly. We had by this time slithered our way to the familiar blue sand box. Instead of opening the box, however, Simon sat on it and looked at me earnestly for a few moments. I felt distinctly uneasy. My nostrils were by this time glued to each other and sealed off with icicles. I had long since lost the feeling in my feet.

Simon cleared his throat. "Look, Joyce, why don't you and I go to England together? You know I want to be with you. Could build up a really good life together there. Yes, there's growing unemployment in the country, but I'm sure we could find jobs. Wouldn't want for anything. I'd go like a shot if you'd come with me."

Simon mistook my tense silence as an encouraging sign. He continued: "Imagine, we'd be able to do all the things we miss here so much: pubs, more active social life, speak English, relive childhood memories, laugh at our own humour, watch decent television for a change..."

"No, Simon," I said gently. This wasn't what I wanted at all, it would be a complete disaster. I seemed to have a strong idea about what I didn't want; but what did I want?

A week later, I'd made up my mind. "Axel," I said firmly, staring intently through the window at the majestic pine-trees laden with snow in the garden, "I'm leaving to go to England in the summer."

Axel looked unperturbed and carried on sorting out papers in his study. "Well, you usually do," he replied.

I took a deep breath. "No, I mean I'm going to stay there," I said.

Axel's eyes narrowed but he continued filing papers away into boxes.

"What do you mean, stay there?"

"Just for a year," I hastened to reassure him. "Look, I haven't really lived in England since I was a child. I want to go and discover my country. It's a remarkable place. I don't know it and yet my entire childhood and adolescence is buried there."

Axel stopped what he was doing and swivelled round in his chair to face me. "How will you manage? Where will you live? What will you do...?"

"These are details," I answered. "I've been asking you for years if we can do this and you've always put me off. I know that I will never get this out of my system unless I make the move to go. I'd prefer you to come with me but if you won't, then I'm going anyway."

Axel saw that I was really determined. "What could I do in England? How could I leave my job just like that?" His voice sounded strained.

"I'm not going for another 6 months," I told him, "And it is, as I said, only for a year." The pine-trees looked sceptical. "You have plenty of time to sort something out if you really want to. You could take a sabbatical, get a scholarship to study comparative law. We could let this house. I have some money saved up. I'm determined to get a job. You could study or simply have a holiday." My enthusiasm gained momentum. "You speak perfect English, you like London, you wouldn't have to lose your job in Stockholm. Here I am," I grinned at him "offering to make you my kept man and you are putting up barriers. Many men would leap at the chance." I had rehearsed the arguments many times.

Axel sighed deeply and looked troubled. There was silence for a few minutes. Then he said: "Why do you want to go so badly?"

"Axel, I honestly don't know if you can understand this, but when I get into my nice warm car and drive home after a day's teaching and wait for you to return so that we can have dinner together and then watch television before going to bed early because we have to get up early the next morning to go to work again, I think to myself: is this all life has to offer? You are a wonderful husband and I love you dearly but I feel..." I could hardly continue. "I feel so restless, I feel so restless," I sobbed.

I got up and looked for a handkerchief, the movement calming me down. I put my arm around Axel. "I can't go on feeling this emptiness for the rest of my life. I know I'm ungrateful, I don't deserve a lovely person like you, this makes it all the worse. If you beat me or treated me with contempt, it would be easier." Axel stared at the floor. "Axel, help me overcome this crisis. I'm still young. I want to do something with my life, I want to grow. I don't feel I'm being unreasonable, I'm not suggesting we give up all our assets in exchange for a mud hut in Borneo to campaign for insects' rights for the rest of our lives. I just need to do something different at this point, otherwise I'm going to explode."

At first, it was out of the question. Little by little, however, my action and determination goaded Axel into making enquiries. He found that it was indeed possible for him to take a sabbatical so that he could go back to his job afterwards and also that there was an interesting course of study at the London School of Economics. He would only commit himself to 6 months, however, so it was agreed that I would go for 3 months, then he would come and join me for 6 months, then I would stay there for the remaining 3 months.

I told Simon about my plans. He looked devastated and also, I thought, a little envious.

"You'll never come back," he prophesied.

"Oh, I will, I will," I said fervently, "it's only for a year." I think I really believed this myself, or else felt that I had to believe it. So I left Sweden to live in London. Jamal's case was handed to Group No. 50 in Stockholm. This illustrious group included Hasse and Gunilla Alfredsson, Märta-Stina and the late Tage Danielsson, Gösta Ekman, Lennart and Berit Aspegren, Birgitta and Per Gedin, most of whom are very well known in Sweden in the film and entertainment world, in publishing and in the Civil Service. I knew them to be totally committed people who had used their talents to provide considerable funds for Amnesty, who had a strong sense of social justice and many resources at their fingertips. I was delighted and relieved that Jamal's case was going to be left in such capable hands.

Once in London, my main preoccupation was to find a flat and a job. I soon found a flat in Highgate, quite adequate but unheated and rather damp. Finding a job was much more of a problem. Unemployment had started to hit record levels, even though worse was to follow. One of my main difficulties was my lack of any work experience in this country and the fact that my degree was not from a British University. I didn't want a job so much for economic reasons, although this was, of course, a consideration (it was very expensive to live in London), but more because I don't think you get to know a place without making some sort of contribution to it.

Axel came in October, left in April and I still hadn't been able to get a job. I told him I would not be returning to Sweden until Christmas at the earliest. I think we both felt our relationship coming to an end, although we wouldn't admit it even to ourselves, as there was such a bond of affection between us. Then one day, when I was expecting him to come to London for a short holiday, I got a telegram instead, saying that he couldn't go through with it.

Axel was more realistic than I was. He couldn't bear us growing farther and farther apart. This was his way of saying we must face up to the facts. My response to this was to cut contact with him completely. This was done not in anger but in sadness and great pain. I think it was my only way to survive.

I renewed my efforts to find a job. I was becoming desperate, I had never imagined it could be as difficult as this. I longed for a 9 to 5 job, with real colleagues, fulfilling work, office politics, Christmas lunches, giggles, fights, a sense of achievement. I applied for countless jobs, in vain. I became interested in photography and bought some dark room equipment. My camera became my friend, never leaving my side and experiencing with me the England of the eighties. I had never been involved in art before but my newly developed passion for photography opened my eyes. I began to love the National Gallery, which I visited about 3 times a week, often participating in their guided tours. Wandering among the great masterpieces there gave me a sense of history and perspective which I had lacked in Sweden.

My thoughts often turned to Morocco. Although I was no longer Jamal's caseworker, the bond already established between us was so strong that there was no question of our ceasing the correspondence. Jamal had stopped being a 'case' and had turned into a human being. And what a human being! Warm, tender, open, interesting, intelligent. We carried on writing all through 1981 and 1982, our letters to each other growing in warmth and length. He responded with great interest to my everyday problems which, by comparison, must have seemed banal. He wrote all about his life in prison in Kenitra, his past, his beliefs and convictions, his relationships with friends, family and co-prisoners. He touched upon what he called his *affreuse solitude*, he spoke of his studies, of the prison guards both good and bad, everything written with a great maturity and sensitivity which belied his youth. There was no self pity, no heroic self-portrayal, no bitterness or recrimination, even the most horrifying events were described in quite a factual

103

way, some with glimpses of humour.

One letter in particular had a powerful impact on me. It was about the rats in the prison. They had been especially in evidence when the prisoners were on hunger-strikes. With nothing going into the sewers, the rats were emerging to look for their food. Jamal described in vivid detail what it felt like to be locked up in a dark cell at night, suddenly to find that you had some uninvited guests. There were only two courses of action in such a situation: either pull the covers over your head and try to ignore the rat dancing on your stomach (hardly the best inducement to a good night's sleep) or else try to kill it. This latter course is obviously not easy. Rats are intelligent creatures with strong survival instincts and Jamal's only weapon was a wooden shoe. Snuggled up in my soft warm bed, I tried to imagine what it was like to chase a vicious and cunning rat around a tiny cell in the pitch dark, brandishing a shoe. Even if Jamal won the battle, he would then be left with all the mess of dead squashed rat. Yet he seemed to take it all in his stride, recounting the details with a sort of detached humour.

His letters were otherwise so full of feeling and so personal that, when I was reading them, I got an overwhelming sense of his being there: his presence filled the room and pervaded my body and soul.

"Kenitra 29-11-80
Dearest friend
I can't explain the joy which overcame me when I received your long letter. I had been waiting for it impatiently, but with a great hope of getting your news. Sometimes I even wondered if something had happened to you but now that the contact has been re-established between us, I hope it will never be cut again. I was relieved to get your letter telling me everything which had happened since the summer. I was very sad to learn that you have a lot of problems. It made me think of some memories. I too have known what it is like to be unemployed. Since 1972, my life became more and more unstable, I had

104

several jobs, but never any fixed employment. I was sometimes sacked because of my activism with the working-class people. Finding accommodation is also something which has caused me a lot of trouble. Before my arrest, I was responsible in my organisation for renting hideouts for our secret meetings. I was often renting flats in different towns and each time with a false identity. I got a bit fed up after a while with this 'job' which I was doing every day. It took up so much time and the changing identities caused me to 'play act' constantly: one day I'd be using the accent of an officer just arrived from the South, the next day I'd be a travelling salesman and so on...

I wrote two letters to you in Sweden and I was just about to write to your address in London, given to me by your friend Lennart. In fact, I never received the letter you wrote me a few weeks ago. The last letter I got from you was dated the end of April. It seems, too, that letters from Lennart have not been arriving, either. It appears that management is increasing the censorship on my letters but at the same time, my other colleagues do not have any such problems. I don't know what is going on. I am thinking of sending a letter of protest to the Director General of Prisons to see if that will help. I think it's better if you put your address on the envelope, it could be the lack of address which is making them stop the letters.

I'm happy to know about your friends Joelle and Nadine. I also remember everything you have told me about your Lebanese friend Siham. If you write to her please send her my regards. I too had lots of friends of different nationalities, but when I was arrested, they all forgot me as if I had never existed, even though we had been very close. I will enlarge on this in another letter.

I should also tell you that I would like to have a Spanish pen friend. I like the Spanish very much with their customs, their songs and their way of life. I was born in an area inhabited solely by the Spanish, which meant that I speak their language, as does all my family. I follow the political situation in Spain with great interest. This is why I would be very pleased if one of your friends would consider corresponding with me, if that is possible.

I must tell you that since the beginning of the summer, I have received two letters from Mr. Lennart Aspegren who told me that he was in the group looking after my case and that he would be the one to write to me. In my last letter I had asked him about the activities of this Amnesty group but in fact you have now told me what I wanted to know. I was also very touched by everything you have done for me, knowing the great interest you take in my case.

There are rumours from official sources that there will soon be a general amnesty here. I actually believe that we are a political card which the regime may use in very well defined circumstances. Everyone confirms that Amnesty International has had a very influential role, the King has admitted several times that he is very sensitive to international opinion.

I would love to get a recent photo of you. I must tell you about a project which I had been preparing for a long time. I am congratulating myself that it has been successful. It is that I have managed to smuggle a camera secretly into the prison. I have taken a few photos in my cell and a few others with my colleagues in the yard after making sure there were no guards around. I will send you some soon when I've got them printed.

On International Human Rights Day, our families are going to stage a 24-hour hunger-strike, occupying the Human Rights Association building, to protest against the incarceration of political prisoners. We are going to make a communiqué denouncing the violation of human rights in Morocco, and I myself am going to do the text.

Please excuse my bad writing but I am hurrying to finish this letter. If I don't finish it within a few minutes I won't be able to get it sent for another four days or perhaps a week.

I must tell you that my family has received some material aid from Lennart, a sum of money to cover the journey to

Kenitra. My family is very grateful for this act of solidarity.

So now dear friend, I will leave you for the moment and hope you will solve your problems about living in London and that you will find yourself more and more at ease there.

Love from Jamal"

"Prison Centrale de Kenitra 4-1-81
Dear friend

Although I have not yet received a response to the last letter I sent you, I am writing to you now to give you my very best wishes for the New Year.

We have celebrated the beginning of the New Year, but only during the day, of course, because in the evenings we are shut away and isolated in our cells. This time, we have been able to celebrate with some musical instruments: a beautiful guitar and two recorders, real instruments brought to us by our families. In order for us to get these, we have carried on quite a battle with the prison governor. During the whole of the month of December, we've kept up the pressure, in order to get this simple request granted. After many 'discussions' with the Governor, we were at last permitted to have a few instruments, for this occasion only.

It was good to celebrate, we sang, danced, laughed and told jokes. But it is on such occasions that you are made most sharply aware of your imprisonment. In the evening, the only company I had was my little radio to console myself with. I spent the evening reflecting on many things, a whole pile of confused ideas went through my head: the five long years I had spent in prison, pictures of my past as a militant, my emotional life, and then I thought of my family. Their material situation is becoming more and more difficult since the death of my father. What gave me a little more courage, however, was the realisation that I am not alone in the world in my sufferings, I share this with all oppressed people, wherever they may be in the world. Another thing which keeps me going is the realisation that, if I am now behind bars, it is because I have fought a just cause.

There are five long years yet to go, years of suffering and deprivation, unless there is a general amnesty. But I must expect the worst, and keep up my morale in every possible way.

Dear friend, I don't know if you have succeeded in resolving any of your problems, I hope that at least you have managed to find a job. I hope also that you have spent a Happy New Year together with your friends.

That is all for now. I will write more the next time. Once again, Happy New Year for 1981.

Jamal

P.S. 1. I don't know whether you have received the little present I gave to my family to send you. It is a piece of handicraft made by one of the common-law prisoners here. I wanted to send you something, but this was the only thing I could find here in prison.

2. I am sending you an article I found in the French magazine L'Express. It's about a well known French comedian who is running for President next time round!

3. Please tell me when your birthday is."

"London. 25-1-81
My dear friend Jamal

At last, I am writing you a letter. I have to accept that, this year, I am finding it very difficult to write letters. I always have a bad conscience when I see time passing and I have not replied to your sweet letters which I am so pleased to read. I hope you will forgive me.

First of all, I must thank you for the lovely present you sent me. I really liked it, as well as being very touched by the gesture. I don't know if it is a jewellery box or not, but as I don't wear jewellery, I will use it as a box for letters which are dear to me and which I want to keep.

I am sending you two photos with this letter: one is of the house where I am living at the moment on the ground floor, there is another family on the first floor; the other is of me with my violin. I have printed these photos myself. I like photography very much, and I like to go through the whole process myself. While on the subject of photos, I would be very happy indeed to receive the photos you spoke to me about.

I was pleased to read that your family has received some material aid for their journeys to visit you in Kenitra, as this was at my suggestion - I spoke about this to the group before leaving Sweden. I am, however, concerned that your family is suffering hardship after your father's death, which makes me all the more touched that they sent me the present.

Before I reply to your latest letter of 4/1, I will tell you a little about my situation here. I still haven't managed to find a job, which is causing financial problems, among others. From time to time, I get some work at the office of my friend Val, but this is very sporadic. I also carried out a Swedish/English translation which was extremely well-paid, but it was a one-off, unfortunately. Apart from this, I am going to do a broadcast, where I will be playing the piano on Welsh radio. I am going to accompany a voice and a viola in two songs by Brahms. The singer has a really beautiful voice, which makes it all the more pleasant to do.

You asked me the date of my birthday: it is this Saturday, the 31st January, and we are going to have a party here in London, mostly only for my family, especially as my father's birthday is on the following day.

Now I have re-read your letter of 4/1, which I found very moving. I feel how brave you are to keep up your spirits after all these years of being under lock and key. This makes my problems seem so minute and it also gives me a lot of courage. I am, moreover, proud to know and to write to someone who has had the courage to fight for a more just society. I have *been thinking of you very much these past few days when the media has been full of the American hostages just freed in Iran. A lot has been said about their sufferings; everything has been done to protect them against all the psychological consequences of their imprisonment; an enormous sum of money has been put at their disposal, they are going to have the best doctors, the best care, everything money can buy will be going to the hostages. Everyone is bursting with indignation at the treatment they have received, they have become the heroes of the century. People are right to be indignant and I am horrified at the plight of these innocent people. However, I cannot help comparing all this publicity with what has happened to you and to many other prisoners of conscience who are treated in a manner much more awful than the worst treatment suffered by the Americans, and who - far from being heroes, are treated like criminals; and - even if they do manage to survive the torture and imprisonment - they emerge from their captivity without money, without work and without confidence. I wonder how you have viewed this affair in Kenitra?*

There was a rather good cartoon in a newspaper here about all this. One of the hostages, having arrived in Germany before going back to the USA, is recounting his experiences to a psychiatrist. He says: 'But the worst torture of all was when they kept telling me that Ronald Reagan had been elected as President...'

Many thanks for the article in L'Express - I read it with great interest and amusement.

Now, my dear friend, I must finish. Many thanks once more for the lovely present.

I hope to hear from you soon.

> *Love from*
> *Joyce"*

Chapter 15

Letters to and from Jamal were sporadic. The correspondence meant a lot to me and evidently to him as well but there were often long gaps between letters. This was partly caused by the inevitable difficulties in getting letters smuggled to and from prison. We could, of course, have corresponded directly through prison but even if our letters hadn't contained any particularly revolutionary material, it would obviously have placed restraints on us. We wanted our dialogue to be spontaneous and free, which would be impossible if letters had to pass the beady eye of a censor. Jamal had become a friend I felt I could confide in.

"London, 5 May 1981.
My dear friend

I was really pleased to get your letter as it was such a long time since I had heard from you. People were also getting worried in Sweden: in fact, Märta-Stina from your group rang me to see if I had heard anything. I did what you suggested about mailing: I sent a registered letter to you addressed to Kenitra Prison about two weeks ago, a simple birthday card, to see if you were given it or not.

I am alone here in England now. Axel has left for Sweden. I think I will stay in England until the end of the year; after that, I will return to Sweden. I have a lot of financial difficulties here - Axel sends me what he can but that isn't even enough to pay the rent. I therefore live a very frugal life - this isn't such a bad thing, it helps me to understand those living in much worse circumstances than myself. Even if I have very little money, I have my family and friends as support; even if I have to make a lot of sacrifices, I am so happy to be in England that I really don't mind. I've put an advert in the paper for some lodgers to help me share the costs of the rent and bills: I hope I will get some replies. I earn a little money when I work in the office of my friend Val - what I earn is just enough to feed me and cover my daily expenses such as travel, stamps, newspapers etc. - but it is a very irregular and unreliable income. I also give piano lessons but I have only two pupils. All in all, however, I prefer to be in England even with my problems of work and finance than to be in Sweden living a comfortable life with regular work and a good salary.

It's strange, when I read your letters, I feel very close to you, even though we have never met. I feel a warmth for you when I read your opinions which are nearly always shared by myself, and when I read about your life and the understanding you have for other people, for example when you speak about your old friends: I see your humanity shine like a big sun! Everything you tell me interests me and I note all the details.

You tell me about worsening economic conditions in Morocco. It is similar here. There are 2½ million unemployed, that is to say 10.6%, a figure which is growing steadily. It is a catastrophic situation caused by the policy (or lack of policy) of the Conservative Government. There is money here but only for an elite group of people. I read recently that 6% of the population here owns 83% of its wealth! Among that 6% are those who could pay off the national debt without ever noticing it disappear from their bank balance. Thatcher has cut practically half of the social service; in addition to this, she has made drastic cuts in education, medicine, culture, transport etc. The cuts have helped to pour all the more money into the police force and defence. The personal tragedies for the unemployed never cease to touch me: when you are unemployed at the age of 40, your chances of finding another job in your life are quite minimal. Imagine finishing your working life at the age of 40! Thatcher's response to this is: use your own initiative and everything will be all right! Use your personal resources and you will manage! It is just as bad for young people finishing school and who want nothing more than to work but there is nothing for them. In a situation like this, you can imagine that the crime wave has risen. . Thatcher's response to this is: More police! We will eliminate these criminals! Yes, Jamal, I know that England is not alone in having such a cruel uncaring government and that, compared with a lot of countries, the situation here is probably quite mild. This thought makes me depressed and pessimistic.

So the political climate here is not the best, I have little money, no work and I have also problems with my marriage which are too long and complicated to expound on here. But apart from that, I am happy to be here and do not regret coming one bit. Even if things are bad here, I feel that I am part of it all, it touches me, I am participating in life rather than observing it.

Is your family able to come and see you regularly? How often are you allowed visits?

Now, my dear friend, I must leave you because it is very late. I want you to know that I am thinking of you. Take care of yourself.

Joyce"

"Prison Centrale de Kenitra 12-8-81
Dear friend Joyce

I write you this letter with a lot of enthusiasm but also with shame because of the long time which has elapsed since I last wrote. I must tell you that I only got your letter yesterday. The people who were to bring me the letter have only been to the prison on two occasions during this period, and each time they forgot to bring me my letters. I have been really upset about this, but there is nothing I can do. I love getting letters, especially those coming from you; it is a sort of relief to know that there are still people in the world who have their hearts in the right place and who are full of humanity, people who show sincere friendship.

Believe me, I have felt it deeply not to be able to get your letters, I have been so impatient to know what is happening in your life. What I like most about your letters, and on a wider level in our friendship generally, is that you write to me in such a spontaneous way which makes me feel closer to you, especially as I feel more and more that we have similarities in character and even more on an intellectual level. During all my life, I have only been able to get really close to people like you, who are very open in both character and spirit. I have never been able to stand people who put up all sorts of barriers and who wear masks. Moreover, I am quite frank and prepared to show what I am really feeling at any moment and find it difficult to hide my feelings and become two-faced. It is for these reasons that, on reading your letters, I feel very much at ease. I dream of being able to read them every week, but with these constant delays in getting the mail, it is impossible, of course, and anyway I don't know if you have either the time or the patience to write.

This month, I have awarded myself a little 'holiday'. A holiday here in prison is somewhat different from a holiday on the outside! For the whole of June I worked almost day and night on my exams, which I managed to pass. During this past term, I have given myself no rest. I stayed shut up in my cell, a third of which was covered in books and documents. I was sure I was going to pass because I worked on this exam like never before, in spite of the conditions in prison which are so unfavourable. Indeed, the essay I wrote was considered by the teachers at the Sociology Department at the Faculty, to be the best one this year. They are all encouraging me to go on to do a doctorate. Unfortunately, the possibilities of doing this in Morocco are very limited. So I am trying to contact a university in France and I am awaiting the reply of a friend who is going

114

to make some enquiries on my behalf. I would like to study sociology of work or industrial sociology.

There are a lot of practical difficulties against pursuing studies (though the main thing is that I am very willing as, for one thing, I would be studying subjects which have fascinated me for a long time). Then there is another problem. I have 4 years and a few months left before I am freed, if I am not lucky enough to be let out before, and I must from now on prepare myself for the difficulties I will probably encounter in trying to earn my living. In the hotel trade, I am too well-known, no-one would take me on there any more. I don't know if I told you that, after my arrest, a whole squad of police officers and inspectors were reprimanded and relocated. This was because they didn't discover my clandestine activities when I was barman in a 5-star hotel, where most of the time I was serving royalty, ministers and top civil servants. Anyway, after all these years in prison, I feel too old and tired to take on any more strenuous work. And then, here in prison, I read at least 8 hours a day, which means that the only work I would enjoy would be in education, devoting my time to reading and with a lot of free time. Don't understand by this that I have become lazy. I would never tolerate the idea of someone else doing the housework and cooking for me.

My holiday means that my daily routine has now changed. I do much more sport, I read novels: Emile Ajar, Gorky, Alfonso Sastre and some Arab novelists. One of the most interesting things I have read lately has been the accounts written by former Communist prisoners in the prisons of Sadat in Egypt.

During my holiday I am eating a bit more and sport gives me a greater appetite. I'm beginning to get fatter; before, I was 65 kilos, now I have reached 68-70 kilos; I'm very pleased about that. Before my arrest, I was terribly thin, only 55 kilos, as I was working so hard, what with my job as a barman and the interminable meetings, leafletting and journeying. But it was also because I used to smoke such a lot, often as many as 35 cigarettes a day. Three years ago, however, I stopped smoking. There were 30 of us prisoners who decided to kick the habit, but by the end of a month, I was the only one who hadn't started again. Now I have completely forgotten my old habit. I count this as one of the best things I have achieved in my life.

Concerning visits, I have already told you that we could receive visits twice a week. Now we are allowed visitors four times a week, but not the same ones; each member of a prisoner's family can visit him twice a week. When my sister Khadija is in Rabat studying, she comes to see me every week. My mother and my other brothers and sisters come in turns once every 5 or 6 weeks, but when they are in financial difficulties, it can go as long as once every 2 or 3 months. The visit is the most precious thing there is for a prisoner. After each visit, I feel tired and get headaches. This is because we are suddenly confronted by people who are, for us, from a completely different life, and we try to remember what we can about the visit once it is over.

In your letters, you have already written about the unemployment crisis. I think that the waves of violence from the skinheads which have hit several English towns is the logical and objective result of a social and economic situation which gets worse by the day. In Morocco, there have been some bloody events recently. On June 1st, an announcement was made about dramatic increases in the costs of basic foodstuffs, increases of 50%, 60% and sometimes even 90%. These price increases were insufferable for a population already living below poverty level. On June 20, the town of Casablanca registered its protests, at first peacefully; but after they were met by violent armed repression from the police, the situation turned into a full-scale riot. The demonstrators used sticks, stones and knives and sometimes bare hands against soldiers armed to the teeth. Women threw boiling water over the forces and children went and stole arms from those who had been injured. The following day, similar riots took place in Rabat. A wave of repression then hit the provinces. Fortunately for us, there was no change for the worse in conditions inside the prison.

I would like you to tell me if you have now decided about returning to Sweden, and what you do by yourself when you are not working. My family would be so pleased if you wanted to come and spend a holiday with them. We have a flat in the centre of Tetuan where you could stay as long as you like. Moroccans show a lot of respect for guests, especially those coming from a long distance. I'm sure you would like it here, where people are simple and sincere and very informal.

Please tell me about the music studies you have undertaken. Music will always be my great passion, I can't tell you how happy it makes me to hear old songs on the radio sung by Jacques Brel, Joan Baez and Georges Moustaki. I dislike rock music, which I find too aggressive and childish; on the other hand, I love listening to some of the masterpieces of classical music. With ideas like these, I imagine most people of my age would find me old-fashioned and conservative!

I've spent 2 nights on this letter; I've spoken to you as if you were here in front of me. When I am writing, I don't feel my terrible loneliness quite so strongly, which encourages me to write more. Now, dear friend, I hope to hear from you soon. In the meantime, my very best wishes

Jamal"

"London 4-11-81

I was distressed to see, my dear Jamal, that from your last letter, it seems that you have never received my last letter, and it was such a long and important letter in which I really poured out my soul to you. I think we have experienced a certain amount of anguish during our correspondence, not from the letters themselves (your letters are among the most beautiful I have ever received) but during the silences and the worries in between letters. It is a proof of the strength of our friendship that we are still in contact with each other, wouldn't you say?

My goodness, Jamal, I was touched when you wrote about the similarity of our characters, as I had exactly the same feeling, that we share the same values in life and that we react in a similar way. I also find that my most unfavourite people are those who wear masks...

I read with interest everything you wrote about your studies. I have just received a letter from Märta-Stina Danielsson in your Amnesty group, who is going to get in touch with a contact at the University of Aix in France to try and assist you. It was a lovely letter from Märta-Stina, who wrote that you had a 'fantastic personality' and that she felt privileged to know you. I feel just like she does - you have enriched my life.

This cannot be a long letter this time, dear Jamal, but I must tell you my most important news - I have got a job, a job which I like very much. It's at the Commission for Racial Equality, set up and funded by the Government, to try and combat racism and racist practices. It's a type of work which I have never done before -research work into race and housing - but I find it really interesting and I am working with such nice colleagues, who are helpful, knowledgeable and have a well developed sense of humour! This means that I will certainly be staying in England for at least another year.

How tempted I feel to take up your invitation to come to Morocco! At the moment, I don't have the time, but it is a dream which I know will be realised one day, and not in the too distant future...

I hope to hear from you soon. In the meantime, sleep well, take care of yourself, my sweet and warm friend, and much love to you.

Joyce"

Kenitra le 6-2-82

Chère amie

Je viens de recevoir ta merveilleuse carte-lettre du 22-1- toute pleine de tendresse et de sentiments affectueux. Comment des mots toujours limités par leurs propres dimensions alphabétiques pourraient-ils traduire mon émotion, ma joie, mon affection et ma reconnaissance pour toi ? Quand je lis tes lettres je ne sais comment te décrire combien je me sens heureux, et aussi inquiet et impatient quand je les attends.

Je suis très content de tes nouvelles, je te partage ta joie pour tes nouvelles conditions de travail. J'espère que tu ne retrouverais plus jamais tes anciens problèmes. Je vois bien que beaucoup de choses de la vie quotidienne t'empêchent de me répondre immédiatement je ne douterai jamais de ta sincère amitié et des nobles sentiments que tu éprouves envers moi. Seulement saches bien que même si je recevrais chaque jour des dizaines de lettres de qui que ce soit elles ne feront sûrement pas sur moi les mêmes effets de tes charmantes lettres. C'est avec tes lettres que je me sens le plus à l'aise, je te l'ai déjà dit je me trouve plus proche de ton caractère et de ton comportement social surtout parce que nous partageons les mêmes valeurs dans la vie. En plus de ça, à travers tes lettres, je vois en toi un nouveau model de femme que je n'ai eu l'occasion de rencontrer que très rarement, je veux dire le type de femme cultivé, combative, indépendante et de forte personnalité. Il faut le dire je n'ai toujours trouvé dans mes entourages que ce type de femme objet, de femme soumise et de faible personnalité. Même pour nos militantes la règle générale était la femme militante, émancipée, communiste, parfaite, mais seulement dans les réunions... mais dans les complications et les petits détails de la vie courante elle n'échappe pas aux traits généraux de toutes les femmes dans la société: soumission et dépendance totale au mari aux différents niveaux; leur manque de personnalité propre et de conscience en tant que femme... J'espère qu'on aura l'occasion de parler du problème de la femme dans la société, c'est un sujet très large et important.

Letter from Jamal to the author, 16 February 1982

119

Mon très cher ami - Cette fois je n'ai pas de mauvaise conscience quand je t'écris, car c'est ce matin même que j'ai reçu ta gentille lettre, une lettre avec toute l'humanité, la tendresse et la sincérité qui marquent toutes tes lettres, et jamais plus que cette dernière. La chaleur de ton esprit me va directement au cœur et me touche plus que je peux te dire.

Je suis très inquiète en ce qui concerne la maladie - une ulcère d'estomac, c'est une chose grave, je n'ai pas beaucoup de confiance dans les médicaments pour ce genre d'affliction. Seulement si c'est au début que ça peut être moins dangereux. Même si j'ai beaucoup de respect pour les motifs derrière la grève de faim, je suis encore plus anxieuse pour ton état de santé, une grève comme ça doit irriter beaucoup l'estomac. Dis-moi que tu ne souffres pas, je suis bien inquiète.

Demain je vais donner les photos à un magasin de photo. Dommage qu'ils ne sont pas en noir/blanc, peut-être, dans ce cas ci, j'aurais pu les faire moi-même, avec des agrandissements aussi grands que tu aurais voulu, et j'aurais pu accentuer les détails intéressants. Je suis très curieuse à voir ces photos, j'espère qu'on peut les copier bientôt, je te les enverrai aussitôt qu'ils soient prêts, avec les négatifs aussi, bien sûr.

Je suis désolée que la cassette ne t'a pas atteinte. J'ai peur maintenant de t'envoyer des paquets; une chose c'est sûr, c'est que je ne t'envoie plus des lettres dans un paquet, elles doivent être séparées après la disparition de la fameuse lettre/biographie que j'ai envoyé dans un paquet.

C'est avec beaucoup d'intérêt que j'ai lu ce que tu avais à raconter au sujet de ta famille et je suis été choquée contente que tu m'as fait cette confiance. C'est difficile pour moi de comprendre que vous êtes de la même famille. Je ne peux pas être de l'opinion que les gens sont comme ci ou comme ça parce-que c'est "dans leur caractère." C'est trop simple, même si il y a quelque chose qui s'appelle le caractère, c'est tout à fait l'environnement qui fait que le caractère se développe de la même façon, à mon avis. Oui, vous êtes de la même famille, mais les circonstances sont toujours différents. Le premier à la naissance d'un enfant d'abord; en tout, ça peut être une grande joie, à donner à cet enfant, on a beaucoup de temps, chaque mouvement, chaque sourire. Ou bien ça peut être le contraire, c'était un accident, les parents ne sont pas prêts émotionnellement ou économiques, on avait voulu attendre un peu plus, on a des difficultés très sensibles etc. Je suis sûre que les bébés sont très sensibles aux circonstances qui entourent leur(s) parent(s) qui se reflètent en tout sentiment qu'ils montrent aux enfants. J'ai beaucoup plus à dire sur le sujet mais pas ici, c'est trop longue et compliqué. Je veux seulement dire que le caractère n'y a pas une chose concrète qui s'appelle le caractère, comme il y a le nez ou la bouche, le caractère est une chose formée par les circonstances en petit, (comme les parents, la présence de sœur ou frère, l'amour ou manque de l'amour) ainsi que les circonstances en grand comme la culture dans laquelle on est né, l'époque etc. Tu m'as donné peut-être la clef en ce qui concerne ton frère, en me disant que c'est l'aîné dans la famille

P.-S. Ce n'est pas "dangereux" d'écrire ton nom comme ça sur l'enveloppe (?)

Letter from the author to Jamal, 1 June 1982

One day, enclosed in one of his letters, Jamal sent me a photo of himself, the one he had promised me, taken for his identity card at University, a small photo and not very clear. It showed an interesting-looking face, but what made a deep impression on me were the eyes - big soft gentle eyes looking up at me with feeling. These eyes started to follow me wherever I went, always soft and compassionate; but if I had delayed in answering a letter, they would take on an expression of gentle reproach. If I was happy, they laughed with me; if I was sad, they were full of sympathy.

One night, I had a dream which left me feeling quite shaken. I was making love with the owner of those eyes. Oh, and it was the sweetest and tenderest experience! In surrealist surroundings, we were floating on a cloud and our bodies and souls submerged with the soft air around us.

When I had to awaken from this vision of Paradise, with half my soul still remaining there, my immediate instinct was to write down what I had experienced through the night and send it to Jamal. When finally body *and* soul came down to earth, however, and my natural reserve took over, I could see this was out of the question. To send an intimate account of a deeply erotic experience to someone I had never met and who moreover was locked up, without the remotest chance of even approaching any of the scenes in that dream was, of course, unthinkable and seemed almost cruel. So I contented myself with the memory of it and tried to go on writing to Jamal as before.

"London 22-1-82
My dear friend
 I was pleased to get your letter before Christmas; I am really sorry that time passes by so quickly that I don't get the chance to reply, and this letter will only be short, too. As I am now working full-time, there's a limit on my free time which I spend keeping up with friends, being politically involved, doing photography, going to concerts etc. At the same time, I feel so

attached to you and want to write to you and receive your beautifully written, very interesting and lovely letters.

I hope to devote myself to you for one whole evening next week; in the meantime, I just wanted to send you a sign of life. I hope you have received the cassettes I sent you and that you have been able to listen to them. I have the Vivaldi on record. I like the freshness of his music, and especially the beauty of the slow movement of the piccolo concerto in C major. What do you think of it? I also hope that you like the Joan Baez. I know many of these songs on the cassette and I like her singing very much.

Otherwise, all is well with me, and I am so much enjoying my job.

Dear Jamal, please excuse this short, badly-written card, I am really ashamed of my silence when I know how lonely you are; I only hope that your group in Sweden have been a little more efficient than me. Never doubt my friendship, nor the strong warm feelings I have for you. You are one in a million.

Joyce"

"Prison Centrale de Kenitra 6-2-82
Dear friend

I have just received your marvellous card-letter of 22 January, full of tenderness and care. How can words, always limited by their alphabetic dimensions, possibly convey my emotion, my joy, my affection and my gratitude towards you? When I read your letters, I just can't describe to you my feelings of happiness, nor can I describe my feelings of anxiety and impatience when I am waiting for them.

I do see that there are many things in your life which prevent you from replying to my letters immediately. I would never doubt your sincere friendship, nor the honest feelings you have for me. You must just know that, even if I received

122

dozens of letters each day from all sorts of other people, they would never have the same effect on me that your lovely letters do. It is with your letters that I feel so much at ease. I have already told you that I feel very close to you in character and behaviour because we share the same values in life. More than that, through your letters I see a new type of woman emerging, the type I have only encountered very rarely - I mean the cultured, active, independent woman with a strong personality. In my circles, the only sort of woman I have met previously has been the woman as an object, submissive and with very little personality of her own. Even in meetings in militant circles, when the woman has seemed active, emancipated and politicised, this only lasts for the duration of the meeting - as soon as she is back among the daily concerns of ordinary life, she becomes like all the other women in this society: submissive, totally dependent on her husband on all sorts of different levels, and with no will of her own. I hope we will discuss the problems of women in society in the future; it is a very large and important subject.

I can't thank you enough for the cassettes you sent me. I listen to them very often, as they are the only ones I have. I was delighted to hear the Vivaldi, especially his piccolo concerto in C major, it is really marvellous. The piece I know best by him is 'The Four Seasons', which I still remember, in spite of my long years in prison. I also loved the Joan Baez, I haven't heard some of these songs for a very long time. I can't tell you the happiness which this gesture of yours has brought me. I am continuing to learn the solfa system. I am also trying to sing songs which I like very much. Could you possibly send me the words to 'Imagine' and 'Yesterday' by the Beatles? We have also managed to get hold of one alto and several soprano recorders. We would love to get some music for this, either for one instrument or else to play together.

Please could you send the enclosed letter to Algiers for

me. It's a letter which I have written to this institute to ask for copies of documents presented at a seminar by well-known historians and sociologists on a subject which interests me very much (social history of the working class in Arab countries). I didn't want to send the letter from here because I can't be certain that it would arrive. As relations between Morocco and Algeria are still very strained, more and more of the mail is getting censured. Could I also please use your address in future for such correspondence?

Well, dearest Joyce, I will write you a very long letter next time. I hope that you will answer all the questions I asked you in my last letter. How happy I will be to get your letter soon. That is all for now, and I send you much love.

Jamal"

"London 24 February 1982
My very dear friend

I was very touched to receive your lovely letter this morning. It was good to read that you had received the cassettes which you liked. By this same post but in a different packet, I am sending you another cassette, one which I made together with two others for Welsh Radio. I am the one who is playing the piano. I can't tell you how happy I am that you are able to play cassettes; this must add an important dimension to your otherwise monotonous prison life. I am really so happy for you.

Here, everything is fine but I have been very busy. I don't mean my work at the Commission, but that I am involved in a campaign to fight against an idiotic decision which will have the effect of causing the collapse of the local transport system here. I am enclosing here details of our campaign, I have translated some of it for you into French.

I am so much enjoying my work at the Commission. I

have a very interesting job with lovely colleagues. My boss - a Sikh called Gurbux Singh - is really nice. He is on the left, very fair minded, dynamic and with a great sense of humour, my God! how we laugh, also with my two nearest colleagues, Richard Seager (English) and Lionel Goddard (from Barbados). I am so fortunate to have tumbled on colleagues like this, who are also very dedicated. The situation for the black population in this country is rather serious, especially now that there are more than 3 million people unemployed. The black people get it worse from all sides: firstly because unemployment hits them more and secondly because they get the blame, which encourages racist movements like the National Front. The political climate here has reached an all-time low, it is even condemned by many Conservatives themselves. The gap between rich and poor increases daily: taxes for those earning 5 times the average national salary have been increased by 50%, while taxes for those earning half the average national salary have increased by all of 92%! We are buying more and more expensive and dangerous nuclear arms; reductions in educational spending are such that it is becoming almost impossible to teach in the schools, while University Principals - even the most conservative - are speaking of a 'dead generation'. The BBC is increasingly becoming the voice of the Establishment. When I saw the 'news' this evening, I felt like throwing up: first of all we saw a day in the life of Prince Charles and Princess Diana on an exotic island in the Bahamas; after that piece of enlightenment, we were able to follow the Pope carrying out his daily blessings; a visit by Margaret Thatcher to her old school was next on the agenda, and then Ronald Reagan spent 5 minutes reassuring us that his contribution to world peace consisted of donating 200 million dollars to Latin America to tackle Communism! Then we were able to see the football results, and finally, the real serious news of the day: it is going to be even colder tomorrow than it has been today.

I will try and get hold of the words of the Beatle songs for you and also some music for recorders. Jamal dear, I feel a very great empathy between us - a lot of what you write to me goes straight to my heart. I have the feeling that I can say anything to you, tell you the whole of my life story. I have great trust in you, you are a very dear friend, an irreplaceable one. I can't tell you how happy I am to know you.

Yes, you can obviously use my address whenever you want, you don't even have to ask me. I will post your letter to Algeria right away. It is a curious thing, but I have an Algerian friend who lives exactly at Ben Aknoun El-Biar. I will put him in touch with you. I am quite sure he will help you in anything you want to do. I've told him about you, so he sort of knows you anyway. He gave me a cassette of a Berber singer named 'Idir' do you know him? He sings 'A vava inou va' and other equally lovely songs.

Jamal, my dear friend, I must leave you now. I await your news with impatience. Look after yourself, it's very important.

Lots of hugs from Joyce"

"Prison Centrale de Kenitra 15-3-82
Dear Joyce

As usual, I was delighted to receive your letter. I am so happy to get your news and to know that things are going well for you, especially your working conditions and your friends... Believe me, I share in your happiness. I congratulate you for your activism in fighting against the local transport issue. What you sent me about this has given me a lively impression of your sincere and fighting spirit.

Today has been an exceptional day, not monotonous like the other days. I am still recovering from the effects of two

126

events which have overwhelmed me. Today, I didn't go straight back to my cell to read after dinner as usual. I assembled along with all the other political prisoners in the prison yard to say goodbye to a colleague who finished his sentence of 10 years today. He was arrested at the age of 24, just after having finished his studies in France to become a telecommunications engineer. Now he is 34, but looks as if he is over 40 with everything he has suffered in prison since 1972. All of us were shaking with emotion, greeting him for the last time. He was the one who was the most deeply touched, however, as he would be leaving his colleagues behind bars, colleagues with whom he had shared the past 10 years, with all its sorrows and joys. In this prison, the release of a prisoner is really an exceptional event, as all prisoners, political and common-law, have sentences ranging from 10 years to life or the death penalty. Some of the common-law prisoners have been there since the 1950s. This week, three old prisoners died in prison after having served 12, 15 and 20 years respectively.*

I don't know if I told you that this prison is the largest and most horrible in the whole of Morocco (some people say it is the largest in the whole of Africa, but I'm not sure) and the common- law prisoners are badly exploited.

From 3 o'clock and until 6 o'clock, there occurred the second historical event: for the first time, and after many battles with the prison administration, we - the political prisoners - won the right to have a television set, though only occasionally, for an important football match. There were about 100 of us squashed one against the other, desperately trying to see the tiny screen in a poky unventilated room. But in spite of this, we were jubilant, because, as well as being able to see television again for the first time in 6 years, for me, and up to 10 years for others, it also represented yet another victory over the system. We looked at this television set as if it were the first time ever. We squeezed together and elbowed

*each other out of the way in the attempt to see the tiny screen
with its hazy picture. The comments from the enthralled
audience were so many and so loud that it was impossible to
hear a thing. We giggled and joked together just like children.*

*I am going to interrupt this letter to continue it tomorrow.
Good night!*

16-3-82

*I am taking up my pen to write once again, it is 8 o'clock
in the evening. I have spent this afternoon in a hospital in
Rabat (about 40 kilometres from Kenitra). I was taken there
for a medical examination - there was nothing serious, but
this trip for me was a veritable excursion! I can't remember
the last time I saw trees, the horizon, the sea, the mountains...
all of which I saw now through the windows of the prison van.
There were 10 of us prisoners in the van, with about 15 guards.
Four of the prisoners were common-law, all under life
sentences. They are quite dangerous. In prison they have their
own Mafia networks and are only allowed medical treatment
at the hospital if their power and social standing permit it.
Here, in order to get medical attention, you either have to be a
political prisoner or a very rich common-law prisoner and
uncontested head of some league or other. It is very rarely we
get a chance to speak to these men; it is forbidden, in case we
'contaminate' them with our ideas. I see these prisoners as
victims of an unjust society, the progeny of the entire socio-
economic and moral system, people who should be treated as
human beings. It is not with oppression and whips that you
educate people, you have to find other more humane means to
prepare for their reintegration into society and to draw them
out of their marginalisation.*

*In the waiting-room of the hospital, I started talking to
some of the nurses and patients; my handcuffs had been
removed so as not to attract attention. I was fairly well dressed,*

even if it was only in prison clothes of poor quality material; my suit had been made to measure for me by a friend in prison. The guard accompanying me spoke to me like a close friend as we chatted and joked together. When I then told the people in the waiting- room that I was an inmate at the infamous Kenitra, they refused to believe me and even chastised me for making tasteless jokes. In the end, the guard had to produce some papers to show that I was telling the truth. When they saw that I was in my seventh year of prison, two nurses burst out crying and the whole waiting-room was stunned with emotion. I had overturned their preconceptions of what a prisoner was like, they said I was far too young, I spoke to them politely etc.

I have managed to get a camera smuggled into prison! Taking photos with it is a little more difficult as the guards are everywhere. Every time we want to take a photo, we have to create a scene. On one occasion, a colleague provoked a dispute with a guard - all the other guards came rushing over to try and stop the prisoner, who looked to all intents and purposes as if he were going to hit the poor guard. This gave me plenty of time to take several shots in the yard, with other colleagues keeping a look-out and keeping up a running commentary on the progress of the dispute. On another occasion, a colleague feigned a heart attack, which gave us the opportunity to take shots of the corridors. My next task is to smuggle both camera and film out of prison, and get some prints made. As soon as this is done, I'll send you some copies.

Tell me about your family - do you meet them often? Please send me some more photos of yourself, to replace those which disappeared en route.

I forgot to tell you about my family, as I promised last time; I will do so in my next letter. I have so many things to tell you, and with the great confidence I have in you, I will be able to tell you all about it without any reserve.

Dearest Joyce, I must leave you with my pen but not with my heart. I think of you a lot, I am proud to know you. I'm awaiting your reply with such impatience!

Much love from
Jamal "

Chapter 16

Looking back on it, the first time I felt my attachment becoming serious was when I wrote the following in the summer of 1982: "Tell me dear friend, when you are going to be freed and whether one can hope for an amnesty or a reduction in your sentence."

Jamal answered this point in a characteristic way:

"I was arrested on 9-1-76 and sentenced to 10 years imprisonment. I should therefore be freed on the 9-1-86. But it is quite possible that we will all be freed soon, you never know when that could be. However, it's not sure. Since our arrest, there have always been rumours of release but nothing has happened. I don't therefore attach any importance to these rumours. I have planned out the three-and-a-half years I still have to serve. A few years ago, some state officials told us to write to the King to ask for a pardon, in which case we would be released immediately. They are still telling us that this is the only solution. My response is and remains categoric: there is no way I could ever ask pardon from a tyrant, a murderer! I have told them that I would prefer to spend another 10 years in jail than to humble myself before the oppressor of my people!"

On 1 September, I wrote the following postcard to Jamal:

"Dear friend - I'm worried because I haven't heard from you for a long time. I hope there is a perfectly normal reason for this: laziness, a temporary difficulty with the post etc. I really hope that you are in good health."

I remember well that, as I was writing the card, I suddenly became overwhelmed with a feeling of wanting to meet Jamal. My pen began writing these words before my mind had grasped their real significance or possible consequences:

"I've suddenly got a mad idea to come to Morocco, as I have one week's holiday left, but I don't know if I can afford it. It's a beautiful dream. We'll see if it turns into a reality. Whatever happens, I send you lots of love -

Joyce."

As luck - or fate - would have it, I was taken ill shortly after I had sent off this card, with appendicitis. There were some complications, so I spent nearly two weeks in hospital. When I was finally discharged, I was given six weeks off work and the doctor advised me to go for a 'complete rest in a warm climate'. I just had to accept that Fate, Destiny, Providence or whatever had now taken charge and that the doctor was their agent in the conspiracy to send me to Morocco. I told her that, although I thought I could fix the warm climate bit, I wasn't so sure about the complete rest. (I don't think she had a Moroccan prison in mind when she made the suggestion). I wrote to tell Jamal that I was definitely coming for at least two weeks. He wrote back:

30-9-82
Dearest Joyce
"I really can't begin to describe all the happiness, joy and great emotion which have taken hold of me since I learnt that you will soon be coming to Morocco. This wonderful piece of news has completely bowled me over. Since I got your letter 24 hours ago, I have only one thought in mind: you. I haven't stopped going over and over again in my head every little detail that I know about you which I like so much: your character, your generosity, your compassion. I must confess that last night, through force of emotion, I wasn't able to sleep until far into the night. My only thought now is: how can I get through the interminable days which separate us? The day when I see you for the first time will be the most beautiful day of my life, which will make me forget all the horrors I have gone through in prison."

I booked a ticket for 15 October. I had tried to imagine what it would be like to go on this, my first trip to an African country, and under somewhat unusual circumstances. I knew very little about the day-to-day life of Moroccans. I had learnt quite a lot about the political set-up there, the repression, the human rights abuses, but what were ordinary Moroccans like? What did they feel, what did they think, what did they wear, what did they eat? Did they look like us? Did they share the same values and aspirations as we did? Did they laugh at the same things, cry at the same things? Were they educated? Did they have cinemas, theatres, concerts? Did they live in extended families or had Western culture left its indelible mark during the many years of colonial rule? How did they socialise? Were most of them devout Muslims?

As I tried to fill in a few answers to these questions with the help of the little I knew already, with the glimpses Jamal had given me, the accounts of a friend who had been to Morocco once on holiday and the scant information provided by the Moroccan Tourist Office, I started to pitch the questions at a more personal level. I was going to Jamal's family. I was confident that I would be able to accept and assimilate whatever lifestyle I found there. I had travelled quite extensively - albeit mostly within Europe - and my job in Sweden with the education of immigrants had put me in touch with children and families from a range of different ethnic and national backgrounds. My work at the Commission had also made me sensitive to cultural diversities. But what would Jamal's family think of me? None of them had ever been outside Morocco. I tried to picture myself through their eyes and I saw a thin non-Muslim, non-Halal meat-eating woman, divorced, not averse to the odd glass of wine, taking the initiative to travel alone to an unknown country to see a man she only knew through correspondence.

Then there was the question of presents, not vitally important but nevertheless something I wanted to get right, as the only tangible statement I was making about myself. It occurred to me that I would have to take presents for all Jamal's family - no mean feat, considering their numbers. I spent a whole day in a string of department stores and came home empty-handed. Jamal had three sisters and two brothers, all but one of whom were married, and hundreds of cousins although whether these latter qualified for presents was a bit doubtful. Here, they certainly would not, but I knew that cousins were a greater part of the basic family structure in certain societies. It suddenly seemed unrealistic to buy presents for hordes of relatives when I knew nothing about their lifestyles, their tastes or the setup of their homes. I didn't even know the names of most of them. I decided to buy something for Mother only, and of course something for Jamal.

Another day's shopping in the West End of London produced shirts and study materials for Jamal. The choice for Mother was between some hand-decorated porcelain mugs, some stainless steel cutlery, a pretty Scottish tartan mohair rug and a clock-radio. After much indecision I settled for the rug - I guessed that even in Morocco, they must have cold weather sometimes, and if they didn't, the rug could be put up on the wall or used as a drape on a sofa.

When the time came, I packed my things and took the tube to Heathrow Airport, hardly daring to fantasise on what lay ahead of me. I had only light hand-luggage with me as, following my operation, I was not supposed to do any carrying. When I got to the airport, I found that the check-in counter for Royal Air Maroc was Air France. There, a written sign informed us that those passengers carrying only hand luggage need not check in but could go straight to the departure gate. Shortly before the time of departure, I went to the gate. What a shock! There, I learnt that I should have checked in, that the sign I had read applied only to Air France travellers. I was told by a stony Royal Air Maroc official that there was no room for me on the plane. No room?

"But I have my ticket!" I cried.

She looked thoroughly uninterested. "As you failed to turn up at the check-in counter, your ticket was sold to someone else."

"You cannot sell *my ticket* that I have already paid for, to someone else!" I was in tears. What a devastating turn of events! She turned her back on me to indicate that the conversation was over. I sat down on the nearest seat in despair. I then saw what was apparently the pilot, emerging from the direction of the plane. I threw myself at him.

"Please, it's so absolutely vital that I get on to this plane!"

He was more sympathetic, said he'd do what he could but that the plane was in fact full. I waited, not very hopefully. The minutes ticked by. The plane was due to leave in 5 minutes and still no sign of the pilot. The Royal Air Maroc official approached me with great disdain and told me to leave the area, almost as if I were contaminating the place by my very presence. Just at that moment, the pilot reappeared.

"There's a seat for you." With barely-concealed satisfaction, I stood by while he forced the incredulous official to give me a boarding-pass, and I rushed on to the plane with the pilot.

My seat was next to a Moroccan woman travelling with two children under the age of five. She filled in for me what had happened. She had had overweight luggage, so had asked a man in the check-in queue if he would take a couple of suitcases through for her. He had agreed. What he didn't tell her was that, while she herself was getting out at the first stop - Tangiers - he, together with his and now her luggage, was destined for Casablanca. When she understood her mistake, she was already on the plane, so she approached the cabin crew about it. They were apparently not very sympathetic and even accused her of trying to defraud the air-company. However, later, the pilot came up to where she was sitting with her two children, each one occupying a seat. He said that if she would put her two children on to one seat and give up the other seat, he would make sure that all her luggage was restored to her in Tangiers. She agreed to this and that was how I got my seat.

It occurred to me that, (a) my ticket had been sold more

than once and, (b) this woman had really drawn the short straw, as I shared the doubts she voiced that anyone would bother to search the plane at Tangiers for one person's luggage. However, I was so pleased to have got on to the plane that my overall feeling was one of exhaustion and relief. We touched down at Tangiers on schedule and I got my first glimpse of Morocco.

Chapter 17

For a week, Jamal, as I was to learn later, had been in a state of extreme impatience. He had spent half his time day-dreaming about what the first meeting with his English friend would be like, and the other half going through all her letters over and over again, just in case there was some detail which had escaped his notice, some trait of character he hadn't been aware of before. His eyes constantly rested on his favourite photo, that of a smiling Joyce holding a violin in her hand. She was slim, had large dark eyes, long hair with a fringe and a bone structure which appealed to him. He liked the photo very much - the face confirmed his own impressions of Joyce's character, and the presence of the violin strengthened the positive feelings he already had and underlined his own deep love of music, particularly of the violin. He often listened on his secret cassette recorder (which had been smuggled into the prison) to Beethoven's violin concerto, one of his favourite pieces of music, while gazing at the photo and dreaming that it was Joyce playing it for him alone here in his cell. He might be an intellectual, but he was certainly a romantic, too!

He wondered why she wanted to come all this way to see someone in prison, but was very moved that she did, and his impatience grew with the interminable hours of waiting. He had prepared the visit carefully during the past weeks. The main problem was how to get Joyce into the prison, where the rule was family members only and no foreigners. The Head of Guards was a corrupt character, willing to allow himself little lapses of memory about the rules if offered sufficient encouragement. A bribe had therefore taken care of the 'no foreigner' rule and the family member difficulty was resolved by Joyce taking on a new identity: Jamal's rich sister-in-law from London (the 'rich' part was necessary to give the Head Guard hopes for a future filled with promise).

Jamal had no doubts about meeting Joyce. He felt he knew

her so well that it would be as if they were old friends, reunited after a period of separation. His intense excitement, however, at this unusual and longed-for break in the monotony and inhumanity of prison life, caused him sleepless nights and inactive days. His main problem now was how to get through the long tedious days before she arrived.

I had been told by Jamal that his mother would be waiting for me at the airport (his father had died in 1979, when Jamal was in prison). Tangiers has a very small airport and, in the queue for passport control, you can see the whole of it at a glance. I looked out over the waiting area as I stood in the queue. The only people I could see who appeared to be interested in the long line of passengers, most of whom were British tourists, were a rather portly nun together with another younger woman. I looked around for evidence of Jamal's mother, but could find none. I wondered what to do if they didn't turn up. Wait for them? Ask for help? Take a taxi? I looked back at the nun and her companion who seemed to be making signs. I looked behind me to see who they had come to meet, but this wasn't obvious. No-one looked interested in them, as far as I could see. I then realised that they appeared to be trying to attract my attention. I pointed to myself with raised eyebrows and they nodded vigorously. I got through passport control and went to meet Jamal's mother - the 'nun' - and his oldest sister Naziha. It was my first major confrontation with the veil. Mother, a bit on the plump side and with big glasses, was clad in black from top to toe, with headdress and long cloak, and a white veil covered the bottom half of her face. Naziha was dressed in Western-style clothes. She was thin, with sharp features and glasses. Apart from Arabic, Mother could only speak Spanish in some unintelligible dialect, difficult for me with my rather limited Spanish to comprehend. Contact was easier with Naziha, who spoke fluent French.

We took a taxi to the centre of Tangiers and then boarded a bus for Tetuan, where the family lived, about 40 miles away.

138

It was dark by the time we arrived in Tetuan. The family lived just a few yards from the bus station, in a rented flat quite high up with no lift. It was a reasonably spacious and quite pleasant flat, although lack of maintenance over the years had left its mark.

I spent the weekend in the flat, which was simply furnished. Mother and Naziha were hospitable and quite friendly. The rug had been gladly received and I was relieved that I hadn't bought the mugs - Moroccans drink both hot and cold beverages out of glasses - or the cutlery: here, you eat with your fingers. Standing out on one of the walls was a photo of Jamal taken before his arrest. His eyes, smiling down on me, dominated the room and I began for the hundredth time to speculate on the character behind those eyes. Only here, for the first time, I could place it in a definite context. I felt much closer to Jamal now that I was in his own setting, in a way which had nothing to do with geography. I felt elated and exhilarated - it was as if all the pieces in the plot, which had been so carefully prepared over months and years, were now falling into place. The doubts I had had in England over the unrealness of the situation, over whether the promise contained in all the lovely letters could ever achieve fulfilment, over whether the difference in our cultural backgrounds would provide a hurdle too steep to overcome, were all swept away as I stood gazing at Jamal's photo in the flat where he had passed his formative years. I felt a oneness with him, this man I had never met but who had dominated my life for so long.

Jamal's family showed me around Tetuan. I had three powerful first impressions of the place which were subsequently reinforced as I visited other towns in Morocco. Firstly, the huge number of men in uniform - police, soldiers, guards, I didn't know what they all were; secondly, the large number of veiled women, both young and old - for some reason, I had been quite unprepared for this; and thirdly, the extent of the poverty. The number of beggars obviously in dire need seemed to be greater than the rest of the inhabitants put together. Looking around at this misery, I wondered how a ruler could be proud to reign in such a country where, according to figures from the International World Bank - hardly the most revolutionary of sources - 40% of the inhabitants live below poverty level. King Hassan himself leads a sumptuous life. Even his supporters are worried by his excessive indulgence, a great deal of which is contrary to the doctrines of Islam, a faith where he is Allah's self-proclaimed representative on earth. He owns at least a dozen super-luxurious palaces in as many different towns and it is rumoured that his agents kidnap young girls to become part of one of his many harems. The considerable amounts of aid pouring into his country, especially from France and the USA, enable him to maintain his position of luxury while a fair proportion of his people are dying of starvation on the streets.

On Sunday, it was time for travel. I was in a state of feverish excitement where every tiny delay in leaving the flat seemed like a major setback. Mother and I took the bus from Tetuan to Tangiers and then the train from Tangiers to Kenitra, where Jamal was in prison. It was a long journey which lasted for hours and hours - there is no modern railway system in Morocco. The train was old, noisy, uncomfortable and pervaded by a musty smell. There were mostly men on it, all of whom seemed to be heavy smokers, which added to the dankness and feeling of claustrophobia. However, there was a lively atmosphere among the passengers and I even found myself laughing with them a few times, although I had only a vague notion of the essence of the joke.

As we stopped in tiny station after tiny station, darkness began to fall, underlining the length of the journey which had begun at two in the afternoon in bright sunlight. At last, the train pulled up at a station called Kenitra.

I stared for a long time in disbelief at the name of this town I had seen so often in a negative context on paper and had written myself so often on envelopes. I thought I must be dreaming, but Mother's elbow digging in my back indicated that I was awake, that we had arrived at our destination and that I had better get out quick. We took a taxi from the station, which drove along badly-lit, fairly deserted streets until it stopped outside the modest home of an uncle of Jamal's in a rather poor quarter of town. (I have since learnt that Moroccans have relatives *everywhere*. Wherever you go you are bound to find a relative you probably didn't even know existed.) This family consisted of mother, father and five children, the youngest being 14 years old. They were all out of work except for one of the sons - Hassan - whose modest wage had to support the entire family. They gave me a really warm welcome. The flat had been rearranged for our visit, and I was given my own room there, which I understood to be quite a luxury.

That night, I didn't sleep at all as I went over and over again in my head my anticipation of the first meeting with Jamal which would take place the next morning. Would I meet him in his cell? Would he be disappointed in my appearance, would I be disappointed in his? Should I kiss him, would he kiss me? Would it be difficult to find things to talk about? Perhaps I wouldn't be admitted at all.

I had never been inside a prison before. Would I be searched? (Better inspect the contents of my bag and remove any incriminating evidence.) Would the guards note down everything I said? Should I avoid certain topics? Would the presence of Mother feel like a security or a restraint?

I don't know how I managed to feel so clear-headed and full of energy the next morning when I had spent the whole night awake in a fever of intoxication and mental activity. I was completely unable to face breakfast or anything remotely resembling food, so I set off with Mother for the prison with an empty stomach but a full heart.

To enter the prison, you had to go to a small building just inside the first gate to register and collect a pass, then walk down a fairly long drive to the prison itself, protected by a large iron gate with a door in the middle. The guard there opened the door and collected your pass and then you walked over to the main body of the prison, where another guard alerted the prisoner you wished to visit. He would then appear. All the prisoners and their visitors sat together in groups on the floor in a long hallway.

I got through the various hurdles with surprisingly little difficulty and waited with Mother in the hallway for Jamal to arrive. My heart was beating so intensely that I felt sure everyone must be able to hear it. The guard had recognised Mother and he called out Jamal's name, a call which was taken up by what must have been another guard some distance away. As we waited there, two or three other prisoners emerged to meet their loved ones and scenes of joy and emotion began to fill the hall.

After an agony of suspense, Jamal at last appeared. He was bigger than I had been expecting but I recognised the eyes straightaway. He came towards us with long strides and a smile which stretched from ear to ear.

"Joyce!" This first sound of his voice was pure music. "*Finalement!*"

"Jamal!"

I felt I wanted to cry.

He hugged and kissed me and greeted his mother and we all sat down on a rug he had brought from his cell. I was scarcely conscious of Mother's presence.

"How wonderful to see you at long last!" Jamal laughed at me. His face was so lit up, so intensely full of pleasure, it seemed that he just couldn't stop smiling. All I could do was to smile back, feel his warmth.

"How was the journey?" He started to talk about banalities. I could hardly say a word. I answered with short sentences, just drinking in his presence. He filled my whole space.

"Tell me about your life in London," he begged.

"Later, my dear Jamal, later, you'll hear all about it bit by bit. Now I just want to look at you."

"Yes, look at me, Joyce dear. I've been looking at you for years, centuries. Was this what you expected?"

142

I nodded, overcome. I was so happy to be with him, he was so easy to communicate with, it was as if we had known each other for years. But then of course we had.

This first meeting passed in a haze. By the end of it, I felt so much in love with Jamal - the build-up, staggering in its intensity, had not ended in anti-climax - I didn't know what to do. I couldn't express this or see if he felt the same way, as I sensed an inhibiting effect of mother's presence.

I spent a sleepless night followed by a restless Tuesday. I couldn't eat a thing, which I felt guilty about, as I imagined the family I was staying with would be insulted. Indeed, they did everything they could to try and tempt me to eat. I blamed this aversion to food on my operation, but this made them all the more insistent. How could I tell them that, Moroccan food notwithstanding, my system was in a state of shock following an emotional rather than a physical assault and that 'since I am myself my own fever' I could see no immediate remedy.

Tetuan. Building where Jamal's family lived (on top floor)

Tetuan. View of the street from the flat of Jamal's family

Rabat. Mosque in the centre of the city.

Chapter 18

Wednesday came at long last and we went again to the prison. I had thought such a lot about what I was going to say to Jamal. He spoke no English so our communication was in French, but it flowed easily between us. Mother and I sat on the rug, one either side of Jamal. He had to divide his time between us, in two different languages. I didn't mind this as, when he was talking to Mother, this gave me time to look around at the other prisoners, to get an idea of the atmosphere and to reflect on the conversation between the two of us, to pick up clues of his feelings towards me now that we were together.

What a new situation this was for me! I had all these strong feelings but was unable to express them. I sat there, agonising over whether or not I should tell Jamal of my feelings for him. How could I tell him how much I loved him without being able to express it in any sort of body language? I felt constrained by the dominant presence of Mother. Once I went to touch him timidly on the shoulder but somehow the sight of the monastic attire on the other side of the rug, froze the movement and I rubbed my head instead. Then a prisoner came up to where we were sitting, someone who evidently knew Mother and who had no visitors himself. To my delight, he sat himself down and started to engage Mother in conversation. Jamal, his duty towards his mother temporarily absolved, turned to me and smiled tenderly. The smile spoke volumes. We didn't need a spoken language. I felt faint. I looked up at him, stared into those lovely eyes I had dreamt about. Jamal said to me:

"Could you imagine living in Morocco?"

I gave a non-committal answer, terrified of the strength of my feelings. He said: "I would like us to live together, either for a time or else forever." I was so happy, I told him how much I loved him and how I wanted nothing else. Just in time, as the prisoner talking to Mother had been called away and now she was back in control.

I nestled into the rug while Jamal chatted away in Arabic to Mother. I felt calm and serene. There was no turning back now. I was totally committed to this warm gentle Moroccan who had been through such hell. What a relief that things were now out in the open! Subsequent visits reinforced the feelings between us. It was a strange courtship, to say the least. All these feelings of love between us, and we had hardly touched each other! The combined censorship of prison and Mother provided a chaperone of bastion proportions. But once, when Jamal was saying goodbye to us in the habitual French manner of a kiss on each cheek, he did, during the passage from one cheek to the other, daringly land a surreptitious kiss on my lips. This *baiser volé* (stolen kiss), as Jamal called it, penetrated deep into my body and I could still feel it days afterwards.

Prison visits were on Mondays, Wednesdays, Fridays and Saturdays, mornings and afternoons. On the days when there was no visit, I often went to Rabat, the capital city (about 30 miles from Kenitra) together with Mother and Aziz, one of the sons in the flat where we were staying. I loved going to the Medina - the old town - with all its bazaars and lively atmosphere. It was always crowded, with traders enticing people to buy, and customers jostling for bargains. Apart from the display of cassettes and videos in a few stalls, there was such a sense of timelessness as we wandered down the tiny cobbled alleyways amidst the cry of the traders, the sight of the colourful wares, the donkeys and carts, the hooded djellabas, the pungent smell of spices and bread being baked in the large ovens and the deeply sensual Arabic music we heard everywhere.

On one occasion, as we were walking along a packed and noisy alleyway, I remembered Jamal's rather shabby prison clothes, and happened to mention to Aziz that I'd like to buy him some trousers. He reported this to Mother. She stopped so abruptly in her tracks that a man and his donkey close on her heels were almost in need of hospitalisation. From then on the entire matter was taken out of my hands. She marched up to a street seller of trousers (one of the many without a stall, his merchandise being of dubious origin) and said something to him, whereby he took off into a nearby street and we all followed. We must have looked an odd sight: guiding us at the head of the procession was the seller swathed in about ten pairs of multi-coloured trousers, Mother striding purposefully along right behind him, with Aziz and I almost apologetically bringing up the rear. We went up and down several different paths and in and out of a few buildings. In the end, we got to a house with a long hallway culminating in a door which disguised a deep staircase. We descended to a cellar which led to a cellar which led to a cellar. It was pitch dark as we groped our way along. I started to wonder how a simple desire to buy a fairly basic article of clothing had led to a journey through the bowels of the medina into the unknown.

Suddenly, the whole scenario changed. From the blackness of the cellar, our guide threw open a door to reveal such a brightly-lit room that we stood there for a moment or two, dazed and blinking. The room, about the size of a large living-room, was crammed full with jeans, slacks, cords and similar of every conceivable colour, shape and size. It was the trouser department of Aladdin's Cave. Mother propelled herself into the midst of the treasure and ferreted around, hurling rejects in her wake. At last she evidently found something to her liking, a pair of dark blue soft cords. She pounced on them triumphantly, holding them up to the light and fingering the quality of the material. Aziz and I might not have existed.

Then there was the question of price. Voices were raised, pleas were apparently being made and rejected, arms were thrown up and down in despair, hands were clutching hearts with the intensity of a doomed man pleading for his life. Three times, Mother strode resolutely out of the room, Aziz and I obediently following. Three times we were all dragged back in again. Suddenly, peace reigned, cups of mint tea were produced, everyone was laughing, and I understood that negotiations had been concluded. The only function for me was to pay.

When we went to get the bus back to Kenitra - the last one of the day - it appeared that about a hundred other people had had the same idea, as there was one of the longest queues I have ever seen. And what a journey it was!

The bus - a dirty noisy museum piece of a vehicle - suddenly appeared from round the corner, whereupon any previous attempt at an orderly queue vanished, and there was a mad rush for the door. Mother elbowed her way to the front and she was one of the first on the bus. I hung back, startled by the scrum, and the shy Aziz stayed at my side. As I looked despairingly from the pavement at the relentless surge on to the bus, a friendly-looking man inside caught my eye and signalled that he would reserve two places for us. Delighted at this unexpected assistance, I eventually managed to board the bus with Aziz, and we fought our way to the promised land of the two seats, only to find that two other contenders had just sat down on them. Indignant, our newly-found friend started to shout at these people, who both yelled back at him. Then a man sitting in front turned on the two seat-thieves and began bellowing at them, whereupon two people from behind started to shout at him. Mother forced her way over and added her not inconsiderable voice to the decibels and soon the whole bus was in uproar, everyone taking sides - I'd say about a 50-50 split. The only ones not taking part were those most involved: Aziz and myself, wishing we could both seep through the litter-filled floor into oblivion.

It was hot, crowded and noisy. Suddenly, it seemed as if the whole dispute had been settled - and in our favour - for our new friend and the people he had been screaming at not five minutes earlier, were now hugging each other and the seats were vacated. Aziz and I sank down thankfully on to the leather and the bus started off. It was completely jammed full, I had never seen anything like it. There were about 100 people stacked together in a space probably intended for about 40. Passengers were almost literally sitting on the driver's lap. There was a very jolly atmosphere. A group of young people at the front started to sing some silly songs, first in Arabic, then in French and then in something vaguely recognisable as English. Most people in the bus joined in but couldn't get the words right and everyone was giggling.

It was then I noticed that the road had turned into a track, that it was pitch-black and we seemed to be going through the middle of a farm as, at one point, chickens scattered in all directions. I remarked to Aziz that this bore little resemblance to the main road between Rabat and Kenitra. He told me that the driver had an illegal number of passengers on board, so he had to take this circuitous route to avoid the police.

Our conversation was suddenly shattered by a banging noise which grew in volume and desperation until, in the end, the driver stopped the bus. The exit door was in the front, just opposite his seat, and it opened outwards. In the small space between his seat and the door, about twenty people were all squeezed tightly together, practically melting into each other. The driver pushed a button. The door opened with a shudder and six people immediately fell out. Another ten had to remove themselves before the driver could get anywhere near the exit. A flock of terrified sheep and half a dozen indignant chickens fled to safety.

The banging noise had, it seemed, mysteriously come from the roof. Aziz gave me a blow by blow account of the heated discussion. Apparently five people, unable to get inside the bus, had managed to crawl on to the roof, doubtlessly having decided that a journey exposed to the elements was infinitely preferable to a 30-mile hike in the dark. It was a decision they were now regretting. The cold evening air was penetrating their thin clothing and they wanted to get inside. After a seemingly endless dispute with the driver, the five were then crammed into the bus (Heaven only knows how) to the accompaniment of loud wails from the indigenous population therein. The driver continued on his way, seemingly oblivious to the noise, discomfort and what appeared to be threats from his passengers, and about twenty minutes later we arrived in Kenitra, slightly the worse for wear.

The next day when we went to the prison, Jamal told me about 'hospital visits'. He was arranging some for when there was no visiting at the prison. Hospital visits were a big treat for the prisoners and one of the great anomalies of the system. It was a chance for them - their only chance - to get outside the prison walls and have a look at normal life. They also used this opportunity to meet friends and relatives in the comparative freedom of the hospital gardens, and especially those - such as former prisoners and well-known activists - who were not allowed inside the prison. They had, of course, fought for the right to receive medical treatment during their long hunger-strike. It became relatively easy for the prisoners to go to hospital - being in need of treatment was often the least important criterion.

Jamal told me that once, during an examination, a sympathetic woman doctor had whispered in his ear in a friendly manner. Understanding the importance to the prisoners of these visits, she was going to sign papers requiring Jamal to attend the hospital regularly for a whole course of treatments. Little acts of kindness and solidarity such as this were not infrequent. Even if individuals felt helpless to change a distressing situation, there were always ways to make a personal statement, with whatever means you had at your disposal. So on two different days during my visit, we all met up in the hospital gardens in a relaxed setting, away from the dark sordidness of the prison.

The evenings in Kenitra seemed very long as there wasn't anything to do apart from watching television. And the television news - it had to be seen to be believed! There were rarely any international news reports and the national news centred very heavily on the monarchy and the monarch himself. When I was there, King Hassan was going on a visit to the White House. He was filmed setting out with his enormous cortege to the airport. The whole runway was lined with dignitaries, several hundred of them. As the

King went along the line, every single dignitary kissed his hand. Some of them were so eager that they almost bit it off. The cameras filmed the whole charade. Not one kiss failed to be shown on film.

Then there were long repetitive shots of the White House, all of which looked rather ridiculous. The King, obviously aware he was being filmed, seemed to be making conscious efforts to stand as near the President as possible. Being a short man, he had to keep peering over taller heads to make sure he was in the picture. This so-called news - in Arabic - lasted about one hour, a good 80% of it devoted to the White House visit. I breathed a sigh of relief when it finished, only to discover that there was then a full action replay in French, just in case any non-Arab speaking person had failed to get the message! About three days later, the King returned to Morocco and the whole unbelievable hand-kissing performance was dragged across the screen once more in two languages. The television set was always on, the volume was deafening and it dominated the whole of the small flat. There was nothing to do other than sit there with everyone else and watch the rubbish pouring out of it.

We saw Jamal every other day. It was amazing to me that going to a prison could be such a joyous occasion, and yet I had still hardly touched the man I loved.

One morning, when Mother and I were waiting in the hallway for Jamal to appear, we were aware of a prisoner and girlfriend sitting on the floor kissing. Mother shuddered at the sight, then looked at me and said: "Isn't that disgusting?"

I was taken aback but replied: "No, it's an expression of love." Mother went on as if she hadn't heard me: *"Que no tienen vergüenza!"* (They ought to be ashamed of themselves)

I now felt rather indignant on behalf of the couple. I said: "Look, most couples can express their love in privacy. These prisoners who are denied this are probably in greater need of love and tenderness than most others. They've had enough punishment. Don't deny them love as well."

153

Mother (taken on a beach near Tetuan)

It didn't come out as fluently as this, as it was said in halting Spanish, but I knew she understood what I was trying to say and knew she disapproved strongly. Was the difference in our approach anchored in culture, age or education, or all three? At least I knew Jamal would have the same reaction as myself.

When we had been going to the prison for about a week, and Mother was temporarily distracted from her self-appointed vigilance, Jamal gave me one of his tender looks and said: "I'd love to see you alone."

"Yes," I replied, "I feel that need, too." I waited for him to make a suggestion about how it could be achieved. However, he fell silent, studying his hands. Then he turned his big dark eyes on me and said, "Joyce, could you try and sort it out with my mother?"

I wasn't prepared for this. I started visibly. "What? Me?" I looked at him disbelievingly. "This isn't going to endear me to her particularly."

I felt scared. Jamal was silent. I leaned forward. "Can't *you* speak to her about it?" I implored, frantically searching for an excuse to absolve myself from any suspicion of cowardice. Silence. After a few moments, I said lamely: "You know her better than I do."

This played straight into Jamal's hands. "Yes, that's the problem," he answered convincingly. "In this country, you can't just exclude your mother from anything. It would have to come from her."

I was learning fast. "That's not very likely, Jamal, is it?"

There was no answer. Concerned by Jamal's passivity on this issue, yet wishing to solve the problem and also confirm his faith in me, I heard myself say with a good deal more confidence than I felt: "OK, I'll fix it."

I knew it was going to be no easy task, but I was highly motivated. I had also started feeling restricted by Mother's constant presence and was conscious of a resentment coming from her. I had no idea whether or not she suspected that Jamal and I were anything other than jolly pen-pals.

Mother liked to be at the centre of everything and in total control. I imagined that her main safety valve would be that I wouldn't be allowed into the prison on my own. I therefore decided to remove the basis for this possible objection before it materialised. I prepared the ground.

I had noticed that the Head Guard was a bit of a womaniser. One day, taking advantage of being alone for a few minutes at the prison gate while Mother was talking to a friend after the visit, I approached him directly. There was a small stream of people leaving the prison and he was nodding and exchanging greetings with some of them. He was a tallish man probably in his forties, with a rather stupid expression on his face, and he seemed acutely aware of his own importance.

"Are you the Chief of all the guards?" I asked him, incorporating a slight tone of awe into my voice on the word 'Chief'.

His body expanded to about 150% of its original state and he leaned in my direction. "I am," he beamed.

Edging a bit closer and dropping my voice, I said to him in a confidential tone: "I have something I would like to ask you."

He looked at me with intense curiosity and interest.

"It will be all right, won't it, for me to come here and visit Jamal by myself?"

I had chosen the exact words with care and had even rehearsed them a few times.

The Head Guard considered the question, looked around him and then back to me. He smiled and winked. "Of course."

I had a sleepless night that night (yet again) thinking over what I was going to say to Mother. I really did want to be on good terms with her. I realised she had been through a lot. Jamal had told me how she had seen her son disappear, not knowing where he was, what had happened to him or even whether he was alive or dead. When she did discover his fate and saw him after a long period of time, she could hardly recognise him after all the abuse and torture he had suffered. In the early days, visits were allowed

156

only once every so often and for a duration of 10 minutes. The prisoners were lined up between one set of bars and their visitors behind another 3 metres away, with guards marching up and down in the middle. The noise was apparently indescribable. So Mother, who was not in particularly good health, would travel for six hours on a bone-shaker of a bus (train was too expensive) for money she could ill afford, to stand and scream at the apparition barely recognisable as her son for 10 minutes before taking the bus back to Tetuan again.

Even worse was the fate of Jamal's grandmother, who lived with the family and who had always adored Jamal. During the time of the hunger-strike, someone came in to announce the death of Saida Menebhi. "They're all dying off like flies," he had said. Grandmother immediately had a stroke from which she didn't recover, and she never regained her speech before she died some time later.

Until my appearance on the scene, Mother had been the only woman in Jamal's life, so I could understand her resentment of me. I had tried hard to like her, to be understanding of her and to be sensitive to her role in Jamal's life. It was not easy, as her hostility was quite apparent. I knew there would be a battle ahead.

The following day was not a visiting day and I got up fairly late. Mother had gone out to buy some cotton to repair a damaged garment. I felt somewhat relieved at her absence and sat down to have breakfast with the family of seven. They were sweet kindly people whom I liked and respected and we got on well together. After breakfast, I went out with the eldest cousin, Hassan. We were to walk to another part of town to fetch a spare part for the television which, mercifully, had broken down the previous evening, probably infected with all the toxic material it had been forced to digest recently.

We discussed Jamal and his imprisonment. Hassan was neither unintelligent nor unaware and, for a time, chatting away about my involvement with Amnesty, I was taken in by his calm

157

exterior. He was a pleasant man of about 30, but the obvious strain of being the only breadwinner in this large family gave him a constantly worried look and contributed to making him seem older than his years. How could he, faced with such responsibility, even start to think about building a life of his own, getting married, producing his own family? His wage was only enough to cover the rent for his poky little flat and to satisfy the most basic needs of his elderly parents and siblings. And yet he may well have been the envy of many other Moroccans because at least there was one wage among seven and they also had somewhere to live.

It was a mild day, warm enough to wear thin sleeveless cotton. We walked down the road, passing a group of wide-eyed children dressed in rags, barefoot, who stared at us. One of them said something to Hassan but he didn't respond. A painfully thin dog was half-heartedly shooed away from a shop selling tired-looking vegetables. The ugly buildings in Kenitra, completely devoid of any charm or personality, matched the general air of depression in the streets, the listlessness of the inhabitants, and the repulsive ever-present stench of poverty and degradation.

Hassan asked me about my life and listened as I described some of my activities in Sweden.

"One day," I said, "We went and picketed outside the Moroccan Tourist Office. Every time anyone was about to enter, we gave them a leaflet about the political prisoners. We told of the dangers in Morocco. We urged them to get their sun tan in other countries. We told them how thoroughly corrupt the King was. Some people ignored us but some listened and discussed the issues with us and we did manage to turn some away. The Tourist Office staff were furious but there was nothing they could do."

Jamal would have been delighted to hear about our action. I don't know why I expected the same response from Hassan. I suddenly realised he had turned silent and was looking nervously around him. I was at that time blissfully unaware that defaming the King carried with it a jail sentence of at least two years. But I was

158

to remember the conversation when, a couple of days later, I was asked politely and apologetically if I would mind moving into a hotel. Feeding six members of your family is, after all, an awesome responsibility.

Later on that day, Mother and I went with some cousins to the local market to buy some fresh fruit and vegetables. Plucking up courage on the way home, I told Mother that I wished to see Jamal alone. I braced myself for the inevitable dispute. I actually felt terrified. There was, of course, a strong reaction.

"Alone? Alone? Alone with Jamal? You mean, just the two of you? Without me?" When the tautology had finally burnt itself out, Mother fixed me with a steady eye. "Why should that be necessary?"

"It's not that it is necessary. I just think it would be, well, rather nice," I said feebly. We were walking down the main street in Kenitra, skirting round some noisy roadworks.

Mother was certainly not going to let this pass. "So what's wrong with me being there?"

"There's nothing wrong. I just feel it would be easier to talk to Jamal if there were only the two of us."

Mother snorted. A drill started slicing its way through the highway. Ra-ta-ta, ra-ta-taaaaa. Bellowing above the noise, she cried: "You mean you want to sit down together like that couple the other day!"

Angry with Jamal for putting me in this position, I nevertheless stuck to my guns and stood up against Mother's undisputed authority in a way which almost surprised me. During a moment of respite from the drill I said firmly: "We feel a need to be alone together."

Mother nearly exploded. The drill started up again louder than ever. The combined staccato of the machine and her indignant voice punctured the air almost visibly. "Are you trying to stop me from seeing *my* son?" (The word *my* was heavily accented, just to show whose property Jamal really was).

159

"No, of course not." I countered, trying hard to compete with the percussive side effects, "You will have many opportunities to see him when I am back in London, but for my last few days here, I would ask that we could be alone, please." (Hadn't Mother ever been in love herself, for goodness sake?)

There was a pause while she considered her next move. Then she said: "Well, that may be what you prefer but the guards will never let you into the prison alone. You need me to be able to get you in."

Mother looked triumphant. The drill spluttered to a halt as we rounded the corner and Hassan's flat came into view. Nearly home and dry. It was the cue for me to produce my trump card. I took a deep breath.

"No, I have already discussed it with the Head Guard. He said there would be no problems about me going there alone."

Mother's eyes widened in utter astonishment and I think she realised for the first time how she had underestimated the strength and determination of her adversary.

What a long and exhausting battle it was. I had come prepared to take on the prison guards and the whole of the police force if necessary, but Mother? That was definitely something else. I did win in the end and for the last couple of visiting days, I enjoyed the unbelievable luxury of seeing Jamal alone. We sat on rugs on the floor together in a corner of the hallway where we were not so conspicuous. I put my arms around Jamal and hugged and hugged him, wanting nothing more than to spend the rest of my life here in this warmth. Jamal held me as if he were never going to let go. He caressed my face, outlining all my features with his lovely soft hands. He kissed me, nuzzled me, hugged me, ran his hands over my body. Between each kiss, I uttered his name over and over again, such a beautiful musical name: "Jamal, Jamal, Jamal." Prison walls, prison guards, Mother, ceased to exist. We were alone in our precious world.

Just before I left to go back to London, Jamal gave me a

document he wanted me to take to Amnesty. It was a paper, rolled up in a scroll, signed by all the prisoners in which they explained in great legal detail how their imprisonment was not only against international law, but also against Morocco's own laws. I put it inside my suitcase.

When I went through Customs at Tangiers Airport, I was surprised to have my luggage searched. To my absolute horror, the Customs Officer picked up the scroll and began to open it. In desperation, I asked him a banal question which required a fairly lengthy answer. He rose to the occasion and started to reply, using the scroll in his hand to emphasise his statements. I felt a cold sweat break out as, helplessly, I watched the scroll going up and down. Then to my utter relief, he rolled it up, put it back in the suitcase, wished me a pleasant flight and hoped I would return to Morocco again soon!

Chapter 19

It was difficult to settle into a normal routine in England after the past hectic weeks in Morocco. Yet this was only a diluted foretaste of what was to come.

I had a mixed reaction to my news from family and friends. Some colleagues were enthusiastic about the relationship, while others were more sceptical. "What's wrong with Englishmen?" asked one male colleague, sniffily. "You don't have to go to either the North Pole or the Equator, you know."

I had a lot of support from people close to me: my friend in London, Val, was encouraging and my lovely sister Jean - always my best ally - was also supportive. She became interested in Jamal and started to write to him in prison, sending him gifts. Another big mainstay of support came from my friend in Cardiff, Beryl Rubens, who had been a militant in the USA during the McCarthy era. She was playing (along with Jean) in Welsh National Opera - anything less militant has to be imagined! She, too, started writing to Jamal and sent him - among other things - a Welsh National Opera T-shirt which Jamal wore in the prison yard, provoking comments from co-prisoners. It was an area of publicity not previously tapped by Welsh National Opera. However, I don't believe it had a large impact on their ticket sales.

The reaction from my father was less favourable. He wrote to me saying I had "given the relationship a fairy-tale flavour" which apparently belied my intelligence and maturity. Jamal, if he should ever think of coming to live in the UK (Heaven forbid) would not, it seemed, ever get a job, a work permit or even (perhaps wishful thinking?) a residence permit. I could understand my father's doubts, and so could Jamal. The difference between a successful Swedish lawyer and an unknown Arab in a Moroccan jail is not inconsiderable.

Letters between Kenitra and London took on a slightly

different complexion. From Jamal:

"Joyce, my love. I just don't know how to begin this letter. It was only about 5 or 6 hours ago that we were together and here I am now alone. I really cannot describe the state of depression, sadness and grief that I am experiencing at this moment. I find it difficult to accept this awful reality. I can hardly hold the pen steady in my hands, I am really in a lamentable state. I must tell you that with you, I have experienced the happiest of days but now that you have left, I am also experiencing the darkest days of my life as a prisoner. I wanted to write you a long letter to tell you all about my feelings and my impressions of you since our meeting, but because of the state I am in, I am unable to continue writing. Please excuse me, my darling, my beloved, I just want you to know that you don't leave my spirit for a single moment. You are always present in my soul.
I love you – Jamal."

To Jamal, written the day after:

"How can I describe the overwhelming feeling of emptiness inside me, since we separated? How can I fill this void when I can no longer hear your beloved voice, can no longer touch that dear face, can no longer feel the warmth of those beautiful gentle eyes caressing me to the depths of my soul? I just don't know how I can manage without you. After all these months or years of unrest that I have experienced, I can see that I have now found a refuge in you which makes me no longer feel alone. If there are contradictions in what I am writing, it's just a reflection of the state of my feelings of love for you: on the one hand, a feeling of despair at this separation and the bigger one of three years, but at the same time, a great happiness that, even far apart, we share a whole world

164

together, and not any sort of world but a world anchored in sincerity and mutual respect and enveloped in a veil of softness and tenderness. Tu es mon ami, mon aimé, mon amant, mon âme.

When I think that it is visiting day at prison today, I nearly go mad. I want to sit snuggled up to you again, feeling the warmth of your body...

All I do is to think and dream of you, I have relived the wonderful moments we have spent together a million times. Please write to me soon. Your words will be my eau de vie. I am dying with the need to feel your lips, your tongue, your body pressed closely to mine.

I love you passionately – Joyce

I had thought a lot about how to give publicity to the violations of human rights happening in Morocco. It was important, as King Hassan was sensitive to public opinion and there was never any mention of the atrocities in the British media. Not even the most well-educated and knowledgeable of my friends had any idea about it. They imagined, as I had previously, that Morocco was some sort of liberal democracy.

A colleague with press connections, got me an interview with Rosemary Righter at the Sunday Times. It was arranged almost before I knew what was happening. I had never spoken directly to the press before, and I felt nervous. If they interviewed me and then wrote an article about the substance of the interview, I would be "going public". Yet wasn't this what I wanted? Yes, of course I wanted publicity and lots of it, but with the reservation that I would not have to figure anywhere. It was difficult to shake off this cloak of self-consciousness, carefully learned throughout the years, which was in stark contrast to the strength of my feelings, bursting for expression.

As I walked down Fleet Street, I thought about what to say and how to say it. I had an uneasy feeling that, when the time came, I wouldn't have the courage to speak out as I wanted.

I was shown straightaway to the office of Rosemary Righter. She looked at me with a certain curiosity, shook hands and said she wanted a colleague to be present as well. She went to find him, returning a few minutes later with a man vaguely resembling Cary Grant past his prime. I said: "I've come here to draw attention to the appalling human rights situation in Morocco and to encourage you to write about it." I then launched into an account of the horrors being endured by innocent Moroccan citizens - the disappearances, long jail sentences for prisoners of conscience, the torture, secret detention centres, detention without trial etc. It wasn't so difficult to speak after all, but I got the impression they weren't interested. However, they heard me out. Then the Cary Grant understudy said: "My dear, there are all sorts of ghastly things happening all over the world. We can't write about everything."

"But you never write anything about Morocco," I said reproachfully.

"Who's interested in Morocco? Who even knows where it is?"

"If you wrote about it, people would learn. You can't expect them to be interested in something they have no knowledge about."

Cary Senior looked at his watch. "We don't have the space."

At this point, the strength of my feelings overcame my natural reserve.

"You newspapers make me sick!" I heard myself shouting at them. "You write about countries which happen to be 'in fashion'. Innocent people in Morocco are dying of torture, lengthy incarceration in stinking jails, and extreme ill-treatment, but because Morocco is not trendy, the abuse of human rights there can pass completely unnoticed by the media."

The two journalists looked startled at the outburst but didn't deny the charges, which emboldened Counsel for the Prosecution to continue: "You've been writing about Poland for about two years. Why should we be interested in Poland particularly? It's not much nearer than Morocco, it's a different culture, we don't speak their language. But it's trendy. It's also good for a bit of Commie-bashing!"

I felt myself getting carried away but was unable to stop. "The press recently wrote a shock-horror story about a political prisoner in the Soviet Union who got the whole of four years in jail. There were no allegations of ill-treatment. Four years would be a *holiday* for a Moroccan prisoner! The 'lucky' ones get 10 years, the others get 20 or 30 years or life for having done no more than distribute a few leaflets and organise the odd peaceful demonstration. It's your duty to inform people of *everything* that is going on, not just pick out a few trendy countries!"

There was a long silence. I sensed that the interview was at an end. They could understand why I felt the way I did, I shouldn't take it to heart, they would look into it and do what they could. They would contact me.

I dreamt of seeing Jamal again as soon as possible. It seemed all the more imperative in view of the difficulties we were experiencing in getting letters to each other. I wrote to him about twice a week yet, as this card written by Jamal on 31 December 1982 shows, letters just weren't getting through.

"I am really distressed and worried that I haven't heard from you. The last letter I received was dated 16th November. I wrote you a short letter on 2nd December, a very long one two days later, and then two other letters put into the same envelope, one of them giving you details of a new address we can use for future correspondence.

Today, it is New Year's Eve. I suppose everyone is celebrating outside, but I am locked up alone here in my tiny cell, my only compensation being the wonderful memories of the happy times we have spent together and the hope to see you again as soon as possible. To console myself and to provide some relief for the pain of your absence during this evening, I have put up all the photos of you I have around me and I am looking at them now and dreaming.

I am dying to see you again and to hug you in my arms. It is my only thought and desire. My God, how I long for you, always charming and smiling and so delicious and tender! I am seeing you this time with your new haircut which I like so much.

It is now midnight. I am seeing in the New Year writing you this letter. I hope we will be able to celebrate the next New Year together and that this New Year will be the year when we can meet in freedom to give a new dimension to our love and our being united.

I kiss you with much warmth and tenderness.

Happy New Year – Jamal"

I was preparing to go to Morocco again in January 1983. I wanted to be with Jamal on my birthday. I was at the time doing a research project with no fixed working hours, which meant I could work very hard and then take time off - an arrangement which suited my new life very well.

I was still not in contact with Axel at this time. I thought about him a great deal but was convinced that a clean break was best. He apparently felt the same as he made no attempt to contact me either. I knew this silence would not last forever but at the moment, it seemed the only way. We each needed to discover ourselves, to realise our potential, we needed to let go of each other, to grow. We had known each other practically from childhood.

Our house in Sweden had been sold. With my share of the proceeds, I had bought a house in North London. There was money left over to finance what would probably be a fairly expensive period ahead. My prime concern was to go and see Jamal as often as possible and provide him with every comfort life could offer and the prison system would allow (or even not allow, as was to be seen) during the remainder of his imprisonment.

I thought of our next meeting constantly. Would it match up to the first one? Would we still feel the same deep love, the same bond? Jamal's letters had shown his feelings towards me to be as strong as ever and I had not the slightest doubt about my own but I was a little apprehensive, even so. In a normal relationship, where you meet your partner every day or so, any changes take place gradually so that you can adapt, assimilate them. But this was not a normal relationship.

When Jamal and I had parted, each of us went back to completely different worlds. I went back to an interesting and worthwhile job, to caring colleagues, to Jean, Beryl and Val with all their love and support. I could go to the cinema at a moment's notice, could travel, invite friends round for a meal, meet up in a pub with colleagues after work, could be ill and be cared for, could have a bath whenever I felt like it. Jamal's quota was one hot shower every Thursday morning. He was locked up with a body of other men, was forced daily to confront and live in close proximity with men he didn't like and never wanted to see again, was surrounded by all sorts of humiliating restrictions, by corruption; and in the midst of this large community of prisoners, he felt the most overwhelming solitude. His was a cold hard world where self-interest and opportunism were the order of the day, a world where the oxygen of love had been virtually cut off, a world of at best indifference, at worst hate.

Chapter 20

It was cold when I arrived at Casablanca Airport on a Sunday afternoon in January and I made my way to Kenitra, where I'd planned to register at a hotel. Jamal's relatives didn't want me to stay with them any more. They thought I was a dangerous militant and they were frightened of repercussions. I don't blame them - to me, it was just indicative of the general atmosphere of fear perpetrated by a repressive regime. They had to consider their own safety first, especially with one son supporting a family of seven. To my delight, Jamal and I were going to be 'alone' during the whole of my stay. He had told his mother he didn't want visits from anyone.

I booked into a modest hotel in Kenitra, near the prison and where I had my own bathroom. I wanted to be clean and fresh for each visit!

My presence at the hotel attracted some attention: whatever was a European woman, travelling alone, doing in a hole like Kenitra, a most boring town without a single positive attraction? Could it be drugs? One employee, no doubt trying to provoke me, said this was the first time he had seen *any* tourist in Kenitra, let alone one from abroad who moreover was planning to stay by herself for three whole weeks! The attention was unwelcome but I was glowing so much inside at the thought of spending a long concentrated period alone with Jamal, that it did not cause me too much anxiety.

I went to bed early trying to make Monday morning arrive as soon as possible, yet sleep seemed out of the question. Even when Nature did finally take over, I kept on waking up in panic in case I had overslept.

Breakfast the next morning wasn't to be thought of - I was much too full up to put anything else inside me. The air was chilly as I started out on the 15-minute walk to the prison, and I was glad of the thick brown cardigan I had brought with me. Last time, it had been warm and mostly sunny. Now, with this weather which was very cold by Moroccan standards, it was as if the whole identity of the country had changed. The chill in the air somehow got through to my heart and I suddenly felt alone and curiously apprehensive as I walked along the dusty cart-track. Even the thought that I would soon be with Jamal failed to thaw the chill. There were too many hurdles to overcome before I could get to his warmth. Supposing I was refused entry to see him? What recourse would I have? Presumably none.

To encourage myself, I went through all the happy moments of my previous visit and dwelt on the longing Jamal had expressed in his last letter.

I got to the prison gate. A guard whom I had not seen before was in the hut, issuing entry permits. I stood in the small queue of visitors to get my permit. I felt in a quandary as the queue moved slowly forward. The guard would ask me who I was. I usually had to present my passport as proof of identity. Should I go on being a sister-in-law in spite of my most unsister-in-law like behaviour once inside the prison gates? Or should I now be a fiancée, risking not being admitted as I was not a family member, and risking their discovery of my last alias?

Confused at my double identity, I couldn't speak for a minute when the unfriendly guard asked me what relation I bore to Jamal. His use of the word 'relation', however, prompted me to stammer that I was his sister-in-law.

"Sister-in-law? Married to his brother, eh?"

I hadn't thought out the exact details. I gave a sort of grunt, then fell silent. I was the last in the queue. There was dead silence as the guard studied my passport. An aggressively buzzing fly suddenly entered and broke the silence. What was I to say? Of course, if I were really married to Jamal's brother, I would presumably have the same surname as Jamal himself. Or were things different in Morocco? Feeling in a slight panic, as so much was at stake for me, I said: "Well, actually now I am Jamal's fiancée."

The guard sat there impassive. I tried desperately to think up a likely story. Should it be sudden death or rapid divorce for the unfortunate unloved husband/brother who had hitherto selfishly been standing in the way of our unrequited passion? I realised, too late, that I should have stuck to one coherent story told with conviction rather than hedge about with other possibilities. I should have been better prepared. The guard was young, inexperienced, unpleasant. He didn't know what to do as he sat there leafing through my passport, as if hoping to find some clue to guide him towards a decision. I don't think he had ever seen a foreign passport before - I noticed he had tried to open it in the Arabic way (which meant from back to front as we know it) and had looked surprised to be met with blank pages. The decision was evidently outside his framework of reference. He left the hut to confer with another colleague. The precious minutes ticked by. The buzzing fly worked itself into a frenzy, hit the tiny window with great force and either dropped down dead or knocked itself out, because the buzzing ceased. It was replaced with the fervent activity of my own thoughts. The other visitors - doubtless all *bona fide* Moroccan wives, in-laws, siblings or parents, with impeccable pedigree - had gone in some time ago.

I stood outside the hut, fuming with impatience. Why hadn't I thought this out beforehand? Would Jamal be worried when he saw that I wasn't arriving with the others? Would he understand there were problems? And if so, would he be able to do anything about it? I scoured the prison yard, trying to see where the young guard had disappeared to. Then, to my relief, I saw him talking to another older guard whom I knew, and who was sympathetic. The latter looked across at me, smiled and nodded. I could have hugged him. The younger guard came back to the hut and gave me my passport and entry pass without a word. I rushed to the prison door, to make up for lost time and also in case he changed his mind.

Now I was inside the prison and they were calling out Jamal's name. It was a wonderfully familiar situation. We threw ourselves into each other's arms, full of joy, emotion and relief and brimming over with things to tell. What bliss to be with him again! We sat on the rugs hugging and hugging each other, oblivious to the twenty or so other people around us.

We had a whole lifetime of experiences to share. It struck me that Jamal had already been through at least one life-time, as he told me in great detail about his political career, his hotel experiences, his arrest, the police stations, hunger-strikes, torture. As I sat snuggled up to him in the prison hall, I often gazed at the young body which had suffered such extreme abuse. His toes, peeping through his sandals, bore the marks of the whippings he had been forced to endure, and his posture bore witness to the abnormal positions he had been subjected to for long periods of time. I wanted to obliterate all this inhumanity, wanted the strength of my love to make it null and void.

I had taken a lot of things with me for Jamal this time: clothes, toilet articles, books and study materials. Jamal had completed his studies in prison. He had gained the equivalent of a B.A. and M.A. and had now - by hard work and good fortune - managed to get himself enrolled at two different faculties at the University of Paris, to take an M. Phil and a doctorate. His subjects were Sociology and Contemporary History. His two professors - André Adam at the Sorbonne and René Gallissot at Paris VII (both well-known and distinguished academics) as well as Jacques Couland at Paris VII and VIII - gave him the most astonishing help and support. Their friendliness was overwhelming. Other support came from Jamal's Amnesty group in Sweden. His main caseworker - Lennart Aspegren - moved heaven and earth to get him expensive photocopies of material from an exclusive library in Paris, material which he badly needed for his studies. The group also periodically sent money to Jamal's family to facilitate their trips to Kenitra.

I asked Jamal about the contact with his Amnesty group. He giggled and said:

174

"This is something I have found out fairly recently, based on gossip reported to me by a friendly guard and also by Lennart himself. Apparently one night, Lennart rang the prison and asked to be put through to the Prison Director. I dare say his amazement at being contacted by someone from Sweden hypnotised him into taking the call. I believe Lennart enquired after my health. He said they were concerned about me and hoped I was getting every care. I didn't learn about this phone-call until much later, but thinking back on it, I remember noticing at the time that conditions suddenly got better for no particular reason."

"In what way?" I wondered.

"Well, I'd been asking to receive certain books and the answer was always no. Suddenly, I was told I could have the books. There were one or two other small improvements, too."

"Jamal, that's really heartening!" I hugged him and we both blessed Lennart for the initiative. It's a small detail, but one worth noting: how could the authorities let anything happen to a prisoner who was known in such a remote place as Sweden? It is one of the many strengths of Amnesty.

The importance of Amnesty's work cannot be too highly stressed as a reason why the conditions of the *Ilal Amam* prisoners of conscience gradually improved.

For other political prisoners, whose cases were not known or brought to the attention of the public, conditions often deteriorate. There's a distinction between a prisoner of conscience and a political prisoner. Jamal was a typical prisoner of conscience, i.e. one imprisoned for the non-violent expression of his beliefs. He was also a political prisoner, the basis for his actions being political, but was adopted by Amnesty as a prisoner of conscience, having neither used nor advocated violence. Other political prisoners may have used violent methods to achieve political aims. Amnesty would not adopt such prisoners but could be concerned if, for example, they were refused trial or were subject to torture or other cruel and degrading treatment. The difference in practice is that if Amnesty

175

adopts a prisoner, it can demand his or her release; otherwise, it can only express concern at unacceptable treatment.

I asked Jamal about the existence of political prisoners in Morocco, who were not prisoners of conscience. He gave me the following appalling account:

"There are many political prisoners who have received the most horrible treatment by Moroccan authorities, without it ever attracting public attention - they were not Amnesty adoption cases. For example, the group of army officers who attempted military coups in 1971 and 1972. The treatment of these officers was by any standards medieval. Firstly, the alleged ringleaders were picked out and executed by firing squad, an event which was given full television coverage in all its grisly detail."

"On television - how gruesome!" I exclaimed. "I suppose today's television is yesterday's public square."

"Yes, but how more powerful! A public square execution reaches a small number of people living in the region, television reaches into every home. And a television programme gives close-ups, freezes some pictures, dwells on others and also provides a running commentary."

I gazed at him, trying to imagine my feelings if I had switched on television and witnessed such an event. I shuddered.

"What happened to the other officers?"

"The hundred or so who managed to escape the extra-judicial executions were tried, sentenced and sent to this prison. In 1973, in a clandestine operation, they were moved from here to a destination unknown. For all their families they just disappeared. There was total silence about their fate for nearly seven years. Seven whole years, can you imagine? Then one of them managed to smuggle out a letter, which was published in *Le Monde*."

"Where were they?"

"They had been incarcerated at a prison in Tazmamart, a small place near the Sahara Desert where there are stiflingly hot summers and icily freezing winters. What has happened and is still happening to them now ten years later, makes the public square butchering look almost acceptable by comparison. I actually cried when I read the letters they managed to smuggle out."*

I sat up in indignation. "Why is this not known? Is something being done about it?"

"Not as far as I am aware. They are not prisoners of conscience and therefore they are not Amnesty cases."

* The Tazmamart letters are reproduced in Appendix II

Chapter 21

Circumstances for the prisoners at this point in time in Kenitra Prison were very different from those of Tazmamart. By this stage in their imprisonment, conditions had relaxed in many ways and I was impressed by how fit and dignified Jamal and some of the other prisoners looked, against all odds. This was due to the access to medical treatment, to the nutritious food and smart clothes brought to them by their families, to sporting events which they staged for themselves in the prison yard and to the possibility of study and intellectual debate. But most of all, it was due to their determination to survive and overcome all the grim treatment of the past.

I found myself able to contribute towards Jamal's studies in many ways, bringing him paper-clips, a hole-puncher, stapler, file - these were untold luxuries for him. I also bought him a dictionary - *Le Petit Robert* - invaluable for his studies.

All books had to pass through the prison censor. Once, I had a book for Jamal which I did not wish the censors to see. I bought myself a green velvet djellaba - the traditional long sort of coat which Moroccans wear over their clothes (also known as cache-misère) and very useful for hiding not only the rags underneath but also many other secrets. I tucked the book into my trousers, threw over my djellaba, and made my way to the prison. I had some nasty moments when, on the long walk between the two prison gates, I felt the book slipping, but fortunately, I got it through intact.

Then Jamal said he'd like some whisky! Not only was alcohol strictly forbidden in prison but it is also against the laws of Islam. Revelling in the double crime, I managed to smuggle in half a bottle. I tried to give it to Jamal surreptitiously but he took it openly and after the visit, he carried it with him unabashed right under the noses of the guards. His theory was that if you do things openly, no one will imagine you have anything to hide. I heard later that the bottle had been shared by 20 prisoners.

My birthday - spent at the prison - was a memorable occasion for me. Jamal had organised a little party *à deux* and I found some presents waiting, as well as a sort of cake, a flower and a lit candle. It all looked very festive and provided a powerful contrast to the bleak prison interior. The presents included a box made by some common-law prisoners and some photo-frames - wood surrounding glass, also made by the prisoners. What a lovely surprise it was! We ate the cake with one spoon between us, kissing at each mouthful and Jamal gave a sonorous rendition of 'Happy Birthday to You' in Arabic. I felt thoroughly spoilt and delirious with joy.

Unfortunately, however, there had been an incident that morning at the prison. Relatives of a prisoner had been caught trying to smuggle out some prison clothes, distinctive for their black and white stripes. It was a harmless offence - the prisoner was soon to be released and he wanted a 'memento'. However, it provided a bit of excitement and meant that everyone's belongings were being searched on leaving. Blissfully unaware of this, I left the central part of the prison carrying my bag of birthday gifts, a smile on my lips and a song in my heart. I was looking up at the sky and dreaming of the lovely morning we had spent together, and was reflecting on how Jamal had managed to get a cake, small as it was. I was thinking what I would use the box for and wondering which photos I would put into the photo-frames. These were made of thick dark-brown wood. I had never used frames before when mounting my photos, only plain glass and clips. Would it be good to insert a portrait photo or a landscape? Such thoughts were going through my head as unsuspectingly, I turned the corner. A mass of blue uniform pounced on me. The bag was wrenched from my grasp, and the single flower fell to the ground and lay there in its beauty and innocence, smiling up at the symbols of oppression.

A vision sprung to my mind. It was of Welsh National Opera's production of Fidelio, Beethoven's moving opera about a political prisoner. The production was set in a concentration camp milieu and flowers were used as a symbol for growth. Whenever a guard or other representative of repression appeared, the flowers got trampled on. In this particular case here in Morocco, however, the flower was not born to blush unseen. One of the guards, red-faced, picked it up and handed it back to me. It was an exquisite touch.

I got word to Jamal about the incident. He told me afterwards that he had gone to see the Prison Director and asked him angrily what was meant by it, couldn't he give some birthday presents to his intended wife? (We had by this time completely ditched the sister-in-law). The Director was apparently apologetic. He explained that his main worry was the glass on the photo-frames. It appeared that, in the whole of the prison, there was not a single complete window-pane left - they had all served to provide the common-law prisoners with a free supply of raw material to manufacture goods and supplement their income by selling the end products. The Director didn't even like to think about where the wood might have come from. By the end of the afternoon, I had the presents returned to me intact. I was amazed. It was evidence of the respect which the political prisoners could command from an individual prison director, an educated man who may well - who knows?- have been appalled at the imprisonment of so many young, intelligent and obviously non-criminal men.

I got to know some of these prisoners. They were sympathetic, interesting, warm and creative people, just rotting their young lives away in prison. And for what reason? Who benefited? The sheer human waste, how appalling it was, how depressing. I wanted to shout about the injustice from the roof-tops.

Jamal told me about one particularly touching case which he had learnt about once the prison regime had been relaxed. It was that of a prisoner we'll call Najib. When he was at Derb Moulay Cherif in Casablanca, he was recognised one day by a guard who belonged to the same tribe, from the same village. The guard, obviously moved by seeing a tribesman in such a lamentable state, managed to talk to Najib without being overheard. He asked if there was anything he could do; he said he couldn't free Najib but he was willing to do anything else in his power to make life easy for him within his own very limited role. Najib replied he wanted nothing for himself, but he was worried about his parents' feelings, as he had just disappeared without trace. Could the guard please tell them he was OK? Well, he was starving, battered, blindfolded, handcuffed and tortured but he was at least still alive. The guard promised to speak to Najib's parents.

He accordingly went to the village in the mountains and gave them the news. They were dumbfounded at first - the whole scenario was light years away from anything remotely resembling their terms of reference. They were a sweet, simple old couple, peasants who had hardly been outside the confines of their own village. They loved their son dearly and after the initial shock, felt a desperate need to do something for him. By questioning the guard closely, they got a clue where Derb Moulay Cherif was situated. Without telling a soul, they decided to go and visit their son. It must have been daunting for them to make the long journey to a town of 6 million inhabitants. However, they were brave and also highly motivated after the months of anguish following the disappearance of Najib, months of speculation, worry and torment. They packed a food hamper containing a chicken, some of Najib's favourite cakes, roast peanuts and some cigarettes, and they set off for Casablanca.

After some trouble, they managed to find the notorious detention centre. They knocked on the gate, probably looking every bit as if they were paying a social call to a sick relative. The gate opened and the astonished-looking policeman on the other side heard the old folk say: "Hello, we've come to visit our son and bring him a few things he may need." Before the words were even out of their mouths, they were dragged inside, and subjected to heavy interrogation about the source of their information.

Realising they had made a mistake but not quite knowing

what it was, they sat there too petrified to speak. This dear old couple were then taken to the torture chamber where they spent a month being tortured until they finally broke down. What happened subsequently to the erring guard is not recorded.

It was during this visit to Morocco that I managed to take a lot of photos of Jamal. My handbag was big enough to hide a camera, but not too big to attract attention. I took it with me on the hospital visits. Other prisoners distracted the attention of the guards while - considering the haste of the whole operation - I got some good shots of Jamal, especially one where, having just arrived at the hospital he was still wearing handcuffs but is giving a defiant 'V' for victory sign. A prisoner on another occasion also took photos of us together. Set there among the foliage of the hospital garden, it looked to all intents and purposes as if we were a couple of honeymooners on the Riviera. Sometimes it actually felt like that, when we were able to forget the real situation and just concentrate on being the two of us. The guards were around but were mostly discreet. I spoke to Jamal dreamily of the house I'd just bought which we would one day, hopefully, share, and I asked him his preference about colours, furniture etc. He had some very definite ideas.

"The bedroom walls should be blue, the same colour as your eyes," he told me, as we stood on a lawn together, half hidden by a spreading bush. This was the cue for him to kiss them and caress the rest of my face.

After a long moment of softness and tenderness, he said gently: "How I am longing to get to know you better." He ran his hand up my arm and along my throat. I shivered with emotion. He pulled the top of my T-shirt and peered down inside. I giggled at his unashamed curiosity. "Do you approve of the movie?" I asked him.

"Oh, most definitely," he replied. "The best I've seen. When is the next performance?" The sound of a guard behind us reminded us where we were and I straightened my T-shirt.

"Pity about the censor," I murmured.

Soft moments like this, the taking of photos, the fact that I was against all odds allowed to be with Jamal, felt like minor victories against a system intent on degrading and dehumanising. For the prisoners, victories such as these served to camouflage a lot of the inner anguish. This was present on an individual level but also in the one-to-one contact and group dynamic, and the way in which these were affected by outward events. Sadly, I heard from Jamal that the improvement in actual prison conditions was often, paradoxically, directly proportionate to the deterioration of some inter-personal relationships in the 'discipline block.' One day on a prison visit, I asked Jamal what it was like living locked up together with over 100 colleagues, all involved in a failed attempt to bring about social change.

"There are some positive aspects of this communal life, if you look away from the prison environment. All the prisoners - whatever their differences on a personal or political level, and there are certainly a lot of those - keep community life together and show complete solidarity in any confrontation with authority. It is an organised life following socialist principles. We pool all resources."

"How does that function?" I asked, shivering a bit in the cold damp air of the prison. Jamal rubbed my back and arms. He was eager to tell me how the prisoners organised life.

"We set up a committee to share out food, books, money, cigarettes, clothes, study materials and such things. Anything brought into the prison by the prisoners' families goes straight to this committee."

"Are you allowed newspapers in the prison?" I wondered.

"Yes" said Jamal. "When the censorship rules relaxed, we also wrote to magazines in France, Spain, the UK, Lebanon and the USA. Everyone gave us free subscriptions which was really good."

"What subjects?" I asked.

Jamal and the author during a "hospital visit" Feb. 1983

Jamal and the author, February 1983

"Oh, all sorts of topics: history, science, technology, music, cinema, sport. We also organised intellectual debates within the prison."

I looked around at the other prisoners, all engrossed in family visits, then back at Jamal and said something I had been pondering on.

"I imagine you have to be something of an individualist in order to survive prison life. And you always strike me as being very much an individualist. I wonder how that equates with your socialist ideals."

"An individualist?" said Jamal. The thought silenced him for a few minutes. Then he said slowly: "Yes, even if there's a framework of socialist living, there's also a strong element of ego. The frustrations are enormous." Jamal sighed. " They're overpowering and it needs every bit of our individual fighting spirit to be able to deal with them."

I could well imagine this, what it must be like to cope with everyday problems within the confined space of a prison. I asked Jamal to expand a bit; his pent up-feelings and years of loneliness appeared to free his tongue and he responded openly and passionately.

"There are frustrations with our families: small ones such as not receiving mail, goods or visits, but also serious ones such as wives wanting a divorce, alienated children, accidents, deaths - all tragedies which you can cope with if you have support from family and friends, but which become unbearable if you are cut off from this support and have to face the shock in isolation."

Jamal paused and a pained expression crossed his face. Looking at the wall, he said: "I well remember the devastation I felt when I learnt in prison that my father had died."

He turned his head back and then covered it with his hands. I understood how much his father had meant to him, how alone and helpless he must have felt upon hearing the news and what restrictions such conditions place on grieving when you cannot grieve with your family or even be present at the funeral. I took one of his hands and held it against my face, squeezing it gently and brushing it against my lips. We sat like that for a few moments. Then Jamal continued:

"There are also the frustrations of prison life itself: just being locked up and everyone living on top of each other, prison guards switching off the lights just when you begin to study, being refused simple requests out of sheer awkwardness, primitive eating conditions, noise. Petty quarrels are blown up into feuds. Trends suddenly surface only to quietly peter out, but arousing high levels of emotion while they last."

One such case which Jamal described in humorous detail had been the call for tennis. It was started by a prisoner who had become fascinated by the game. After a long drawn-out battle with the Prison Director, he was finally allowed to receive a tennis racket brought to him by his family. He then got a detailed book about the sport which gave him the measurements of a proper tennis court.

He found that the prison yard, meant for the exercise of about 150 prisoners, could just about be stretched to house a mini tennis court. However, there was one major drawback and what a drawback! The only tree in the yard was standing in the way. It wasn't any old tree, either. It had been planted there and nurtured by a keen gardener among the prisoners, who had also fought long and hard to get permission to receive it. It had constituted a great moral victory for him and he had spent hours planning where it was to go and then planting it with tender care. He watered it, sat by it, spoke to it, dreamt of it. When he first heard rumours to the effect that his cherished creation was under attack, he refused to believe them. His tree? No, impossible. Then, as the rumours grew stronger, to give way to heartless talk about whether to chop the tree into pieces or to burn it whole in a triumphant funeral pyre, his disbelief changed to anger and indignation. The full force of his scorn was turned upon the would-be attacker: this little upstart prisoner from the slums in Casablanca who had never played tennis before in his life but who was now trying to turn the prison yard into the Centre Court at the expense of his most valued possession! He started looking around for support and found that it was forthcoming from a number of prisoners, who condemned tennis as a thoroughly bourgeois pastime.

The budding Wimbledon star in his turn solicited allies from the more sport-orientated of the prisoners, who did some research on the subject, finding and distributing theories among the hitherto fainthearts, theories which proclaimed tennis to be the most developed sport in the world. The tennis lobby then got themselves armed with rackets by any means available - the hard currency was mainly Marlboro cigarettes.

The ecology lobby had to rely more on the psychological and philosophical approach and they spoke eloquently and fervently of the need for trees, especially where there are otherwise only walls. A tree symbolised growth and therefore hope, a badly-needed attribute among prisoners with long jail sentences. Then, as more and more tennis rackets and tennis balls appeared, the loud thuds of the game began to distract those trying to study. Soon, the sound became unbearable, so the ecology lobby found itself reinforced by the anti-noise lobby. In response, the tennis lobby sat themselves down defiantly in the middle of the yard and began ostentatiously knitting a primitive tennis net.

It became a real battle of wits and will, each new day scoring points for one or the other side, each side losing or gaining a supporter amidst cheers or boos, depending upon whether you favoured growth or motion. Each side had its heavies and its passive supporters, and the former put a lot of resources into attracting the floating voters: i.e. the majority of the prisoners who weren't too bothered either way but who just wanted to see an end to the anguished disputes.

One day, the tree mysteriously disappeared. A covered-over hole with newly-dug earth was the only evidence that it had been there at all. The anger of the ecologists was matched only by the grief of the gardener. For two days, the prison was in a state of shock. Just before any threatened violent revenge took place, however, the tree just as mysteriously reappeared in a part of the yard not affected by the court. It was over - the tennis lobby had won. For a week, the prison yard was transformed into a triumphant arena of feverish tennis playing. Then someone discovered Judo. As if by magic, rackets, balls and nets vanished as quickly as they had come and the tree, looking somewhat forlorn after its journey, was to witness a new phase in the era of sport.

Jamal told me how the highly-charged emotional atmosphere, together with the amount of energy generated by this comparatively small matter, were indicative of the general levels of frustration and boredom experienced by these young intellectuals who were seeing their dreams of a more just society slowly turning into nightmares. Prison life aggravated these frustrations to an almost intolerable level - being locked up with ex-colleagues was a constant reminder of the past and most particularly of the mistakes of that shared past.

A group of people consisting of a prisoner and his visitors were sitting right by us, talking in a loud agitated fashion. The visiting area was never quiet but it seemed particularly noisy today. I picked up on a certain level of distress coming from the group, although I didn't know what they were talking about. Jamal was obliged to raise his voice.

"Would you believe that the more the prison conditions improved, the more the problems between us increased? Well, that's what happened." His face was alight now, reliving what had obviously been painful developments inside the featureless walls. "You might also be surprised to learn that prison was at first the Headquarters of radical opposition and, from there, many outside groups were set up and organised. But theorising behind locked doors doesn't work out in practice," he continued grimly, "and even worse, it led to the arrest of many other people."

A sudden swell of emotion from the noisy group forced us to break off talking for a while. I tried to snuggle up to Jamal, but he seemed unusually tense and distant. The noise abated after a few minutes and, although I wanted to talk to him about a few problems I'd had at my hotel, I felt how important it was for Jamal to continue describing the prison atmosphere and how it had affected him.

"Did you talk much about the aims and ideas of the organisation?" I asked.

A shadow passed Jamal's face and I understood that this was a difficult issue for him.

"Oh yes, it never stopped. The questions were numerous and often painful to confront."

"What were some of the questions?" I asked.

"What were the questions?" he repeated slowly. "I've gone over this many times. I've even written a paper on it which I was thinking of trying to get published." Jamal sat lost in thought.

"Tell me some of the questions," I persisted.

"Well, here are some of the ones I remember writing in my article:

- Had we overestimated our influence and weight within society?

- Had we similarly underestimated the King's cleverness, especially in his ability to turn any situation to his own advantage?

- Were we sectarian in our approach to the conflicting relationship with the traditional parties?

- Were we dogmatic in our treatment of European political theories?

- To what extent had we researched and understood the Moroccan reality?"

Just as Jamal uttered these last two words, I was startled by an agonised howl which ripped into our conversation, shattering it to pieces. It had come from the group sitting by us. I swung round, just in time to see the prisoner breaking into violent sobs. Others in

191

the group started comforting him and also each other. I turned back to Jamal for an explanation. He told me he had learnt earlier that this prisoner's father had just died and now members of his immediate family had come to mourn with him. The man's grief clung to the entire visiting area, enveloping us all.

Jamal and I were silent for some time, almost as if to speak would have been blasphemous. I could feel Jamal re-enacting his own grief. After a while, the feeling lifted and I encouraged him to continue explaining why their organisation, powerful though I believed it was, had not succeeded.

"Socialist theories and experiences from other countries did not, as we'd discovered to our cost, translate into everyday Moroccan life. We'd overlooked the strength of Islam as well as tribal solidarity," he told me.

"I imagine that outside events, like the collapse of socialist models in other countries, must have been a large part of the debate," I ventured.

"Oh, this certainly added to the general feeling of despair," Jamal agreed. "Many members had believed fervently in what was going on abroad and when we saw whole systems disintegrate, you can imagine what it felt like."

Jamal went on to enumerate major events which had shaken them all, such as the invasion of Afghanistan; the workers' revolt in Poland, with the workers fighting the Communists; the new pragmatic 'Capitalist' orientated approach of the current leadership in post Mao China; the leaning of former Socialist parties towards social democracy, e.g. in France and Germany.

He told me how much debate all this had given rise to in prison, and how their hitherto monolithic movement had started experiencing major divisions, familiar to most political groupings but especially those on the left.

"There were, broadly speaking, two different strains," Jamal explained. "Those who wanted to define a new approach, more realistic and less dogmatic: the 'renovatory' group; and those who wanted to continue just as before: the 'orthodox' group."

"Which group were you in? no, let me guess, it's not difficult. The renovatory group, of course."

Jamal nodded.

"Were most people in your group?"

"No, we were in a clear minority. In both groups, each prisoner felt very strongly about his own viewpoint and it caused a lot of bitter feelings which led to some excesses from the majority to the minority."

Again, Jamal looked tense and distant. I started to ask him the nature of these excesses but just then, the bereaved prisoner started sobbing again as his family was preparing to leave. Two others in the group started crying, as well. The air felt heavy with sorrow. It underlined, too, the difficulties I had sometimes felt about communicating in this often crowded visiting area, where other people's emotions intruded into your space. (I remember in particular the constant loud laughs of a certain regular visitor which could be very irritating if I was discussing a serious subject with Jamal). It brought home to me the pressures of everyday life in the prison, from which there was no escape.

Visiting time was drawing to a close and people were getting up to leave. I still hadn't spoken to Jamal about whether I should move hotel or not but suddenly, this whole issue seemed trivial. I also wanted to hear what the orthodoxy had done to the renovators. I prompted Jamal and he obliged.

"A few of them became suspicious of their progressive counterparts and started to spy on them and plot against them. Imagine my shock when I learned that the cell of one of the minority group had been searched by one of the majority group. I thought, was this what prison life had reduced us to, from a movement set up to fight any sort of oppression?"

As I got up to leave, I tried to visualise how this must have affected a sensitive person like Jamal. Usually, the end of visiting time meant some long tender moments together. However, the seriousness of our discussion, combined with the heavy family drama being played out a few feet away, precluded any such moments on this day. Instead, I asked Jamal whether he thought it would have been different if he had not been in prison, or whether he considered it to be an inherent failing in orthodox ideologies.

Helping me pick up my things, he said: "I think that the frustrations of prison life and the fact that we were all locked up together and apart from normal life probably intensified the problems."

"What happened in the end?" I asked, walking with him towards the door and trying to ignore a guard harassing me to leave.

"The renovators worked on the orthodoxy, backed up by outside events showing need for change. The result was that the orthodox group became the minority, but the smaller it became, the more fanatical its remaining adherents became until in the end, the whole thing collapsed."

I walked out into the sunlight. I was more than usually conscious of leaving Jamal behind in the darkness.

Chapter 22

How painful it must have been for Jamal to contrast all this with the fervent optimism of his youthful political activity! During my journey back to England, I went over and over again this and other discussions we had shared. I also dwelt on the sweet and tender moments we had spent together. I had such a desire to be with him. Almost as soon as I got back to London, I began planning my third trip to Morocco, the one on which the trouble began.

The preparation for the trip was therapeutic, helping me overcome the anxiety of my separation from Jamal and distracting me from other frustrating problems, such as our getting letters to each other. I had the idea of writing a daily diary to be sent off once a week, and Jamal started to do the same. Thus, we could be acquainted with each other's daily life, how we coped with it, our hopes and fears. This gave a more complete picture, rather than reflecting the prevailing mood of one occasion a week, and it was also less effort writing little and often, especially as I was writing in French.

Jamal had no difficulty in smuggling letters out of the prison to me, but the difficulty of getting uncensored letters into him was a source of constant worry and frustration. The main problem was the address. We had had to change it frequently, the most usual reason being fear on the part of the person receiving the mail. Then there were problems about the reliability of the recipient, our dependence on that person going to the prison once in a while to deliver the mail into Jamal's hands, the fear that his or her address might be watched by the police, the problem of the times when that person was away from home and, on returning, forgot to take the accumulated mail on the next visit, and then the insurmountable and worrying problem of the letters which just disappeared without trace, both from Jamal and myself.

This situation was reflected constantly in our correspondence.

Once, I wrote Jamal the following:

"I have just received your last letter where I see that I never received the one before that. And now when you write in this letter that one of my letters has gone missing - yet again - I feel really disturbed. I always feel a sort of despair when this happens, but to learn at one and the same time that two letters have gone missing, one in each direction, I find quite devastating. I must tell you quite frankly that my gut reaction was to go on strike: no more letters to Morocco. But what am I saying? Punish my dearest one, whose sole crime has been to send me the most beautiful letters, full of love and tenderness, and who moreover lives for my letters? This would be horribly unjust and would also be a victory for those bastards who are stealing our correspondence."

We did what we could to alleviate the situation. Jamal spent hours and hours trying to find a safe and reliable address and to get in touch with a friendly soul at the Post Office, not the easiest of tasks from behind bars. I started to write a resumé of my last letter/ diary on the top of each new one. I also photo-copied every letter I sent so that I could send it again if it got lost. I wrote in the tiniest possible writing on the thinnest possible notepaper, hoping that thin envelopes would attract less attention than thick. I also sealed around the whole of the letter itself with sellotape. Even with all this energy and precaution, letters still disappeared and some which did arrive had the sellotape broken by the time they got into Jamal's hands. It was just one of the many frustrations of the entire situation.

We wrote to each other about everything - any and every detail in the life of the other one was of great interest, and was read over and over again.

"London, February 1983
Darling Jamal, how difficult it was to leave you! Going out of the prison on Saturday, it seemed that my steps were

leading me farther and farther into the darkness instead of the opposite. I have a very ambivalent relationship with that prison. It is the symbol of repression, the instrument of power run by a criminal regime, the place of incarceration of the victims of this criminality and the place which is separating me from my beloved. But at the same time, I feel an irresistible nostalgia for that prison, as it is there that I have spent the most tender and sweet of times, it is there that my love is.

I've had a virus since my return, so have been in bed more than usual. I haven't been able to chase away this picture from my imagination: that in a minute, the bedroom door will open and I will see the dark intelligent head of my beloved. You are coming towards me with a pudding which you have just made and you sit on the bed and we eat the pudding together with one spoon. What a beautiful dream!

Val came to see me this evening and we shared a bottle of wine and a meal together. I showed her some of the photos: the one where you have your arm around me and two others of you in handcuffs. She said jokingly that you looked very mischievous! I gave her the card you had written her, which she was pleased to get. As she was leaving, she said what nice handwriting you have, how happy she was about our relationship and how impatient she was to meet you. She sends you her love. I will be proud to introduce you to Val, I'm sure you are going to like each other a lot. Some people have said that she and I are alike, not necessarily physically, but in character, and Val and I ourselves have noticed that we often have the same reactions to things. I'm really happy to have such a friend as Val - a sincere and loyal friend, very open and spontaneous.

Jamal, my love, I can't stop thinking about the happiness before us when our relationship can be conducted away from prisons and hospitals. Just imagine, a walk in the park, an evening together with friends, a trip to Montreal, a day in the country, a concert, a demonstration, a film! But the sweetest of all will be the bed for two where our caresses will help us forget all the unhappiness of the past, where our kisses will whisper the deep secrets of our souls and where our bodies will show all the tenderness of a love made in Paradise.

Joyce"

"Kenitra February-March 1983
My dearest Joyce

Ever since you left me, I have not been able to re-adapt to everyday life. Sitting together with you, I felt myself to be on an island of love and happiness surrounded by an ocean of horror and hate. I am like a drowning man, clutching on to a piece of wood, fighting to get to the shore of security and hope. I confront all the waves of horror and intolerance to cling on to you, you who symbolise for me everything that has to do with humanity. Imagine what you represent for me! Your softness and tenderness is so much the opposite of my situation here.

I should tell you a piece of news: the death of General Dlimi in a car accident (?!) Dlimi was second-in-command after the King, a military officer with lots of power. Many newspapers (Le Monde, El Pais etc.) speak about an abortive coup attempt but the details remain very obscure. No smoke without fire, however! The 'opposition' are delighted at the removal of this General, the most fascist individual of the regime. It is history repeating itself: the man who is closest to the King always ends up by rising up against him (e.g. in 1971 General Medbouh, and in 1972 General Oufkir, both of whom attempted South American style coups).

I read with great pleasure what you had to say about Val. I will be delighted to get to know her and I am sure we will be the best of friends. Please send me her photo.

I have been thinking about conversations we have had about friends, and I must tell you that, when there have been problems, I am always in favour of reconciliation, whatever has happened in the past. I will give you a significant example: when we were arrested, some colleagues taken to secret detention by the police ended up by collaborating with them in moments of moral weakness. Some of these colleagues were brought to the torture-chamber while I was being tortured and they started to denounce me there and then, something which was almost the worst torture for me - it was unbearable to see these former militants participating in the interrogation. I thought that I would never be able to bring myself to talk to them again. During the long periods of solitude and silence in secret detention, however, I thought a great deal about these militants who had capitulated before the police and I found that I shouldn't harbour any resentment against them. It is very difficult to explain their case in subjective terms. Their capitulation is a political matter which reflects many things outside their individual cases and which touches upon our political and ideological ideas, including perhaps deficiencies or even errors. Even if these colleagues did give in to the police, now that they are with us in prison, we have to help them recover their morale and get over these lapses instead of entrenching them all the more. I should add that this attitude of mine caused me a lot of problems with colleagues who were of the opposite opinion.

I must stop writing now, because the guard (!) who has promised to post this letter for me (to avoid the censor) is waiting for it now. My dearest wife: lots of love and kisses.

Jamal"

"London, March 1983

Jamal, you are always in my thoughts, darling, you follow me everywhere. I don't know how many times I have read and reread your letters. Usually, I only read letters about once or twice, but your letters are my source of life, I am

199

devouring them like a hungry wolf!

I have just seen the film 'Ghandi' which had been recommended to me by several people so my expectations were high. However, I was a little disappointed - I found it a bit superficial, a sort of 'Hollywood does Ghandi' type of film. We were thrown straight into 1893 with no historical perspective, all the women in the film were feeble stereotypes and there was very little portrayal of ordinary Indian people. Having said this, the photography was quite beautiful and the actor playing Ghandi was superb. But I didn't have a lot to take home with me. I am very demanding when it comes to the cinema!

It is good to be back at work again where there is such a nice atmosphere. My senior, Gurbux Singh, is the very best of line-managers: he knows how to get the best out of people, he is so understanding and easy to talk to, and such fun to be with. He is exactly what a manager should be. When I started there in his office, he said to me: 'You have a job to do, Joyce, and we expect it to get done in reasonable time. Having said this, I am not going to stand over you with a stop-watch, but if the work doesn't get done, I will want to know why.' It was exactly the right attitude -this non-authoritarian approach makes me want to work twice as hard and I feel twice as loyal as I would do under a strict disciplinarian character. My other two colleagues, Richard and Lionel are lots of fun. Yesterday, when Lionel had been teasing me rather a lot, I finally got a bit exasperated and said: 'Lino, can't you go and be rude to someone else?' He replied: 'Well, I could, but you would feel so left out!'

Next week, I have to go to Bolton to address the Community Relations Council with a paper I have compiled on race and housing in that area. Afterwards, I will be going on to Liverpool where my sister Jean is playing with the Welsh National Opera, and I hope to see my favourite opera, the only one written by Beethoven, called 'Fidelio'. I have always loved this opera with its beautiful music but now it has taken on a new dimension for me as it is about a political prisoner, indeed, the whole opera takes place in a prison. Liberty is a very dear subject for Beethoven, this opera is about freedom and this WNO production is an extremely interesting one, full of compassion and symbols. Beethoven is for me the Shakespeare of music, because his work contains something for everyone: passion, tenderness, philosophy, humility, dignity, poetry, everything.

I'm really pleased that you are taking such an interest in Western classical music, which is so important to me - I assure you it will create a new side of your life which will enrich you for always. I remember that the first time I spoke to Jean about you, spoke of your character and all you had been through, her immediate reaction was that she wanted to take you to a concert. This might seem banal, but I saw at once the feeling behind the remark. She wanted to share the most precious thing in her life with you: music. It was the deepest expression of solidarity and the most meaningful present she could give you. Jean is such a lovely person. You wrote that you were disappointed in your own sisters. Well, let me share Jean with you, only not too much, as I've seen what happens to your sisters-in-law!

I'm longing for your letter, dearest Jamal. While waiting, I hug you and re-hug you and hug you again even stronger and I feel I have the whole universe in my arms."

This letter revealed a background in total contrast to most things which Jamal had experienced in his life. It showed a life where there was room for fun at work, even with your boss, a life of music and films, of love, care and dignity.

Jamal, as he recounted to me in detail later, began to go through the events of his past, wondering what such experiences had done for him, where they had left him. Had they been enriching or annihilating, stimulating or decimating? Or a mixture of all of this? What about his colleagues?

His thoughts turned to Youssef and Mahmoud, the two men who had collaborated with the police in return for a promise of their release. The irony of it was that the *de facto* separation then became much longer than Youssef could possibly have imagined in his worst nightmare. He - along with Mahmoud - was given a 12 year jail sentence, the same as Jamal, who had always stuck to his original standpoint of refusing to disclose any information whatsoever. So much for police promises.

Youssef and Mahmoud then had to live in the confined atmosphere of prison with all the colleagues they had betrayed. One can well imagine the feelings of those who had been picked up by the police on the strength of information given to them by these men, as well as those who had endured severe torture for refusing to give information leading to the arrest of these same two men and others.

A shroud of silence and contempt surrounded the two. Some of the other prisoners even spread (false) rumours that they were police agents who had been put into prison solely to spy on the activities of the others. Their isolation was as complete as if they had been in solitary confinement. It was the greatest punishment of all, to have to live with this knowledge of what they had done and most of all, to have constant reminders of this from the accusing stares and contemptuous remarks or articulate silences of their former friends and colleagues. *'L'enfer'*, says Sartre, *'c'est les autres.'* These men had been afforded their day of judgement well in advance of their demise here in prison, where every single day was Doomsday.

Although Jamal was one of those whose ill-treatment and very presence in prison was directly due to information passed on by these men, he nevertheless watched with growing concern as he saw them being destroyed before his eyes. They had become recluses, they were given to fits of violence, they awoke screaming the place down from nightmares, their cries reverberating over the whole prison. They were slowly and systematically growing mad. Now Jamal felt remorse. After all, they had been colleagues in the past, they had worked together well. There was such a lot of suffering everywhere, all around him, most of it imposed by hostile people in positions of authority, where he was powerless to intervene - indeed, his very attempts to do so had extracted such a high price. How could he have it on his conscience to be party to the inflicted insanity of a fellow human being, whatever his wrongdoings? One or two of the other prisoners were of the same mind as Jamal, but they were all met with much opposition from the majority of prisoners, who held these two men entirely responsible for their scars, their destitute wives and families, their broken marriages, their brokenhearted parents etc. They found it easier to project their feelings on to the smaller, identifiable enemy in front of them than on to the much larger, faceless one at a distance.

Little by little, however, Jamal and a few of his colleagues managed to persuade most of the other prisoners to forgive and try to forget, and thus an uneasy truce was obtained which arrested these men on the brink of madness.

Chapter 23

My next trip to Morocco was in April 1983. I had decided this time to stay in Rabat rather than Kenitra, the latter being such an uninteresting town. Rabat is the capital and has a lot of charm, especially the old town (the Medina) with all its bazaars and old walls, still trying to retain their majesty in spite of their crumbling condition. So I booked into a modest hotel in Rabat and took the communal taxi to Kenitra, half-an-hour away. I encountered slight difficulty in getting into the prison this time. The former Head Guard had been dismissed (for corruption!) and there was a new one called Hadj D'ghoghi. He was one of the most unpleasant characters I have ever come across, he seemed to make an art out of his sheer nastiness. In the days to come, I was to witness the tears of several women because of the way he treated them, and it was also reported that he had assaulted a child. It was not for nothing that I nicknamed him *Le Sadique* and soon other prisoners and their visitors were doing likewise. I could well imagine him carrying out torture. The authorities knew what they were doing when they put him in the post: he was completely loyal to the system. Give me a good old-fashioned corrupt guard any time!

On this first meeting with *Le Sadique*, he refused me entry. With the help of other visitors, I got word through to Jamal, and the following piece of drama was enacted, to be repeated at nearly every visit: I would wait outside until Jamal realised I hadn't appeared with the other visitors; he would then contact the Prison Director, who agreed I should be let in. I would subsequently hear the telephone ring in the wooden hut from where Sadique operated. A few minutes later, after much grumbling and many insults, he would sling a pass at me and I would enter. He always knew that he would have to let me in eventually; his constant initial refusal was in order to display his little bit of power and to humiliate me. Being together with Jamal was the sweetest of all antidotes against this treatment. It was like a vision of Hell and then Heaven, all within the space of half-an-hour.

During my second visiting day to the prison, Jamal formulated the most daring plan I had yet heard. He would arrange, as usual, to go on a hospital visit but this time, instead of my going to him, he would come to me! Once at the hospital, he would persuade the guards to let him 'disappear' for an hour, with the assurance of his return and the encouragement of a packet of duty-free cigarettes I had brought with me, with this sort of purpose in mind - a much-loved American brand, far beyond the reach of the normal wage of a humble prison officer. (The only time in my life when I was glad of the existence of cigarettes.) *My* task was to move to a hotel near the hospital and chat up the receptionist.

On my next visit to the prison, I brought with me a map of Rabat. Jamal identified the hospital, as it was one of the - by now very few - hospitals in Rabat I was not acquainted with, and we located a hotel nearby.

The next day (the day before Jamal's proposed visit) I went to book a room. I had thought a lot about my role and decided I was going to be a writer, researching a tourist-book about Morocco (and especially its hotels) and wildly enthusiastic about the country. Accordingly, I turned up in bright cheerful clothes, a couple of cameras slung around my neck, and spun my story. I was immediately given the best room in the hotel and assured of the most superior service. I became friendly with the receptionist, but found it difficult to speak in more personal terms as he was always behind the counter and there were other people around.

As I was wondering how to get him to move from behind the counter so that we could talk away from the presence of others, my eye alighted on a map of Morocco on the wall. I asked if he could come and point out where Agadir was, which I was thinking of visiting next in the quest for material for my book. He fell for it and dislodged himself from the counter. I then asked about all the other places in Morocco, where he himself came from, his family etc. I asked him if he liked travelling. Yes, he loved it. In that case, he was welcome to come and visit me in London and I would give him my address.

I hardly slept at all that night. Half of me was dying of longing for the opportunity to spend some precious moments alone with Jamal; the other half was alive with anxiety in case it all went wrong and there was some terrible price to pay. A notice reminding everyone that guests were strictly forbidden to have visitors in their hotel room didn't do much to reassure me.

The following morning I was up early. Jamal had said he would arrive after 10 o'clock. At 9.30, I went nervously down the stairs. My feelings were running so high that I half expected the hotel to be in uproar. However, the lobby was calm and the receptionist was behind the counter as usual. He looked pleased to see me and we exchanged a few words. Then in a casual tone more appropriate to a request to put out the cat than permission to receive a political prisoner in my room, I said: "Oh, by the way, I'm expecting a visit today from a well-known researcher - Dr. Benomar - who is going to discuss some material for my book with me. Just show him up to my room, will you?"

I started to return up the stairs, my heart pounding. The movement was arrested by the voice of the receptionist. In a tone with an edge to it, he said: "Un moment, s'il vous plaît".

This was it. He was going to refuse. Jamal would appear in blissful ignorance. The receptionist was a spy. He would call the police. Jamal would walk straight into the trap. His sentence would be doubled. I would be deported.

I turned round, my heart feeling as if it were going to leap right out of my body and hit the receptionist between the eyes.

"Oui?"

He fumbled with some papers and then glanced around him. There was no-one else in the lobby. In a lowered voice and without looking up, he said: "Is it really necessary that he comes to your room?" From my assumed elevated position of Western liberalism,

I feigned great surprise at the question.

I heard myself say: "Well, of course. We need to discuss business in peace and quiet. There's no difficulty, is there?" I heard my voice convey slight irritation. To my great relief, he smiled and shook me by the hand.

"OK, no problems."

It seemed to have worked! I went back to my room and waited in anxious anticipation for the arrival of Jamal.

I lay on the bed and tried to picture what it would be like to be alone with Jamal, but completely alone this time! I had grown attached to him through his human qualities, his intellect and his integrity, his gentleness and courage, even before I had ever met him. When sitting close beside him in prison, I could also feel a strong emotional attachment and a physical longing, the longing of the dream yet to be fulfilled, the dream of the past penetrating into the reality of the present. I smiled broadly, savouring the moment in delighted anticipation.

After a while, however, the smile left my lips and I began to feel uneasy. I wondered if he would appear. I had prepared myself for the negative. I told myself that the obstacles were too many and too difficult to overcome. What guard in his right mind would dare let a political prisoner in his charge disappear, with no guarantee that he would return? It was absurd even to think of it. Surely the hospital would be surrounded by police, as everywhere else in this country appeared to be, and Jamal would be seen straightaway? The terrible fear then went through my mind that he might be picked up and charged with attempted escape, which would - horror of horrors - perhaps even get him a life sentence. Was it really worth the risk? Even if he did get to the hotel, I couldn't be sure he would be allowed entry, with a suspicious employee maybe telephoning the police (who have their spies everywhere). I began to feel pangs of regret at having agreed to Jamal's visit. At least it wasn't my idea and Jamal had been so eager, but it was sheer madness. It would lead to disaster.

Not far away from the hotel, as I was to learn later, Jamal's preoccupations were quite different as he was preparing for his clandestine appointment. He was relieved that two friendly guards had been put in charge of the prisoners. Now that they were within the confines of the hospital grounds, he approached them where they were sitting lazily on a bench in the warm April sunshine and started chatting to them about a scene which had taken place in the prison a few days ago, then he asked them about their families and started talking about his. Having delivered the hors d'oeuvre, it was at last time to speak out.

"I'm just going for a little walk around. Should be back within the hour."

It could have been someone sitting in his office chatting to his work-mates, who suddenly felt the need to go and stretch his legs during the lunch-hour. One of the guards said: "Well, I'm not sure if that..."

"You're not going to be difficult about it, are you?" Jamal said, then he grinned and added, "In that case, I shall stay away for two hours instead of one and there is just the chance I might not come back at all!"

The guards laughed uneasily, then looked at each other and hesitated. Jamal sensed that half the battle was won. Time to produce the next round of ammunition.

"Here's something to help you overcome the vacuum caused by my absence. Oh, and another packet for your family."

The obviously expensive gold-coloured cigarette packets sparkled in the sunshine. There was a silence, broken abruptly by one patient shouting to another across the forecourt. Another silence, and then one of the guards said: "Well better make sure it's not more than an hour." The cigarettes changed hands, marking the conclusion of the deal.

Two minutes later, Jamal was standing outside the hospital gates, overcome by a sense of elation and dizziness. Here he was in central Rabat, alone on a street for the first time in over 6 years!

209

His immediate feeling was that he just wanted to run and run! Then he smiled and even laughed out loud. A couple of passers-by surveyed him in astonishment and then looked at the hospital behind him, as if the key to his behaviour lay behind those walls. Jamal wanted to grab the people, shake them, dance with them, share this feeling of elation with them. He wanted to tell them he was free and how wonderful it felt and how important it was!

The sight of a policeman walking along the street in his direction, quickly brought him to his senses and reminded him of the vulnerability of his situation. He composed himself in order to face the mammoth task of crossing the road. This was a major undertaking after all those years locked up. There were so many cars, all of them travelling at what seemed to be a dangerously high speed. For some precious minutes, Jamal shrank at the daunting prospect of slicing his way through the thick volume of traffic, almost like an uncertain swimmer who, having found his way to the top diving board, now stands there in dismay and disbelief at the vast distance between the safety of the diving-board and the unknown perils of the water. Like the swimmer, he knew there was no going back, only forward.

After a long hesitation, he finally took the plunge and dived into the sea of traffic. The relief at reaching the other side unscathed was intense and the reward was sweet - he could now actually see the hotel where Joyce was waiting for him.

Before entering the hotel, he went to a stationery shop with money I had given him, and bought an impressive-looking file, his first purchase for so many years. The bored shop-assistant would undoubtedly have had his day livened up if he had known who he was serving! A few minutes later, 'Dr. Benomar' duly turned up at the hotel, really looking the part. His relatively tall frame and general air commanding respect was complemented by his clothes: he was wearing a smart black suede jacket - a present from a cousin - and a pair of dark trousers. He looked very business-like with his file in one hand and a packet of the duty-free cigarettes in the other. He addressed the receptionist in French rather than Arabic, waved his Paris University study-pass at him and offered him a cigarette. Anything further from the concept of a miserable prisoner doing time could not be imagined.

Two flights of stairs up, I sat waiting. I didn't dare go to reception to see if he had arrived - I knew anyway that if he had, my face would give me away.

Suddenly, there was a knock at the door. Unbelievable! Jamal stood there. For one whole minute, we just stood and looked at each other, wide-eyed. Then Jamal strode across the threshold, the door somehow got closed and we hugged and hugged each other like never before.

We spent a delicious hour together. Amazing that this was Jamal's first sexual contact for over seven years. There was absolutely no constraint between us, it was as if we had been lovers for years. The pent-up longing and the sense of it being Jamal and me versus the rest of the world, added to the delirious sweetness which just flowed between us.

The joy of that coming together was in the starkest contrast to what happened next.

Chapter 24

The following day, another hospital visit had been arranged in a hospital in Sale, near Rabat. As usual, I turned up first. Unusually, however, there was a guard on duty at the hospital gate who refused to let me enter. I felt uneasy at this new development as I waited for Jamal to arrive in the prison van. There had never been any problems before and this was an ordinary hospital where we had met several times previously, not a jail.

The prison van arrived and Jamal got out, along with five other prisoners and two guards. I rushed up to him and told him what had happened. He took me by the hand and went up to the hospital guard.

"What's the problem?"

The guard said he had been given instructions not to let me in. Jamal replied:

"I will only accept such instructions if they are given by the Director of the hospital himself. Now will you please let us in so that we can discuss it with him?"

Amazingly, the guard stood aside.

Once more I had witnessed the quiet air of authority Jamal had, which commanded respect wherever he went. We entered the hospital garden and sat down on a seat. We tried to chat together in the usual way, but there was a tension in the air which defied normal conversation.

The hospital gardens looked deceptively calm and the fragrant smell of Spring flowers wafted over to us. It was a lovely time to be in Morocco, while everything was still green and fresh-looking and before the fiery heat of the summer sun had singed the landscape brown and dry.

The soft green foliage framed different areas in the grounds, almost like screens dividing different rooms. The garden in this Hospital for Rheumatics was well-cared for. A few patients hobbled past and smiled at us as we sat there in the warm and gentle sunshine, and a gardener started to plant a new shrub nearby. The setting was so much at variance with the unease which we both sensed that I knew some sort of explosion was inevitable.

The gardener finished planting the shrub and stood back to survey his work with pride. Two men dressed in white djellabas sat on a seat opposite us and started chattering in Arabic. We got up to look for the guard, who had disappeared from view. I always brought a supply of fruit yoghurts with me, including one for the guard. We would then eat them all together. This, said Jamal, followed an old Arab tradition that you cannot harm anyone you have eaten with. We found the guard and transacted the edible insurance policy with him. He was a kindly man in his forties who didn't look as if he could harm a fly. He and Jamal had a good relationship; in fact, when Jamal had introduced me to him, he'd said: "This is one of my best friends", and the guard had looked delighted. He was relaxed, seemingly quite unconscious of the fact that this was a prisoner in his custody.

We finished eating and went back to the bench. The two men had left, so we were quite alone there as we listened to the bees buzzing round the flowers in harmony and freedom.

Then suddenly, a car drew up at great speed in the driveway and screeched to a halt, shattering the peace. Four armed policemen jumped out and came over to where we were sitting. They were all quite big and seemed to know exactly what they were looking for and what they were going to do when they found it.

Jamal stood up and started talking to them in Arabic. The talk seemed to centre on me but I had no idea what they were saying. Jamal appeared to be protesting. As I stood there, strongly frustrated at not being able to understand a word or join in what was obviously a discussion about my future, if I were now going to be allowed to have one, I suddenly became aware of a consensus on the part of the police, and held my breath for what was to come next. Without any warning, two of them grabbed my arms and half

214

dragged me down the drive. I was bundled into the waiting car which then drove off at speed.

Jamal, as I was to hear later, stared for a long time after the car, unable to believe what had happened. The abruptness with which a potentially lovely morning had suddenly erupted into fear was overwhelming. There was this constant juxtaposition of softness and warmth with cruelty and repression. The sweetness of the warmth made the harshness of the repression all the more powerful.

The friendly guard came over to speak to Jamal, who did not, however, feel like talking. He wanted to be alone with his thoughts. On the long silent journey back to the prison and then locked up in his cell, these thoughts were in confusion. His feeling of impotence was unbearable. For a moment he cast his mind back to the previous day and the precious moments he had spent with his love but he could not dwell on it. It was afterwards he was thinking about, when he had left the hotel and had gone back to the hospital, back to his chains, back to the repression he had fought for so long. Was this really Jamal Benomar, the activist, who had spent two years working underground before being finally caught? Was the man who had stood up to the authorities with such defiance now creeping back to captivity after his pathetic little spell of freedom, with his tail between his legs? What a coward! What a fool!

The first time he had been taken to prison, he was blindfolded and handcuffed to his captors, in a police van with the sirens at full blast and a couple of guns digging into his ribs. He had felt no shame: on the contrary, had felt pride to have fought for the social justice he believed in, right until the end; he had not, like most others, just paid lip service. This time, however, he was going to his cell voluntarily, out of his own free will! Oh, it hurt and hurt badly. Had he, like the trapped bird, become so conditioned to his situation that when the cage-door was casually left ajar, he could only fly a short distance before returning to the protection of the bars?

No, no, it wasn't true. He wanted to escape. He rolled the word around his lips, letting the essence of it pervade his body. Escape! The word flew round his dark and cold cell, hitting the walls with strength and determination. It was a magic word, it conjured up freedom, courage, ability, action, victory over repression.

For a long time, he lay there in the darkness, in a fever of excitement. Escape! He was already in his mind half way across the country when he was brought back to harsh reality by the screams of a fellow prisoner gripped by a nightmare, a fairly common occurrence along this corridor of despair.

Then depression set in. Jamal had often thought of escape - a prisoner's recurrent fantasy - but escape to where? How? In such a police-controlled state, with spies and informers everywhere, there was no way in which he would not be caught sooner or later, and anyway, he did not wish to live like a hunted animal for the rest of his life. He would have to flee the country, but that required preparation and resources, even if it were feasible at all.

His humiliation was complete now that the unthinkable had happened, and edged with a feeling of guilt. This was his country, Joyce had come all this way to see him, and he couldn't even offer her the minimum of protection!

The next day was Thursday, so no prison visits. He would have to wait until Friday - it seemed like an eternity - before there could be any contact with the outside world. He dared not dwell upon what might be happening to Joyce. It was a situation which, strangely enough, they had not envisaged so it had never been discussed. Anyway, even assuming it had been anticipated, what could he have done? How could he have stopped it? His impotence about the whole situation, his past, his strong views, about Morocco, was really driven home to him by this turn of events.

He picked up a book to provide some distraction for himself, but he saw the words through a haze - his mind was faraway.

What could he do except wait for Friday - visiting day - when he was sure he would hear something, whatever it was.

After a sleepless Thursday night, Jamal was the first person in the visiting-hall on Friday morning. Visitors started to appear, and names of prisoners were called out to announce the arrival of their people. Jamal eagerly scanned the visitors to see if there were any sign of Joyce or anyone who could bring him news. After about an hour, it became obvious that Joyce would not be putting in an appearance but Jamal stayed in the hall just in case.

Then it was lunch-time and the visitors left, with Jamal in a fever of impatience for the afternoon visit. At last it came, and with it, another stream of visitors. It was depressing watching the prisoners greeting their loved ones with joy and delight, and it was downright painful every time his eye happened to alight on the corner where he and Joyce had spent such happy moments together, now occupied by another blissful couple.

So Friday came and went with no news about his beloved. Surely he must get some sign tomorrow. Saturday was also visiting day both morning and afternoon. However, Saturday morning dawned and still no sign of Joyce. Jamal went despondently back to his cell to think what to do. It was time for action. He looked through his address book and picked out four names and addresses which Joyce had previously given him. Then he prepared four telegrams: one for Joyce's parents, one for Jean, one for Beryl and one for Val. He would give the text and directions to an afternoon visitor who could be trusted to transmit it. The message on each was the same: "Joyce disappeared. Contact British authorities. Jamal."

The last memory I'd had of my abrupt departure from the scene was the sight of Jamal's worried face. I was pushed into the back of the car, where I sat wedged between two policemen. My escorts were silent until we arrived at a police station in Sale, where they told me to get out. We entered the building and went up some stairs. With two policemen in front of me and two behind me with cocked guns, I felt like some dangerous criminal, liable to press the remote control releasing the detonators for a few well-planted bombs.

I was taken to a room where I had to wait seemingly hours, but in fact probably only 10 minutes. I was then taken to a large room, at one end of which sat someone I presumed to be the Chief of Police in Sale, surrounded by bodyguards. I felt how unreal the whole situation was, like the sort of thing you read about in books. It just wasn't happening to me. My captors exchanged some words in Arabic with the Police Chief, who then addressed me in French. He spoke to me with the utmost contempt, almost spitting the words out. He was a smallish man with a crop of very un-Moroccan looking white hair. He sat behind an enormous desk which went round in a curve, upon which were two flags: one Moroccan, the other I didn't recognise. Adorning the wall was a massive photo of King Hassan. The four guards standing to attention were dressed in brightly coloured uniforms which included plumed headgear. It looked like some medieval pageantry.

The Chief of Police sat at the far end of the room, a long distance from me. He glared at me in what I believe was an attempt to intimidate me, although curiously enough, I didn't feel in the least intimidated, just wary.

He asked what I was doing there. I replied that I didn't know, that I had been visiting my fiancé in hospital when suddenly, for no apparent reason, I had been arrested. He said "Your fiancé is a prisoner, isn't he?"

"Yes."

He lost his cool and started shouting at me. "Don't you know about the law which explicitly forbids contact with prisoners outside the prison?"

I was so calm I couldn't recognise myself. I felt almost outside the situation, as if I were an observer. A voice which must have belonged to me replied: "No. I've never heard of this law. But then I'm no expert on the Moroccan legal system."

This infuriated him. He exuded the manner of someone who has just accidentally let a bunch of criminals escape, is being threatened with reprisals and now has been ordered to deal with some foreign woman mixed up with politics, which was the last straw. Well, *he* was certainly not going to accept responsibility. Red-faced with anger, he barked something at the policemen by my side and I was led out of the room.

I was taken from the police station and put into a different car which seemed to be going towards Rabat. I thought I was being taken back to my hotel. There were two policemen in the car as well as the driver and I asked where we were going, but they wouldn't say. I recognised the landscape as we drove along, I was becoming very familiar with this part of Morocco. There was the blue bridge, which I had seen them feverishly painting just before the visit of President Mitterand in January; there was the luxury hotel perched up on the hillside, there was the start of the medina and ah, yes, there was my hotel. The car slowed down and I felt my body relax. They were just driving me back to make sure I got there safely. Decent of them. The questioning at the police station was obviously just routine, it was all over now. They would drop me off. I would wait until they were out of sight and would take the next available collective taxi to Kenitra. What a lot I would have to tell Jamal! I had been inside a police station, been questioned by the Chief of Police. Jamal would be so relieved to see I was OK.

But what was this? The car was gathering speed. On it went, past the hotel, and as it circled the town, I tried to imagine what our destination could be. I have a fairly vivid imagination, a gift which brought me no consolation whatsoever at this moment. Thoughts of Derb Moulay Cherif secret detention centre went through my mind but this was too impossible to be even contemplated. Anyway, I had done absolutely nothing wrong. But then, given Jamal's fate, that did not appear to be a criterion for staying out of the hands of the police. What worried me was that

219

no-one knew my whereabouts. The only person to witness my undignified departure from the hospital had been Jamal, and what could he do, behind bars? I consoled myself with the fact that I was British, not Moroccan. Did that help? I wondered idly.

The car stopped outside a large building and I was taken into what turned out to be National Security Headquarters. For the rest of the day, I was subjected to heavy interrogation. There were two main interrogators: firstly a quiet fatherly sort of man who obviously hoped that in a weak moment, I would take him into my confidence and 'confess all', and then a small hysterical type who shouted and screamed at me, obviously hoping to intimidate me into confession. This latter was a singular looking man - thin, wiry and with frizzy hair - who at one point admitted he had met Jamal. (I learnt later that this was Mr. Kholti, one of Jamal's torturers. The social setting of their 'meeting' had been the torture-chamber).

The police were trying to get me to confess that I was a member of Amnesty, or (to use their exact words) "some other left-wing organisation run by the Zionists". Morocco, along with other countries where there are gross violations of human rights, hates Amnesty and often tries to ridicule and denounce the organisation in public. I knew that if I had admitted to an active involvement in Amnesty, my days in Morocco, not to say on earth, could well have been numbered. I therefore stuck to my original story that I had got to know Jamal through a colleague in Sweden, an acquaintance of Jamal's sister, who had told me they were trying to find an English pen-pal for Jamal as he wanted to learn the language. I had started to write to him and we were now in love, engaged to be married. It sounded so sweet and innocent.

As I was speaking, I suddenly turned hot and cold at the thought of the address-book in my bag. It contained not only the name and address of Amnesty's International Secretariat in London, but also its sections in Sweden, Britain and France. Moreover, and worse still, it contained the name and address of a Minister for

Polisario, the title of a group of Saharans who, since Spain had pulled out of their territory, had been fighting a bloody war with Morocco for their independence. The claim of this brave group of people for self determination (a claim supported by the United Nations) was also a position held by *Ilal Amam,* Jamal's organisation, and one reason why they had received such heavy prison sentences. The Moroccan authorities' national pride had been outraged at the discovery that not every Moroccan agreed to the colonisation of the Sahara and some were prepared to state their opposition publicly. (Once, the Moroccan Ambassador to London -Mr. Znined - said quite seriously that all Moroccans were fervently in favour of a Moroccan Sahara, so that when this *Ilal Amam* group of subversives had spoken against it, the authorities had been obliged to put them all in jail "to protect them from the wrath of their fellow countrymen.")

My thoughts turned back to the address book. I had been given the name of the Polisario Minister written there by a Swedish journalist doing research on Morocco. I had spoken to him when I was trying to increase my knowledge about the country. I'd never in fact followed it up, but there was the name in my book, for anyone to see.

Supposing my bag were searched and this book were found? As I gave monosyllabic answers to the respective pleadings and ravings of my two custodians, my mind was working furiously on how I could emerge unscathed, if the worst came to the worst. Deny knowledge of the existence of the book? Feeble, not to say suspicious. Accept that the book was mine, but play down the importance of its contents? Better, and I could probably have got round it if there were only the Amnesty addresses, but the existence of the Polisario name required an explanation more plausible than any I was able to think up in French at a moment's notice under such conditions.

"Show me your passport and your flight ticket!" ordered the hysterical one suddenly. I delved into my by now red-hot bag and handed them over. My interrogator grabbed them and gave them to the fatherly one, who opened a drawer and - to my consternation - put them inside. He closed the drawer and locked it.

The interrogation continued. "Are you a member of Amnesty International? Have you heard of Amnesty? You might just as well confess. Which organisation do you belong to? What are you doing in Morocco? How do you know Benomar? Who are your contacts here? Where are you staying? Who are you meeting? Admit you've come to see *les politiques*". The questions, flung at me, kept on being repeated in various guises.

One thing which surprised me was the National Security officials referring to Jamal as a 'political prisoner' and even writing it in a *procès-verbal* which I had to sign: *"Jamal Benomar, prisonnier politique..."* I had also noticed at the prison that all guards - including Sadique - referred to the prisoners as *les politiques*. Even more strange that this should be the case at National Security, in a country which vigorously denies the existence of any political prisoners!

After a few hours, there was a pause and Kholti wiped the sweat from his forehead. The two men discussed something in Arabic and nodded.

The fatherly one turned to me. "You can leave now."

I jumped up. "Can I have my belongings, please?"

"No, we will look after them for you."

This was something which really irritated me about Morocco. Nothing was ever spelt out. These two Security men, after spending all these hours bullying me, were now telling me they were going to "look after" my belongings, as if they were doing me a personal favour. These men were not looking after anything; they were expropriating my possessions against my will.

I said slowly: "I'm quite capable of looking after them myself. May I have them back, please?"

They were not to be deterred. "Report here tomorrow

morning and you will get them back."

What choice did I have? At least they weren't detaining me.

I walked out of the dark office and into the strong sunlight, feeling shaken. My most immediate concern was to get rid of the address-book and also some uncensored letters lying around in my hotel room which I had suddenly thought of during the interrogation, letters showing all too plainly my link with Amnesty. Remembering that I had been asked for my room number, I entered the hotel with some feeling of trepidation. However, the receptionist seemed to be just as before and my room did not appear to have been tampered with. I found a hiding-place for my undesirable belongings and settled down for the night, trying to take in the implications of what had happened. The thought of my not being able to contact Jamal hung over me like a heavy weight. I drifted into an uneasy sleep.

Chapter 25

Next morning, I went to National Security Headquarters early. Neither of my two antagonists was to be seen. At about 10 o'clock however, the fatherly one turned up. I approached him eagerly. "Please may I have my belongings back?" He would look into it. I waited and waited and nothing happened. Minutes turned into hours and soon it was lunch-time and no sign of my passport or flight ticket. When I asked why, I was told they were "awaiting instructions from higher up". It was an excuse I was to hear many times. Before I left to go to lunch, the official said he wanted to give me *un petit conseil* "as a friend". The chummy piece of advice was: "Don't go to the prison". I was told to return to National Security that afternoon, when he was sure that there would be no further problems and my belongings would be restored. I went back and hung around for the whole afternoon, staring at the bleak cold interior. It could have been the prison itself, and no Jamal to provide any warmth. I left the office empty-handed. This was the scenario all day Thursday and all day Friday, two precious days of my limited stay in Morocco.

Then it struck me that the passport did not actually belong to me but to the issuing authorities in London. Morocco had been stealing from Her Majesty's Government! I found out where the British Embassy was and went there. I was seen by a woman official remarkably sympathetic to my story. What a great joy that she believed me! I had imagined I would be treated with a large dose of scepticism and that the British authorities would not wish to get involved. However, nothing was further from the facts. The official said that she would make enquiries. This was Friday, and she said that, if I hadn't got my things back by Monday, I was to go to the Embassy before going to National Security. She told me that if it had only been a question of the passport, there would be no problem - the British Embassy could provide me with a new one in 24 hours. But we couldn't see why I should have to lose my flight ticket home and I also did not see why the police should be able to get away with the quite uncalled-for theft of my belongings.

I left her office, feeling that at last I could share my situation with someone. I wasn't alone any more. However, apart from this relief, I felt most depressed about my unexpected and dramatic rupture from Jamal. I imagined that he must be feeling alarmed, too, since the last he had seen of me was being dragged off by 4 armed policemen. Jamal - if anyone - knew only too well the methods of the Moroccan police!

I returned to report to National Security as usual on Saturday morning and was met with the same excuses. This time, however, I had taken a decision. I was going to go to Jamal in the afternoon, friendly advice notwithstanding. The police, during their very detailed questioning, had asked me what form of transport I had been using to get to Kenitra. I replied that I always took the collective taxi. There was only one such taxi-rank in central Rabat, to my knowledge, and I thought there was just a possibility it would be watched. Not wanting to overestimate my importance yet not wanting to take any chances either, I decided to take the train, not usually a recommended form of transport in Morocco owing to the antiquated railway system. However, I reckoned I had no choice.

I turned up in good time at the deserted station and had a long wait on the platform. I looked around constantly to see if I was being followed but, even to my unpractised eye, this did not seem to be the case. When the train eventually put in an appearance, I made my way to an empty compartment and sat down, feeling despondent. The train clanked its way slowly out of the station and into the countryside. During the journey and then the walk to the prison, I thought what a futile exercise this would all turn out to be. Sadique wouldn't even let me in with a passport, so I could imagine his glee when I turned up without one. The police must also surely have contacted the prison by now and given orders that I was not to be admitted.

The sand on the unmade road got into my shoes, adding to my discomfort as I walked towards the prison gate. I was passed by a man savagely whipping a bony donkey and then the street became empty. With a heavy heart, I arrived at the prison gate. I entered and crossed over to the hut, bracing myself for the dreaded showdown with Sadique. There was no queue, the place seemed almost deserted. I was a little late - all the other visitors must have already gone in. Then, what a delight as I crossed the threshold of the hut! I saw that Sadique was not there. In his place was another guard who recognised me from my previous visits and had witnessed - I had thought even with a certain amount of compassion - Sadique's treatment of me. He smiled as he saw me enter, and without even asking to see my passport, handed me an entry pass. I nearly wept at this unexpected kindness, coming at a moment when I needed it so badly.

I rushed into the prison to meet Jamal and we hugged each other long and hard, tears in our eyes. He had just been on the point of handing over the four telegrams he had prepared, to a visitor he knew. We went over all the events of the past few days, and I told him how amazed I was that word hadn't got to the prison not to let me in. He then told me something which I was also to hear later from other sources: namely that police officers hated National Security officials who hated Prison Directors who hated the police and they were always informing on and complaining about one another. In this general atmosphere of hate and suspicion, there was not much room for co-operation!

"Yet another facet of a repressive State," laughed Jamal, "but this time, one we have to be thankful for!"

"But Jamal," I said, sitting upright so that I could see him properly, "I think this episode poses many questions, some of them really worrying. Why did the police choose this particular time and occasion to create trouble? Was it a pure coincidence that it started the day after the famous hotel visit?"

227

"Who knows?" said Jamal, smiling. He seemed much more interested in stroking my face than in conducting a post-mortem about police behaviour. I needed, however, to share the concerns which had been going through my mind during the past few days.

"Was there an informer at the hotel?" I continued. "And were the prison guards involved in any way? What about the hospital staff? Were they weary of seeing the hospital grounds transformed into a secret lovers meeting place?" The questions tumbled out, rhetorical ones, because how could we possibly know?

"We can only speculate," replied Jamal, stroking my hair to calm me. "What a good thing we have the British Embassy behind us! We may well need them in the future..."

"What about the present?" I interrupted him, "I am still without my passport and ticket. It was by sheer luck that I managed to get in here to see you today. Supposing they are going to use my passport to prevent me from seeing you? That would be too awful, I don't think I could stand it. They have no obligation to let me into the prison. Or," I added ominously, "into the country, for that matter."

"Joyce darling," Jamal took my face in his hands and looked at me earnestly, "we love each other dearly. We've come so far. Don't think we're going to let them spoil it. We'll fight them back, all the way!"

I hugged him, delighted, and left the prison that afternoon, prepared to take on the whole of the Moroccan army if necessary, my love was so strong.

That evening, I took the precaution of ringing my friend Beryl. I told her briefly what had happened, giving her the name and telephone number of my contact at the British Embassy. I said I didn't wish to sound melodramatic and I was sure everything was going to be OK but that if I hadn't turned up in London on the date I was due, she was to take action. I knew that Beryl was one of the best people to contact about this. I trusted her and she was also very 'international' - she wouldn't think twice about ringing Morocco or anywhere else and I could even picture her turning up in Rabat. She was always full of ideas and would know what to do.

On Monday morning, I went to the British Embassy. My new friend there gave me a warm welcome. She said, "Go back to National Security. Play their little game once more, but don't hang around all morning. If your things are not there for you when you first ask for them, come straight back here."

As I could have predicted, I was soon back at the Embassy. My friend there said: "I've got to make a few phone-calls. Come back at 3 this afternoon." I duly turned up and we went outside, where an Embassy car was waiting. "I'm coming with you to National Security this afternoon." So to the obvious surprise of my two adversaries, they next saw me appear in a chauffeur-driven car, flying the Union Jack, with company. I introduced my guest and she produced her credentials. She was most impressive. What an asset to the Diplomatic corps! The two police officials looked as shame-faced as if they had been caught out in a lie. They listened to her and then Kholti said: "Well, to tell you the truth, we don't believe in this love-story. What can an educated European woman possibly see in an Arab prisoner serving time behind bars for criminal behaviour?" (He made it sound as if Jamal had been going around mugging old ladies.) My Embassy friend, without actually telling a lie, led them to believe that my first contact with the Embassy had been to get some information about the formalities of marriage (we had actually discussed this).

After about an hour of discussion, the fatherly type unlocked a drawer and handed me a familiar-looking passport and flight ticket to London. To my surprise, he then suddenly confided in the woman that he thought I was *'courageuse'*. I told him, *"Non, pas courageuse. Amoureuse."* There was no hint of any further embargo on future visits to the prison, and Jamal and I enjoyed the last precious few days we had together to the full.

One of these days was spent on an unforgettable hospital visit. It took place in a neurology hospital called *Razi*. It was a clear hot day and in the large expanse of grounds, there was a general feeling of peace and contentment. There were only two guards present, both of them relaxed and friendly with the prisoners.

Jamal and I detached ourselves from the others and strolled around as if we were spending a long weekend together on a country estate.

As we walked along the paths edged with trees and flowers, we caught sight of a disused swimming-pool, empty of water. Our steps almost involuntarily led us to the brink. We peered into it. It was about 6 feet deep, with a few leaves scattered on the bottom. It seemed quite clean. It had been painted turquoise and it glistened enticingly in the soft sunlight.

Jamal and I looked at each other and then, without a word, we jumped down into it. It felt as safe as the grave but much more full of promise! The blue-green colour which surrounded us now on all sides, enhanced the feeling of serenity. We took off all our clothes and fell into each other's arms. There, with the sun kissing our naked bodies and the sky - hopefully - our only witness, we made love with complete abandon. We felt like Adam and Eve. The borders of our Garden of Eden were perhaps a little more closely defined, but the forbidden fruits were there in abundance. It was a memory I was to cherish all the way back to London and beyond.

When I arrived at Heathrow Airport, I was stopped by Customs officials who searched my bags meticulously and asked me many questions about my stay in Morocco. They were particularly sniffy about a pretty wooden box which Jamal had sent as a present for my sister Jean. It was a typical example of Moroccan handicraft and had been made in the prison. I thought it best to omit the detail of its origin, so I said I had bought it in a bazaar. The Customs man thought the lid seemed suspiciously thick. The box disappeared and when it reappeared later, I found the lid complete with drilled holes. So much for the box.

Then it was my turn. Where were the drugs I was hiding? I

protested my innocence most vehemently, but to no avail. When the search through the entire contents of my suitcase had proved fruitless, two women officials took me off and made me undress. Each garment of clothing was held up to the light and studied in detail. It was embarrassing and unpleasant. As I stood there naked and shivering, I was told I might just as well confess, otherwise they were going to insert instruments up my backside and anywhere else they thought fit. I was so horrified and angry that this time, it made some impression and I was apparently believed at last. After a brief consultation with each other, the women told me I could get dressed, pick up my bags and leave.

I have travelled many times to different countries and have never had trouble with British customs. Had they been tipped off by the Moroccan authorities in revenge, or was I just becoming paranoid? Or perhaps it had just been noted that this was my third trip to Morocco in about 6 months. All I wanted was the right to see and spend some time with the man I loved and the authorities - first the Moroccan and now my own - were treating me like a criminal.

I went back to the first Customs official and demanded an explanation and an apology, both of which were forthcoming. I was told that Morocco was the biggest exporter of cannabis and that travellers from this country were therefore particularly under scrutiny. I remember hearing from Jamal and other Moroccans that drug plantations are allowed by the authorities in the north of the country. Whole fields of cannabis are grown. The only restriction on this practice is a law preventing sale outside the region, a limitation which paves the way for heavy black market dealings. The main people involved in raking in enormous profits include the police and high-ranking Government officials.

Chapter 26

None of the unpleasant consequences of my trips to Morocco deterred me from trying to see Jamal as often as possible and trying to lead a normal life under the unusual circumstances. Rather, it strengthened my resolve. Before long, I was back at Heathrow Airport, destination Casablanca.

As I stepped off the plane, I had that elevated feeling I always get coming from a rainy, barely warm climate, spending a few hours on a plane and then being hit by the soft warm air of a different climate. "I'm a Southerner at heart," I said to myself, walking down the steps and drinking in the sweet smelling air of North Africa.

This time, I'd decided to stay in Kenitra to be nearer Jamal. It was a hot Wednesday in July when I once again made the by now very familiar trip to the prison. I had to go through the customary ritual with Sadique at the entrance but I had become hardened to this. It robbed me of about 15 minutes of each visiting-time, but I was always confident of being let in eventually and the joy of seeing Jamal again and knowing that we had three whole weeks before us made up for all the aggravation. At least, that was what we thought then.

It was during the afternoon visit when I felt the first hint of possible trouble. A guard came up to where we were sitting. (A word about the guards is appropriate here. They came in all shapes and sizes and temperaments. Some were like Sadique - thoroughly committed and completely incorruptible, qualities which I would have been the first to admire elsewhere; some were corrupt and would do anything for a reward; some were genuinely pleasant and caring; some had been unshakeably pro-establishment in the beginning, but as they got to know the prisoners and realised they were dealing with intelligent, creative and non-criminal men, they became sympathetic, taking a pro-prisoner stance. All of them except for the Sadique replicas would do things for the prisoners, some for love and others for a more concrete reward. Anyone who imagines that guards are fearsome, and by definition fierce upholders of the law, putting their lives on the line to stick to the rules, may be surprised by this. Here in Kenitra at least, they were just like any other cross-section of society, with their varying degrees of standard, loyalty and conscience.)

The guard who approached us as we were sitting talking together, our arms around each other, was one of the converts. He hung around us before bending down and whispering:

"By the way, you might like to know I've been instructed to listen in to your conversation."

We all laughed about it and then I started to make some facetious remarks in the guard's hearing, such as "Oh, by the way, you know that bomb, well it's timed to go off tomorrow." The jokes we made served to cover up my feeling of unease, a feeling which soon turned out to be justified, as events were to show.

The next day, there was no visiting at the prison and Jamal had been unable to arrange any hospital "outings" so I took the collective taxi to Rabat and spent a day on the beach in the lovely July sunshine. How I pitied Jamal not being able to share such a modest pleasure. ("The sun," I was told by a Moroccan," is the only thing which is free in this country.") As I lay there, I tried to analyse the previous day's feeling of unease, tried to see whether it was justified or whether I had become unnecessarily nervous. Who had instructed the guard to listen in to our conversation? If it was Sadique, then there was nothing to be feared, but suppose it was the Prison Director, acting on orders from the police?

The sea lapped over my feet and I sat up and looked around at the others on the beach. There were, as was to be expected, quite a lot of children, looking and behaving like children do everywhere: some laughing, some crying, some fighting, some playing happily alone, others playing happily together. I looked at the mixture of women on the beach. They were mostly Moroccan, although there were a few tourists, too. What struck my Western eyes was that, although a few Moroccan women - and only the younger ones - were dressed in bathing costumes and occasionally bikinis, the majority of them were sitting in the bright hot sunshine fully covered and with headdresses and veils. It seemed incongruous beach-wear.

My attention then switched towards the men. They were lying in gay abandon, stretched out in skimpy bathing trunks for the most part, their bronzed bare torsos fed by the sun; or they were swimming in the sea or playing games on the sand. It all seemed much more natural, given the place and the temperature. Why did women have to be restrained, or why did they restrain themselves? I am the first to respect customs and traditions of another society, but when it concerns oppressed women my feelings of loyalty to my gender are stronger. I felt indignant at the way men had built up such comfortable lives for themselves, their comfort being founded on the status quo they had established, and often backed up by individual interpretations of religion. For example, the Koran states only that women should be "modestly dressed" (it doesn't put any restrictions on the way in which men dress). It does not say that women have to be veiled and head-covered. A divorced man in Morocco is equal to a single one: indeed, men don't even have to get divorced, they can be married to four wives at once. But for many Moroccans, a divorced woman has a status not much better than a prostitute. Why should men have the monopoly on enjoying a variety of partners? I felt disturbed on behalf of my oppressed sisters.

I fell asleep and dreamt that I had gone up to one of the older women and swept off her veil and head-dress. In one graceful movement, she cast aside her djellaba and there stood a lovely young girl laughing at me, her long dark hair blowing in the wind. This Prince Charming's kiss had delighted her and we hugged each other and started to dance together on the beach. Smiling people made way for us, encouraging us with cheers and claps. Then, as we danced, I suddenly became aware of another transformation, this time a gradual one. As I danced with my partner, her features began to change, her body began to change and become heavier, her hair fell out. She had become a man.

I awoke with a start. I must have slept for a long time, because it didn't feel quite so hot, and I could see the djellabas packing up to go home. I did likewise.

When I got back to the hotel, there was a little reception committee waiting for me. The police. *"Voulez-vous nous accompagner au Commissariat?"*

"Est-ce que j'ai le choix?" (Do I have any choice?)

"Non".

That was clear enough. They looked fairly determined. Sitting in the car, wedged between two stern-looking policemen, I wondered unhappily what was going to happen this time. I felt distinctly uneasy. Were my passport and flight ticket in jeopardy again? Or were they going to do a more thorough job this time?

I understood by now that the authorities were not pleased with my presence in their country, but I hadn't the faintest idea to what lengths they might go to get me removed or just discouraged. A warning, a threat, a little "accident" perhaps? A one way trip to the airport?

I felt strangely calm and unruffled as I was led up the steps to the police station and from there into a room where three police officers were waiting for me.

A two-hour interrogation at the Police Headquarters in Kenitra followed. The police were reasonably polite but firm. It appeared that, before I could go to the prison again, I needed a special authorisation from the Ministry of the Interior.

"But I've been visiting my fiancé for nearly a year now without needing anything other than my passport," I protested.

"The rules have changed."

I knew it was a lie, as they had said this sort of thing before and it hadn't been true. I had been met with blank stares at the Interior Ministry, and been assured that only the Prison Director

236

could give or refuse permission to enter his prison. I decided to go and see Jamal the next morning and then go to the Interior Ministry. The irritation I felt once more about not having things spelt out for me! Why couldn't they just say: "No more prison visits for you" instead of getting me running around the capital in the fierce July heat in vain pursuit of a mythical document? At least I'd know where I stood.

The next morning, I thought I had nothing to lose by trying to get into the prison. So I went there and saw to my delight that Sadique was not on duty. I got in with no difficulty. I reported to Jamal all that had taken place the previous evening at the police station. We sensed that worse was to follow. In fact, the real problems started that afternoon. Encouraged by the ease with which I had got into the prison that morning, I went back in the afternoon in a reasonably optimistic mood. Sadique was waiting for me with a look of relish on his face which should have warned me of the trouble afoot. No, he would not give me a pass and no, he was not prepared to discuss it. He then started shouting at me, but this was usual, so I left his hut and waited just outside the prison as I usually did when Sadique refused me entry.

I was standing there quite calmly when suddenly Sadique came rushing out of the prison towards me, shouting: "Quittez! Quittez! Quittez!" He then grabbed me by the arm and breast, threw me on the ground and kicked me. He disappeared into the prison, cursing me. I was dazed and trembling after this unexpected show of physical violence. I couldn't quite believe it had happened. The pain from my arm, however, which felt jerked out of its socket, was intense and my breast was throbbing. There was no one in sight except the guard at the gate; he had observed the whole scene, but I couldn't imagine him standing witness. I didn't quite know what to do, nor did I feel capable of acting. I felt hurt, angry and bewildered. After a few minutes, I managed to pull myself up from the ground with some effort. I dusted myself down and looked around. I could see some visitors approaching by car. I went up to them, gave them Jamal's name and asked them to tell him I had been attacked by Sadique outside the prison and that I was still there, hoping he could get me in. They promised to pass on the message. After a while, another group of visitors arrived and I told them the same thing, in case the others didn't keep their promise, and also to let Jamal know I was still there.

What happened next was that Sadique sent out a guard, a young man of about 18 years old at most, carrying a gun. He told me aggressively to get out of the place. I told him that they might be able to stop me from entering the prison but they couldn't stop me from standing in the street. I was right on the first count but wrong on the second. Three minutes later, the police arrived in two cars - I never ceased to be amazed at the resources they had for this sort of thing - and I was taken back to Kenitra Police station. All pretence at politeness had by now vanished - they were nasty, aggressive and very aware of their power and duty to their country.

They asked me why I had been trying to get into the prison when they had expressly told me not to enter without a special permit.

I stood my ground. "I understood the permit to mean before my next visit to *Morocco*, not the prison," I improvised.

They were furious and said I was lying. Then they said that if I tried to see Jamal or attempted to communicate with him, or if I even went near the prison, they would arrest me on the spot. In the meantime, they wished to give me *"un petit conseil"* . The friendly advice this time was that I should leave Kenitra, since they didn't want any more trouble. They drove me back to the hotel where I was staying and instead of leaving me at the door as they had done previously, they came in and spoke to the manager who was on reception.

I felt stunned. I went up to my room, trying to digest everything that had happened. About an hour later, I went to the foyer again just in case Jamal had sent someone to the hotel to talk to me. However, no-one was there. After a while, a policeman I recognised appeared, spoke a few words to the manager and then disappeared without looking in my direction.

I had had the good fortune to make friends with a kind soul at the hotel - I'll call him Hamid. I had told him my real reason for being in Kenitra and he had been sympathetic. I told him now that the police were hostile and would probably go on harassing me until I left town. He informed me he had found out that the police had put a plain-clothes man at the hotel to watch and follow me. He also gave me the useful information that this man was there now and would in future be starting duty at 7 each morning.

This latest development turned the whole situation into something akin to a 'B' movie plot. I decided to test the accuracy of Hamid's statement. I sat down in the foyer, with a few other people and began reading. I suddenly jumped to my feet, took a few steps towards the door and then stopped dead in my tracks. I had been monitoring the situation behind me in the reflection on the window-pane. I could see a man (whom Hamid had previously pointed out to me) echo my movements. Later, I went for a walk around the block and saw him behind me, all too painfully obvious. Hamid had also got hold of the information that the police had given orders for any message or visitor to me to be intercepted. I realised they meant business this time.

Next morning, I left the hotel at 6.15! I had two main plans: one was to get a letter through to Jamal telling him what had happened and, with luck, to get a reply telling me what to do; the other was to go to the Interior Ministry for an authorisation. I knew that the latter was a hopeless task, but at least I could tell the police I had tried.

For the first part of my plan, I went to see a young woman called Raja, whose brother was in prison with Jamal. She was a kind, warm-hearted person, the only one of the prisoners' relatives who had ever approached me - all the others seemed afraid of my presence.

Raja was, and still is, a stunningly beautiful woman, with

glistening red-brown hair falling in waves round a smooth olive-skinned face with classically high cheek-bones. A lovely smile often used drew attention to soft, sensuous lips and brilliantly white teeth. Her physical beauty was matched by her delightful warm and caring personality, inner depth and strong sense of social justice. She was trustworthy, loyal and fearless, for all her youth - she was only 19. A better person to help me would have been impossible to find.

She had given me her address the previous day and said that I was to have a meal with her some time (although I don't think she had meant breakfast at 7 the next morning!) She lived in a suburb in the poor quarters, where she rented a room in primitive conditions. Her family were there on holiday, all staying in the one small room: father, mother, one brother, two sisters and Raja herself.

When I drew up in a taxi and banged on her door just before 7, I awoke not only her entire family but all the other people in the house, along with half the street. I was suddenly surrounded by flocks of curious nightdresses and pyjamas. People were touching my clothes and hair and chattering between themselves and to me, although I was unable to understand. Raja's family appeared, and I was pulled into the house and given a cup of disgustingly sweet liquid. Raja was not there - she had spent the night elsewhere - but was expected back later that day. Her family were very friendly. When I left, they insisted that I return as soon as possible.

Then I went to the Interior Ministry. I had to hang around there all morning, until I was taken by two guards to an office on the first floor. I was seen by a small man with glasses, behind an enormous desk. I don't know what work he did, if any; the room seemed curiously devoid of books, files or papers, and the huge, highly polished desk was empty. This reinforced my previous impressions of officials' work-places in Morocco: empty walls, empty desks, empty everything - perhaps a symbol of their function in life. I explained that I had been sent by the police to seek a special authorisation to visit my fiancé in prison. The small man asked a few questions and then told me politely that the Interior

Ministry had no power to grant authorisation. He was sorry, and would like to help, but there was nothing he could do. Well, I hadn't expected anything, either, but at least I could say I had been there.

I went back to Raja's family and found Raja there. She was delighted to see me and promised support. I gave her the letter for Jamal, and she went to the Saturday afternoon visit with it smuggled inside her bra. She met Jamal and smuggled out another letter to me, using the same very effective means. What a friend in my hour of need!

It was heartening to receive a sign of life from Jamal, especially under the circumstances. His letter was a mixture of love, anger and good advice. It began:

"I have just received your note. I am so full of rage, I could explode, against everything that has been done to you!"

He wrote that he had been to see the Prison Director the minute he had got my note, and told him he had to do something. The latter had promised he would get the matter sorted out immediately, but when Jamal returned an hour later, he had left the office. Jamal promised me that there were going to be lots of protests and that he was supported by his colleagues, as an injustice against one was an injustice against all. He went on:

"We must fight this, we will succeed in the end. Each of us will do what we can, me from the inside and you with your Embassy, the police and the Ministry. There is no force on earth which can stop our love, it is made stronger than ever by this test, and stronger than the whole of this hostile environment put together."

One of the most useful pieces of advice he gave me was to go to a specified lawyer.

I stayed the night at Raja's and spent the following day, Sunday, planning my next move. I thought it best to contact the lawyer and then get him to come to the prison with me, so that when all these strict rules of Moroccan law were quoted at me by the police and Sadique, the lawyer would be able to refute them.

I got back to the hotel late. Hamid told me the police had been to the hotel four times, asking lots of questions, such as whether I had received any mail or visitors, where I was, whom I'd met, where I ate etc. They were going to do everything in their power to stop me from seeing Jamal the next morning, they had told Hamid.

Monday morning dawned. By using a back door which Hamid had showed me, I managed to give the police the slip and went to see the lawyer. He was helpful, friendly and efficient. He said he would try to find out what the authorities were up to. He rang the Prison Director, who was either not in or refusing to take the call. The lawyer then rang the Public Prosecutor, who agreed to see us.

He was an oily type, that prosecutor, all teeth and handshakes. However, being Moroccan, he was curious. He promised to summon the Prison Director to his office for consultation and we were to come back later. Upon our return, he told us that the Prison Director was under orders "from Rabat" not to let me into the prison. As for the attack, none of his guards would do a thing like that. It was obviously someone else (probably a foreigner) hanging around in the street. It also appeared that I had been outside the prison distributing leaflets with anti-Moroccan propaganda to everyone going in! The lawyer was then amazed to hear the Prosecutor admit it was true that I had been placed under observation and that the police had received orders to do everything in their power to make life difficult for me. The main message was that there was nothing further to be done at local level, I would have to get authorisation from higher up.

Jamal had advised me to get a medical certificate about my injuries, as he wanted me to sue Sadique. My right arm and breast were still badly bruised and swollen and I couldn't move my shoulder at all. So I went to see a doctor recommended by the lawyer. I didn't want to go into exact details (I imagined the doctor would have seized up completely if he had known that security and the prison system were involved), so I said that I had been the victim of an assault on the beach. The doctor examined me and wrote a detailed certificate covering all the injuries. At the end of the report, I was advised 18 days "complete rest"!

The next day I spent with the lawyer, going to every authority we could think of: the Interior Ministry, where a different official gave a regurgitation of the same boring story; the Minister of Justice (whom Jamal had urged me to see) wouldn't see me as, according to his secretary, he "didn't recognise" fiancées, only wives; and the Prison Directorate, where an official said quite frankly that if the police had told me I could get an authorisation there, they were lying. His office had no power to grant authorisation except when it was a question of the death sentence. The only person who could refuse or grant me entry was the Prison Director. We always seemed to come back to him.

I realised there was nothing further to be gained from pursuing the authorisation angle. I felt depressed. I rang Jamal's mother and family but they weren't interested and either couldn't or wouldn't do anything. I was disappointed at this lack of solidarity at a time when I felt so much in need of it. What did I want from them? I had a feeling that if Mother had been there with me, insisting that I was one of the family, doors might have been opened. But why should she? She had been excluded from visiting Jamal while I was there, and I could still feel her resentment of my intrusion into the family, when before she had had the monopoly of visits to Jamal. I was asking too much. All the same and perhaps this was unjust but in my vulnerable state, I couldn't help contrasting their lack of interest with the warm generosity shown to me by Raja's family. At least I had this support.

The lawyer was going on holiday the next day. This was depressing news. I felt I was losing a friend as well as an invaluable support. He had spent two whole days with me. I dreaded to think what the bill for this might add up to. I met him for the last time at a café halfway between Rabat and Sale. We discussed possible future tactics and he gave me the name of another lawyer in case of further trouble. We finished our coffee and he stood up to go.

"How much do I owe you?" I asked him.

"Nothing."

"Nothing? But it's your job!"

"It's my duty".

Chapter 27

I must move out of this hotel, I thought. I had hesitated before as all the time I was there I would have some idea what the police were up to, and also I wanted to be near the prison in case the way suddenly became clear for me to get back in. However, by now I had really had enough of the police. It was nerve-racking to be shadowed and to know that my every move was being watched and reported. The shadowing was fairly amateurish. (Once, I went up to my shadower in the hotel. I said to him: "Do I walk too fast for you?" He looked startled but didn't say a word. The following day, however, I noticed that he had been replaced by someone else.)

Raja's friendship was indispensable. It was she who suggested that I move into her home.

"Goodness, Raja, it would be such a luxury to be anonymous for a while!" We were walking together through a vast souk near where she lived, her parents behind us, occasionally pausing to check out some food or other goods. It was noisy and lively. Raja stopped dead in front of me.

"Then you'll come?" She put a supportive arm around my shoulders. I hesitated.

"What I'm afraid of is that this will put you and your family at risk. The police might get all sorts of ideas if they discover you are hiding me from them. You would doubtless in their eyes also be part of the left-wing Zionist conspiracy and I rather fear you would have less protection than me."

At that moment, Raja's parents called us excitedly. We went over to the stall where they were negotiating a purchase of some black chalky-looking substance for me. It was a sort of henna which Moroccan women used in their hair to make it gleam. They told me that, out of all the stalls in this market, this one was of the very highest quality. Touched by their kindness, I accepted the bag they gave me and continued the discussion with Raja.

"You have all been so wonderful to me. I couldn't bear it if anything happened to you. I think the worst that could happen to me would be deportation. While that would be catastrophic in terms of my seeing Jamal, at least I don't imagine my life would be in danger." We paused to fend off an enthusiastic stall-holder, trying to sell us some olives. I continued: "Apart from this, there are already six of you sharing your one small room and all of you sharing the sparse facilities in the house with the rest of the tenants."

Raja wouldn't be put off, however. "You are my sister, Joyce. What is the difference between us? We both have two eyes, a nose, a mouth, two legs, two arms. We laugh, we cry. There is no difference. Everything that is mine is yours. If they come for you, then let them come for me too!"

She was very persuasive. I - not unreluctantly - let myself be talked into it. This plan also carried with it another important advantage: Raja promised me that either she or a member of her family would go to the prison every single visiting time to pass messages between Jamal and myself.

I made my decision. I got up extremely early the next morning, packed my things, paid my bill to a sleepy receptionist and got away in a taxi before any chance of reaction.

I stayed at Raja's for 12 days. The 7 of us lived, ate and slept in one small room on the ground floor of a house in multiple occupation. The only toilet serving the whole house, situated in the hall just inside the entrance, was a hole in the floor with no flushing system. The only water supply was one cold water-tap in a kitchen with no door, also located in the communal hall. This also served the whole house. Washing was therefore not the most private of activities.

This was a house full of strange people, where every tiny domestic argument would turn into a matter for the entire house to sort out, and where people would be screaming at each other one minute and then laughing together 10 minutes later. All disputes were thoroughly confusing to me with my 20 words of Arabic, none of which I ever recognised in their slanging matches, and was made worse by people apparently changing sides all the time without warning. Even more nerve-racking was when I was occasionally grabbed by someone evidently to prove a point, when I hadn't the faintest idea of the context, and never quite knew who to smile at and who to glare at or look apologetic towards, amid this constant realignment of loyalties.

A typical case was a big argument that had arisen after I had tried to plug my hair-drier into the only electrical point in the house: in the communal hall. I'd left the hall for a couple of minutes and on my return found the entire population of the house assembled around the point. People I had never seen before were taking hold of me and shouting, some appeared to be on my side, others were in opposition. The opposition were vociferous in laying the charges, using every part of their bodies to punctuate the details of the transgression. I felt I was going to be crucified. Raja's family united behind me and the row lasted for some time. When it had subsided and we had all retired to our respective rooms, I asked Raja what on earth it had all been about.

She had started to explain when her sister disputed some detail. The whole conflict was then re-enacted, this time between Raja's family: father against mother, brother against sister. What struck me was that when the original argument had taken place in the hall, her family were one hundred per cent united against the antagonists in the rest of the house, almost, I'd felt, going to their deaths to defend me for my unknown crime. Now, however, it seemed that a different truth and feelings were emerging. I never did discover the problem with the electricity point, but I made quite sure I didn't go near it again!

On two occasions, there were big disputes originating from within Raja's family. After the initial screaming match, there was a sullen silence, and the family started packing their bags aggressively to leave. (These disputes were often Raja versus her family, and on one occasion, she even threatened her father with a knife!) Everyone would go around hating the situation, but feeling much too proud to do anything about it. The air would be blue for an hour or so, when a chance remark would lead to a chance remark and, finally, almost imperceptibly, bags would start to be unpacked and I understood the immediate crisis was over.

Apart from these two occasions, the evenings were fun. Raja treated me like a sister and for her mother I was a daughter. It was a warm, homely atmosphere. We all sat on the floor around one enormous plate of food from which people ate with their fingers, Moroccan-style. Once, at my request, I was allowed to make dinner. However, word got round about this and everyone in the house turned up with an empty bowl, leaving precious little for the rest of us, so I never repeated it; probably just as well, as it's no easy task to make food for seven from a spirit stove on the floor, with not much hope of getting to the kitchen in view of the stiff competition for the single water-tap.

As for going to bed, it was a work of art! There was hardly enough floor space for us all, so the last two people 'in bed' invariably trod on everyone else, provoking shouts, screams and giggles. I tried to teach them some English songs and a few English words. The word 'sleep' used to send them into hysterics, which puzzled me until I realised that it sounded the same as the French *slip* meaning underpants or briefs.

One night was especially hilarious. Father was doing the talking, and everyone was giggling. I asked Raja what he was saying and she said, between chokes of laughter:

"My father is giving us a vivid and detailed description of a television series he has never seen!" Otherwise, we would talk and laugh and sing to each other until we fell asleep from sheer exhaustion.

Raja's family were the ideal post carriers. There was a constant flow of letters and messages between Jamal and myself. I learnt that Jamal was putting up a big fight inside the prison. An open letter, signed by the prisoners, was sent to the Minister of Justice and copies circulated to the Moroccan newspapers, protesting against the 'cowardly aggression' towards me and demanding that I be allowed back in the prison to see Jamal. In the evenings, Jamal and a few other prisoners 'occupied' the exercise yard, refusing to return to their cells for the night.

In the middle of all this activity, Jamal wrote to me that he was due for a hospital visit in a couple of days and wanted to see me there. Oh no, Jamal, this is far too risky! I thought. I sent a message saying this and pointing out that all eyes would be on him under the circumstances and I did not wish to show myself to the police. However, he was determined we should meet and as I wasn't allowed into the prison, it would have to be outside, so he answered that I should send Raja to the hospital and he would come back to her place and meet me there!

In the meantime, having exhausted all possibilities of action with the Moroccan authorities, I decided to try with my own. I was not very hopeful, as I didn't see how they could intervene in what the Moroccans must have reckoned to be a matter of domestic national security, and what the British must have seen as a purely personal matter. However, I had nothing to lose, so I went to the Embassy, and met the same woman official. She was just as sympathetic and willing to help. She rang the Prison Director who was apparently reticent and merely repeated that without an authorisation, there was nothing he could do.

She put the phone down and stared out of the window as if some fascinating drama was being enacted in the courtyard. Still gazing out of the window, she said with the utmost casualness:

"I suppose you have never considered bribing the officials to get this authorisation?"

I started in my chair. I thought I hadn't heard right.

"Bribing? I couldn't, I wouldn't know..."

She smiled at me reassuringly as if she had been practising this art with impunity all her life.

"Oh, you do it in a perfectly ladylike manner. You take out your purse, finger a couple of hundred dirham notes rather conspicuously, and then say 'Of course, if there is some sort of stamp duty involved...'"

I hardly knew whether to be amazed or amused at receiving lessons in corruption from the British Embassy.

My Embassy friend told me that if Jamal had been British, she would have been in a much stronger position to apply pressure. She remarked, however, that the ease with which I had managed to see Jamal in the past had amazed her. She told me of a British prisoner she visited now and then in Kenitra Prison, convicted for drug-smuggling. Each visit was apparently surrounded by a mass of bureaucracy and had to be applied for well in advance. I could only imagine this was because, being a common-law prisoner and therefore guilty in the eyes of most, he was in a much weaker position. This reinforced my impression that, because of the injustice and outcries in Morocco and other countries about the incarceration of these political prisoners (Amnesty was to a large extent responsible for this) the Moroccan authorities were very circumspect about them.

She wrote two letters: a "To whom it may concern" letter to show the police and other authorities, and one to the Prison Director to be delivered by me personally. The first letter stated that I was British and worked for the British Government. It went on to say: "She is known to this Embassy from her previous visits to Morocco and is considered to be a person of integrity. She is the fiancée of Jamal Benomar, presently imprisoned at Kenitra Prison, and she has come to Morocco with the sole object of visiting her fiancé." The letter ended by saying that Jamal and I intended to marry as soon as we were able to do so and that the Embassy would appreciate any assistance anyone could give me etc.

The second letter - to the Prison Director - was a bit longer and a bit stronger. This time, the Embassy were 'honoured' to introduce me, and now not only was I a person of high integrity, but moreover one of 'excellent reputation'. Any help which the Prison Director might care to put my way would also apparently be much appreciated by the British Embassy.

My friend then told me she was going to the prison to visit the erring British citizen in a couple of days when she would try and have a word with the Prison Director about me. In the meantime, I should go along to the prison the next visiting time and give him her letter.

The next day was the day of Jamal's hospital visit, when he would possibly be coming to see me. Given the current situation, I wondered how I could ever imagine that this would not end in total disaster?

AMBASSADE DE GRANDE-BRETAGNE
RABAT

le 3 août 1983

A QUI DE DROIT

La porteuse du présent certificat est Madame Joyce Edling, de nationalité britannique et fonctionnaire du gouvernement britannique. Elle est connue de cette Ambassade de ses précédentes visites au Maroc et elle est considérée comme une personne de bonne vie et moeurs.

Madame Edling est la fiancée de M. Jamal Eddine Benomar, qui est actuellement emprisonné à la Maison Centrale à Kénitra et elle est venue au Maroc dans le seul but de visiter son fiancé. Nous avons compris que Madame Edling a l'intention d'épouser M. Benomar dès qu'il sera libre pour se marier.

Toute aide nécessaire qui lui sera donnée pendant son séjour au Maroc sera appréciée.

G Murray
Vice-Consul Britannique

AMBASSADE DE GRANDE-BRETAGNE
RABAT

le 3 août 1983

Monsieur le Directeur
Maison Centrale
Kénitra

Monsieur le Directeur,

J'ai l'honneur de vous présenter Mme Joyce Edling, porteuse de cette lettre. Elle est de nationalité britannique et travaille pour le gouvernement britannique. Elle est venue au Maroc pour visiter son fiancé, M. Jamal Eddine Benomar, qui est actuellement emprisonné à la Maison Centrale.

Mme Edling nous est bien connue de ses précédentes visites en Maroc pour voir son fiancé. Elle est considérée comme une personne de bonne vie et moeurs et d'excellente réputation. J'ai compris qu'elle a l'intention de devenir l'épouse de M. Benomar dès que le nécessaire sera fait pour organiser leur mariage.

Je vous serais très obligé si on pouvait donner toute l'aide qui s'avérerait nécessaire à Mme Edling durant sa brève visite au Maroc.

Vous remerciant d'avance de votre aimable assistance, je vous prie d'agréer, Monsieur le Directeur, l'expression de ma haute considération.

Mme G Murray
Vice-Consul Britannique

Embassy letters

Chapter 28

Sleep that night came to me in fits and starts and I awoke with a mingled feeling of apprehension and warm anticipation at the prospect of seeing Jamal.

I discussed the details with Raja. I never ceased to admire her courage and maturity on this issue. She was going to farm out all her relatives and let Jamal and me be alone together in her room. She had no hesitation about going ahead with this plan. Yet it was against everything she had been brought up to believe in, as well as being against Islam and against the law. Extra-marital relations were punished by at least six months in prison. Woe betide a non-married couple who are even out driving together in a car after dark! There was also a famous case involving Maurice Serfaty, son of Abraham Serfaty, the most well-known prisoner in Kenitra. Maurice had been living with a German woman. When this was found out, she was given a year in prison and subsequently deported. Maurice, not at all politically active himself, but who had allegedly been tortured in the past because of the activities of his father, was given a two-year jail sentence, no doubt as revenge on his outspoken father.

Raja's parents were not, of course, too happy about our proposed plan, no doubt for security reasons, apart from anything else. However, they were kind-hearted people and Raja let them understand that this was her decision and her room, and if they didn't like it, they could leave. They accepted the situation partly, I believe, out of respect for Raja, partly out of solidarity with political prisoners and partly out of friendliness towards me.

The time came for Raja to go to the hospital to try and fetch Jamal. We kissed and hugged each other for luck and then she was gone. I had no idea how long I would have to wait before she came back, either alone or with Jamal, or pursued by the police.

I felt a bit like a prisoner myself as I did not wish to show my face outside, and was confined to a bare room not much larger than a prison cell. The other people in the house were already curious about my unannounced arrival there, and the hair-drier incident had created some unwelcome attention. Foreigners always excited a certain amount of curiosity, especially in a poor area like this, which had probably not seen a foreigner at close quarters since the end of French colonisation.

As I waited for Raja's return, my ears sharpened at every footstep. There were plenty of false alarms. I'd made the mistake of leaving the door of the room slightly open. Suddenly to my horror, one of the occupants of the house came down the stairs and tried to talk to me. It was the last thing I needed. He was a rather odd character about 30 years old, with apparently severe learning difficulties, and Raja had told me he had a lot of complexes about having only one arm. He was the son of the owners of the house, an old couple who lived upstairs. I tried to speak to him in French, but he spoke only Arabic, so it was a very one-sided communication. When he saw that he wasn't getting through to me, he started repeating each remark louder and louder, as if my failure to respond adequately was attributable to an advanced condition of acute deafness.

He was quite persistent, and I was loathe to try and get rid of him even if I had known how to; partly because I feared what might happen if he became hostile, and partly because I was so conscious, not of his disability per se, but of his (reported) feelings about it.

He lurched into the room and kicked the door shut behind him. My instinct to scream was immediately replaced by another instinct not to attract attention. The empty shirt-sleeve assumed gigantic proportions, looming in front of me in a forceful way, as threatening as a complete arm wielding a knife. I began to feel frightened and alone. I ached for Jamal. The man held out his one arm to me beseechingly, saying I don't know what. He leant forward and touched my hair. At that moment, someone called him. He shouted something. I heard someone coming down the stairs. He shouted again and to my relief, opened the door and lumbered off up the stairs. What a relief! The minute he had left the room, I got up and shut the door and leant on it, my heart racing. I could hear shouts and thumps coming from upstairs.

A vehicle drew up outside. I could only hear it, not see it, as the two tiny windows in the room were above eye level. I strained my ears anxiously. Could this be the police? A motor vehicle was a rarity in this street, about the width of a small corridor. I held my breath looking for a hiding-place almost subconsciously, but in such a primitive room, there wasn't even a cupboard. Then I heard the vehicle drive away. I wished I could just go to sleep and not wake up until Jamal was there in front of me. The suspense was terrible.

At last, I heard Raja's strong and dramatic voice and then she appeared, followed by Jamal! The joy of seeing each other was almost unbearable. We had so much to say to each other and yet we wanted most of all to give expression to our love. Raja disappeared and this simple room was transformed into a new world.

Jamal was amazingly cheerful and encouraging. I gave him my news. He said we were on the point of winning the battle and that I was to go along to the prison tomorrow with the letter from the Embassy and insist on seeing the Director. He told me what was happening inside the prison. The prisoners had appointed a committee of three people, one of them a well-known political prisoner serving a life sentence, and they had gone with Jamal to see the Director. They had decided beforehand that if the discussions did not lead to any positive results, then all the political prisoners in Kenitra (over a hundred in number) would refuse to return to their cells at night. The confrontation with the Director had apparently been stormy and almost violent. In the end, the Director had promised that the next time I came to the prison, he would receive me and find a solution to the problem. It was obvious to him that he was otherwise laying the way open for a big dispute with all the political prisoners.

There had apparently also been some more unorthodox suggestions about how to deal with the situation, such as one from the élite of the hardened common-law prisoners with life (and death) sentences, who - for a packet of cigarettes of their choice - offered to waylay Sadique and redesign the shape of his body. It was not the solution I would have chosen.

Jamal told me that most of the political prisoners were very supportive. A few, however, were doubtful. There was unfortunately a novel circulating in the prison at that time, a romance about a woman who, saying she was working for Amnesty International, had corresponded with a prisoner in an Egyptian jail. She went to see the prisoner a few times and then it turned out that she was a spy working for the CIA. So a number of Jamal's colleagues had asked him what he really knew about me. It could be like the book and I could be in the pay of the CIA, the KGB or whatever.

We spent two delicious hours together. As my friend the writer Niema Ash wrote: "...as so often happened in Morocco, the benign and the terrible were inextricably woven into a tapestry of surprises and shocks." In the midst of all this violence, repression, prohibitions and police activity, I was able to meet Jamal in peace and freedom. It was one more triumph over the system and yet another of its many anomalies.

The next day, it was time for constructive action again. At Jamal's instigation, I had dressed up in my best clothes and went, complete with the Embassy letter, to the prison gate. I felt shaky but determined.

Instead of going to Sadique's little lair just inside the gate, I approached the guard on duty outside the gate and told him I wished to see the Prison Director. He told me to wait, and he went off. Five minutes passed and the guard did not reappear. However, the police did. There were three of them and they were furious.

"What do you mean by coming to the prison when you have been expressly forbidden to see Mr. Benomar?"

My fingers tightened around the letter in my hand. "I have not come to see Jamal, but to see the Prison Director."

This infuriated them all the more. What could I possibly want with the Prison Director? I told them I had a letter for him, whereupon they demanded to see it. I looked shocked and said, "It is a confidential letter from the British Embassy".

I witnessed a complete change in tactics. Now they wanted to 'help' me to see the Prison Director. In fact we could all go together (what a jolly party!) Just as they were discussing how best to organise the treat, a rather distinguished-looking man appeared.

He asked me my name before introducing himself to me as the Prison Director. His next statement made my heart leap with optimism.

"I have taken the unprecedented step of coming to meet you personally at the prison gate just in case you should experience any slight difficulty getting into the prison!"

He then turned round and indicated that we should follow him. We made the familiar journey down the driveway. There was no sign of Sadique. We entered the main gate, went upstairs to an office and sat down. There was a strange atmosphere. The Director was quiet and non-committal. I gave him the Embassy letter which he read slowly and methodically. The police pounced on the letter and took a copy of it. I had planned to ask the Director if I could see Jamal, even if it were only for a few minutes and in his office, but I felt too inhibited by the intimidating presence of the police to mention it.

The Director addressed his remarks to me in a not unfriendly fashion. "The only way out of this situation is to get official permission to see Mr. Benomar."

He looked apologetic. My heart sank. From the clues I had picked up in the past, it had seemed that the Director was the only

257

person who could make a decision about letting me in, but now it appeared that he, too, had joined the special authorisation club. I told him how hard I had tried to get this but all roads seemed to lead - if not to Rome or Rabat - then certainly to Kenitra Prison. In fact, there was no-one left for me to ask. He looked distressed and said he was sorry. He got up to show me that there was nothing else he could do. The police looked triumphant. One of them took my arm and led me out of the prison into a waiting police-car. I was then driven to the Police station and taken to a room where another long and detailed interrogation took place, all of which was written down as I was speaking. There was a lot of talk about Trade Unions. Did I belong to a Union?

"Yes, in common with many other ordinary working people in Britain."

They wanted to know its name, the dates I'd joined, what it stood for, its aims and objectives, my activities within the Union etc. I explained that ASTMS was a normal Union, its membership being mainly white-collar workers and its aims in common with most other Unions, were to look after the interests and improve the conditions and salaries of its members etc. About half the *procès-verbal* was concerned with ASTMS, not the most revolutionary of organisations. Then a police officer, examining my passport, suddenly turned on me with a triumphant look as if he had found the missing part of the jigsaw.

"Aha! You've been to Ireland!"

I had to admit to this apparently heinous crime, even though I realised it could provide the police with proof of the IRA connection which no doubt in their minds formed part of the Amnesty-Zionist-Algerian conspiracy. However, I was a little surprised that they could discover this from my passport because, although it was true I had visited Ireland, I didn't remember any stamp in my passport. At the end of the interrogation, I was given the whole statement to read through and sign. It was packed with inaccuracies but I signed it just to bring an end to this lengthy and futile exercise.

As soon as I had signed the document, I was taken to an upstairs hall, where a police officer told to me to sit down. He said I was to be taken to the Divisionnaire (the Chief of Police in Kenitra).

After some time had elapsed, I was shown into the Divisionnaire's office, and here followed the strangest interview I had ever experienced. The Divisionnaire was a smartly dressed, fairly pleasant looking man in his early 40s. He asked me what the problem was and I told him all I wanted was to meet my fiancé in peace. He said:

"In that case, you should shoot me. This would be seen as a political deed and you would then be put into prison along with your fiancé. I would agree to this as long as you only pretend to shoot me."

I decided quickly the best tactic would be to humour him so I asked:

"Could you recommend a toy-shop where I could buy a water pistol?"

This seemed to amuse him, and he sat there and chuckled to himself for a few minutes.

The conversation then turned to my work at The Commission for Racial Equality in London. (Jamal had told me the previous day that this had been the object of suspicion among the authorities and it had been alleged that I was working for an international racist organisation). I started, therefore, to explain my work in great detail, going back to the time when Britain was a colonial power, to the recruitment of cheap black labour from the former colonies in the '50s, to the problems of racism and disadvantage faced by immigrant communities which had encouraged the Government to set up a Race Relations Board (I peppered the whole account with the word Government), right through to my own research in the Housing Section.

"OK," he said after listening to this long exposé without interrupting, "I have a proposition to make. I know a very nice doctor who has everything: good looks, money and status." The Divisionnaire paused, undoubtedly to allow me time to marvel at this perfect individual and be impressed at what, in his mind, constituted having 'everything'. Then he continued: "However, he has one big disadvantage: he is black so no-one wants him. He is looking for a European woman to marry, so as you love the blacks so much, can I arrange an introduction?"

I could hardly believe my ears. How unreal it all was! What was actually happening? I politely declined the offer, whereby the Divisionnaire started to chat me up himself, paying me compliments and saying that he wanted to show me the real Morocco. He would put an official car at my disposal and I could go wherever I liked and he would join me when he could.

What a state of confusion I was in when I left his office! I didn't quite know where to go from here. I felt depressed. I had played all my cards, I hadn't got to see Jamal, the Prison Director appeared to be uninterested, the Chief of Police appeared to be a raving lunatic; there was surely nothing else the British Embassy could do for me and there just didn't exist another office where I could hope to get hold of this mythical authorisation. I knew that if I turned up at the prison gate again, I could certainly expect to get arrested, no questions asked (no-one could say I hadn't been warned) and once arrested, I would surely never be allowed near Jamal again. I had started the day reasonably confident that the matter would be resolved, which made me feel the let-down all the more. Hope, as someone once said, makes a good breakfast but a lousy supper. I went straight back to Raja's.

A little while later, a woman appeared in a taxi, sent by Jamal. She brought a short letter from him, just stating that everything had been sorted out, I was to be allowed back into the prison, and he wanted me to go there for the next visit. There was no way I was going to believe this. I sent a letter back saying that it was a trap to get me arrested, and that the only thing which would persuade me to go was a *laissez-passer* written by the Prison Director himself.

260

Chapter 29

That evening, Raja came back from the visit with another longer letter from Jamal, giving a full explanation of events in the prison. He had been summoned to the Prison Director that morning, where he was told that although the Director had seen me and was sympathetic, there was nothing he could do, as it was the police who were opposed to letting me enter. It was a long and agitated discussion, at the end of which Jamal told him that if he didn't solve this problem in our favour, he was in for a few nasty surprises. This apparently worried him and he said he would try to convince the police.

An hour or so later, Jamal was summoned to the Director's office again. The Director had had a long discussion with the Divisionnaire, who had said he had met me and that the Director was to let me back into the prison. (Later, Jamal was to learn from a friendly guard that there were two reasons for this: firstly, the letter from the British Embassy and secondly, the Director took the threats from the prisoners about sit-ins, strikes and other disruptive action seriously.) Jamal told the Director he was sceptical about this latest promise - how could he believe it when so many promises in the past had been broken? In answer, the Director sent for all his chiefs and told them in front of Jamal that from now on, they were to let me into the prison and that furthermore, they were to treat me with the greatest respect (no doubt it was the letter from the Embassy which was responsible for this last sentiment!) It seemed that it was the Divisionnaire (certainly in collusion with the Prison Director) who had authorised the ban on my visits. Jamal wrote:

"In Morocco, it's the police who are in charge!"

He also wrote many times, and heavily underlined, that I was to come to the prison next day without fail.

What had I to lose? I set off the next morning. It was a

Saturday. Raja's mother came with me but walked about 50 yards behind. It wouldn't therefore seem as if we were together, but she would be able to report to Jamal anything she saw happening. As I walked down the road leading to the prison, I thought: This is another trap. After all, how was I supposed to know I was to be let in again? I could only have known through Jamal, and I wasn't supposed to have any contact with him. This could be the final trap. The police would be waiting. They would say: "We have lost patience with you. We have told you again and again there are to be no visits to this prison but you have defied us. Our only option now is to arrest you until we can arrange for you to take a plane out of this country."

It was a dreary prospect. I wasn't afraid - it had never occurred to me they might do me harm - but I so much wanted to see Jamal and I realised that if they deported me now, they would certainly never let me into the country again. I felt depressed and anxious. At least the presence of Raja's lovely mother behind me felt reassuring, and I was touched by her concern and willingness to help; but there would, of course, be nothing she could do if the police were there.

I got to the gate. No sign of police. I walked gingerly to the entrance hut, looking around me cautiously, half-expecting an army of uniform to leap out at me from the bushes. I braced myself for the inevitable encounter with Sadique. I wondered what his attitude would be. Whatever it was, it would tell me everything. If I wasn't going to be let in, he would be looking triumphant, standing very upright and feeling his great sense of power over me; if I were, he would be coldly contemptuous.

I entered the hut. To my delight, there was another guard on duty. He gave me an entry pass with no problems at all. I rushed to the prison building. There was a rapturous reunion with Jamal. We went through all the details of the past few days, alternately serious and laughing. What a fantastic feeling to touch and be touched by his familiar body.

I told him that the police had 'accused' me of going to Ireland, although I had checked, and there was no such stamp in my passport.

"Give me your passport," he said. He thumbed through it. After a couple of minutes, he looked up and said laughingly:

"Here is your journey to Ireland!" Stamped there in my passport, was the name of the international airport of Stockholm: Arlanda!

It seemed now that my every meeting with Jamal was dominated by dealing with the pressures trying to separate us. Gone were the days when we could just relax, talk dreamily together, bask in silence, eat cake with one spoon...

What had happened this time, with all its implications, had been a nasty jolt for us, so Jamal's next idea came as no great surprise. He wanted to escape. It wasn't the first time he had expressed this wish, but in the past I had not been keen on co-operating because of all the risks involved when he 'only' had two-and-a-half years left of his sentence. However, I now realised that I was not going to be left in peace again in Morocco and might well be stopped from seeing Jamal altogether. Also, the group of prisoners at Tazmamart had finished their sentences but the authorities were refusing to release them. It suddenly became much easier to talk about escape. We discussed practicalities in low voices. There were no problems involved in Jamal actually managing to leave the prison. The difficulty would be immediately afterwards. He obviously couldn't stay in Morocco so would need a passport to leave the country immediately. I promised that as soon as I returned home, I would look into all the possibilities of false passports. We decided on a code for communication about this plan. The name of the operation was to be Joyal, the union of our two names. All the details surrounding it would be as in a school: the prison was the school itself, the guards would be the teachers, the prisoners the pupils, the police the school inspectors, the plane the school bus, the passports would be the books, the passport stamps the exam marks etc. We knew that any other details we hadn't covered would be easy to invent and would be understood by the other, now that we had established the school framework.

There weren't many days left of this trip, and we had had a large chunk cut out of our precious hours together. The police, to my great relief, left me alone for a few days. I knew it wouldn't last. After all the energy they had put into following and harassing me, I couldn't believe they would just disappear. Sure enough, about three days before my departure, they were waiting for me outside the prison gate. My heart sank - I knew they had come for me - and I looked desperately round to see if there were any other way out of the prison. Of course, there wasn't. There was just the driveway, with the prison looming large behind me and Sadique's den in front of me. I was particularly apprehensive as I had given the police a false address in Rabat - I didn't want them to know about Raja, both for my and her security. Raja and her family had taken considerable risks on my behalf, solely out of friendship and love, as if I were one of their family, although I was a complete stranger to them and they only knew Jamal distantly.

I walked down the drive with slow measured steps, in the vain hope that if I dragged my heels long enough, the police would lose patience and go away. Needless to say, they were still there when I reached the gate. It was as if they had nothing else to do. Their first question was: "Are you still staying in Rabat?"

"Yes."

"Why haven't you moved to Kenitra?"

The police were amazing. Not so very long ago when I was staying in Kenitra, the tune had been: why didn't I move to Rabat?

"I'm tired of moving all the time," I replied, wanting to add sarcastically "at every little change of heart from the Kenitra police", but decided not to provoke them unnecessarily. Then they asked me why I hadn't "dropped in" to see them, almost as if they were a bunch of caring school-friends who wanted to reminisce about old times. I tried to convey - as diplomatically as possible - that

264

social visits to repressive police forces weren't highest on my list of priorities. I was then asked for exact details of my departure from Morocco - when I was going, time and number of my flight, means of transport to Casablanca Airport etc.

The day I left, Raja came with me to the airbus terminal. We got there early and sat in a café together to have a drink. I had to leave the café briefly, and when I returned, I found Raja talking to a man who was sitting behind her. This shouldn't have made me uneasy. After all, why shouldn't she be talking to someone in a café? Something, however, told me this was not just a casual chit-chat.

It made me reflect upon how much things had changed for me. I had always been a trusting person, had never been suspicious or searched for ulterior motives, and had taken people at face value. I had not generally had cause to regret this - life had been quite kind to me. But now here, thrown into this country of repression, I felt I had to have my wits about me all the time. I could never relax, never confide completely in anybody. I remembered that from what I had seen of other Moroccans and what Jamal had told me, they didn't trust each other either. I couldn't imagine what it was like to live in a society like this. It was just one more facet of being dominated by a repressive regime: people couldn't afford the luxury of trust. I didn't believe it was part of 'the Moroccan nature' - if there is such a thing - to be distrustful. Indeed, I imagined it to be the contrary, with a people who in the past lived in tribes, communities where the concepts of loyalty and solidarity are very strong. What a tragic evolution!

I retook my seat opposite Raja. She turned away from the unknown man and back to me, mouthing the words: "I think he's from the police". Raja was 19 years old. Even at this relatively young age, she could pick out the enemy. She was right. He got on the air-bus with me, although I noticed he didn't have any luggage. He hung around the airport lounge until I had been through passport control. The police were obviously going to make sure I was really off the premises.

I left Morocco with the usual mixed feelings of regret and relief. Only this time, it was tempered with the urgent need for action: ESCAPE.

Chapter 30

Back in London, I got in touch with everyone I could think of to get a forged passport for Jamal. The person who knew most about passports and passport checks was a work colleague, Andy. However, his information was discouraging. He told me that, with all the modern techniques available, a trained immigration official would be able to detect a forgery. Using my passport, he showed me in the minutest detail how any forgery could be detected. He explained how impossible it was to exchange the photo or to redo the personal information page without it being apparent; how different shaped stamps had different meanings, with a whole range of information conveyed to the immigration officer by the use of, for example, a little line or another mark under a letter or figure, in a way quite unintelligible to anyone else. There was also other information contained in the passport, indiscernible to the naked eye but quite visible to an immigration officer using a special light.

Andy knew what he was talking about. He questioned me closely about the immigration setup at the Moroccan airports, which I described as best I could. We focused on Moroccan airports, as it was getting Jamal out of the country which would provide the greatest problem. Once he got to this country, he could apply for refugee status.

It turned out that none of the airports would be safe. Rabat was a small airport with very few international flights and none to London; Tangiers would have been ideal, being unsophisticated and computerless, but the distance between Kenitra and Tangiers was too great, especially in view of the many police checks along the route, which was well-known smuggling territory. That left Casablanca, but this was a brand-new airport, and as I described it to Andy, he could see it contained exactly the sort of modern equipment he had been talking about.

A forged passport seemed out of the question then, and anyway, even if I got hold of the means and the contacts to procure one, how could I or any other lay person know if it were a good forgery or not?

Andy noticed my despair and smiled at me sympathetically. "Don't give up, Joyce," he said. "Go and invest in a copy of *The Day of the Jackal* by Frederick Forsythe."

Intrigued, I followed his advice. This best-seller was a thriller about the attempted assassination of General de Gaulle. The relevant part was where one of the characters needed a passport for a new identity. He went on a tour of graveyards, looking for details of a deceased person of the same age and gender. Having found his unwitting and powerless accomplice, he then sent off for a birth certificate of the dearly departed, applied for a passport and was granted one.

I rang up Andy. "It's ingenious - would it really work?"

"You've got a fair chance," he replied, "They check up in 10% of applications only."

I bought a book about graveyards and went on a few sightseeing tours. My task seemed a bit macabre - checking out corpses to give a new identity to someone escaping from prison, or using the dead to promote life for the living! Graveyards, prisons, hospitals, forged passports... it was all rather far removed from teaching English grammar to Swedish school children.

It proved to be a difficult search. Very few people had, it seemed, been cut off from life at Jamal's tender age. I felt almost angry at all these men who had selfishly insisted on attaining their three score years and ten, and began to develop a positive hatred for octogenarians. Eventually, after much searching, I found a monument erected to a man born in 1953 (Jamal was born in 1957). The extra four years would be a tribute to his maturity, but would the authorities really believe that someone of Jamal's so obviously Semitic appearance could be called Arthur Smith, born 30 years ago in Little Torrington, Devon? Once more, I felt discouraged.

I wrote to Jamal and tried to convey to him by allusion what was happening, along with an implied suggestion that we should perhaps call the whole thing off. He wrote back and let me understand that he had become obsessed with the idea. I could see how attractive a proposition it was for an intelligent active person like Jamal trapped in a cage, and I felt highly motivated to go on looking into the possibilities.

Beryl came to see me frequently - her love and support gave me a lot of strength. We spoke about Jamal often, and I shared the whole situation with her. We spoke about the approaching winter and I told her of the cold and damp conditions prevailing in Kenitra prison, even when the temperature outside was relatively mild.

"I'd like to knit a sweater for Jamal," said Beryl.

"Oh, he'd be really touched, Beryl."

"What size should I make it?"

"I'll have to think about that one," I replied, dreamily conjuring up past moments of love with my arms around Jamal, when the circumference of his body in inches was not a factor I had dwelt upon.

"Well I've just finished a sweater for my son," said Beryl, "and as far as I can see from photos of Jamal, they appear to be about the same size."

We paused for a moment while we pursued one of my favourite pastimes, studying Jamal's photos.

"In fact," Beryl went on, "he looks very much like Jamal altogether!"

There was dead silence. We stared at each other and then chorused "My God, the passport!"

Beryl produced a photo of her son and there was indeed an astonishing resemblance, I could almost have been looking at a photo of Jamal. Perhaps this is not so surprising considering the Semitic origins of both men, Beryl and her family being Jewish. Beryl's son lived in the USA, having been born and brought up there, and he had an American passport. So much the better; the

USA was so cosmopolitan that virtually anyone could pass as an American. We had an excited discussion and Beryl agreed to write to her son to see if he was willing to go to Morocco and 'lose' his passport at an appointed date and time.

In the meantime, life went on. I got a new job which meant further travel and harder work for me. This didn't, however, stop me from writing every day to Jamal.

Then one day came the telephone call.

Chapter 31

The house which I had bought in London just after my first visit to Morocco was in the throes of being repaired, remodelled and redecorated. I had become friendly with Michael the builder, who was interested in Jamal and touched by his fate. All the renovations in the house were being made for Jamal, it had become *his* house. A new kitchen was being fitted where he would cook delicious Moroccan meals, a sash-cord window was removed to make way for a French window so that we could step straight outside into the garden, a spare bedroom was being equipped as a study for Jamal to use for his research.

I sat in this study, and read the following letter from Jamal:

"Kenitra 6-11-83

I can't tell you the state of my emotions when I received a parcel from you this afternoon containing 3 books, a present sent from Holland. I was really very touched by this surprise and also by the thought that my darling thinks of me wherever she goes. This very kind gesture gave me such great pleasure on a day which I was expecting to finish very sombrely and tediously, as usual. I've heard a lot about 'Dedalus' by James Joyce but I'd never read it for the simple reason that I was never able to find a copy. The same thing goes for Solzhenitsyn's 'The First Circle'. I know the author, of course, but not the book. I am therefore delighted by the choice you have made.

I am very, very disappointed not to have received your letter yesterday. I don't know how I can get through a week without hearing from you. The days which separate me from next Saturday seem interminable. I am thinking about you, my adored darling. I love you passionately.

I was just listening to some music which I like very much. It is Ravel's 'Bolero'. How I would have loved to have you here with me listening to this lovely music. I also heard 'Eine kleine Nachtmusik' by Mozart. I liked this very much too, along with his 40th Symphony. I've always been very taken by this symphony since I was very young. Tomorrow, I will borrow Beethoven's Violin Concerto from a colleague. I haven't heard it for a long time and I can't wait much longer to hear it again. I feel such joy listening to this concerto and become ecstatic in the last movement. I am a music fanatic and Fate has wanted my darling wife to be a good musician.

Tuesday 8-11

I spent a very, very dull day. To break the monotony, I started to read 'Dedalus' this afternoon. I've already read about 100 pages. I realise that I can always count on my darling for her choice of book. I've just discovered that you have a very refined taste in literature. I love you very much, my darling. You are unique in the world. I want to devote my whole life to you.

Wednesday 9-11

I was expecting my mother to come today, but again, she didn't. She must be very involved in problems with the house. I've done nothing else the whole day other than read the book by James Joyce. It is very interesting. He is a writer of great talent. The very subtle way in which he describes his childhood gave me a strong reminder of my own childhood. It put me in mind of things which happened when I was only 3 years old! I remember my childhood a lot. It wasn't a very good childhood but it wasn't too unhappy, either. I will tell you all about it for hours and hours, with your arms around me and with your soft and tender look upon me. Oh! how I'm dying to be with you! My life without you has no sense!

Thursday 10-11

After a depressing day, I received the second parcel of

books you had sent me. It contained 'Les bons sentiments'
'Huis Clos' (Sartre) and 'Sons and Lovers' (D.H.Lawrence).
These books from you consoled me no end. I very much liked
your choice of books, I hadn't read them before. I also received
a card and a cassette from my very dear sister-in-law and friend
Jean, which touched me very much. I am very proud to have a
sister-in-law like Jean. I find her sincere and wonderful.

There was also a letter from my professor André Adam
in Paris, which I found moving. He told me that on 4
November, he had written to the King, asking him to pardon
me. In the letter, André Adam evoked the 24 years of service
he had given Morocco and the different posts of responsibility
he had held. He reminded the King of the banquet he, Hassan,
had held for him in 1960 to thank him for his services when he
left Morocco (he was at the time the Director of the Ecole
Nationale d'Administration - most of the highest-ranking civil
servants graduated from this college). He also praised me a
lot in the letter, showing how I had managed to study at a high
level under difficult conditions etc.etc.

I hope that his intervention on my behalf will achieve
the desired result, given his very high standing and his personal
acquaintance with the King himself.

Last time I wrote to Adam, I sent him the famous photo
you had taken of me, with the Victory sign. He told me he had
been very impressed with the photo and thought I had a nice
face! It seems that Adam is growing to like and respect me
more and more and has decided to do anything he can to help
me. I don't actually think that this intervention in my favour
will have any direct effect on my situation, in spite of the great
prominence of his personality and position, but you never know,
this action could have a positive effect if it were followed by
other steps taken by others like him. Indeed, this unexpected
initiative touched me very much, it was really nice of him."

About a week after having received this letter, I was writing to Jamal upstairs. I could hear Michael the builder banging around downstairs when the phone rang. It was Jamal. "Joyce darling, I've been freed!"

The line was atrocious. Not daring to believe what I thought I was hearing, I shouted "What did you say? Speak up, louder!"

"Je suis libre, je suis libre!"

"Jamal, say it again."

"I'm free! I ..."

The phone crackled itself to a halt and I sat there paralysed, staring at the receiver in my hand.

Then I rushed downstairs, grabbed the astonished Michael and hugged him. The kitchen doorway still bears the mark of where my sweater rubbed itself off on to the wet paint. "Michael, Jamal's free!" I then had terrible misgivings. It couldn't be true - Jamal still had over two years of his sentence to serve, and prisoners were never released singly before the end of their sentence. I was imagining things - it was the bad telephone line playing tricks, just telling me what I wanted to hear most of all.

However, later on that evening, Jamal rang back on a better telephone line. It was true! It was obviously on account of Adam's letter. (Note: This letter is reproduced in full in the Appendix). We were both so moved we could hardly talk. I don't even remember what we said and it was probably quite incoherent. .

The next few days passed in a fever of excitement. I telephoned everyone I could think of at home and abroad, starting with Beryl, telling her that we probably wouldn't be needing the services of her son, the little problem had been solved otherwise. She was overjoyed, as was Lennart, Jamal's caseworker, when I phoned him in Sweden.

What did this mean for us? How was our life going to change? How soon would I be able to get Jamal here so that we could live a normal life together? Would there be many difficulties in getting him here? These and similar thoughts passed through my mind, but the overriding emotion was sheer and unutterable joy, an emotion which never left me. I woke in the morning with a song on my lips, went to bed hugging myself in delight and blissful anticipation. Joy was now within reach! It had all been a dream before. Now, instead of years, it was weeks, maybe even days away from being realised.

I put a lot of energy into organising my next trip to Morocco - what a different trip it promised to be! Fortunately, Christmas was near and I had a generous leave entitlement. I booked a ticket for Christmas Eve. The plane was due to leave at 4.30pm and would be in Tangiers three hours later. I got to Heathrow Airport in plenty of time and checked in. At 4 o'clock, a slight delay was announced. This was terrible news for me. Every minute was going to seem like an hour. At 5 o'clock, there was another 'slight delay'. I got myself something to eat to while away the time, but was so excited I found I couldn't swallow more than a couple of mouthfuls.

It was very crowded at Heathrow on this, one of the busiest days of the year. I couldn't imagine that anyone in the whole of the airport could be as desperate to travel as I was, it just wasn't possible; our combined frenzy would have burnt the place down.

At 6 o'clock, another slight delay. At 7 o'clock, the same story. I was by now beside myself with impatience, almost ready to hijack any south-bound plane. Then the worries started. Perhaps there would be no plane today. No, that thought was too horrific to contemplate. There just had to be one. Could I get a private plane, perhaps?

The hours rolled on: 8 o'clock, 9 o'clock. Then at 9.30, the wonderful announcement came: Would all passengers due to fly to Tangiers please proceed to Gate no. 9. I was first in the queue.

We eventually took off at 10p.m. and arrived at Tangiers Airport at 1 o'clock on Christmas morning. A beaming face and a pair of outstretched arms were there to greet me - darling darling Jamal and our first taste of freedom. It was a seemingly unimportant detail, but the fact that I arrived on Christmas morning rather than 24th December was to have dire consequences at a later stage.

Mule trip to Berber village in the Atlas mountains, January 1984

Berber shepherd in the Atlas mountains, January 1984

Chapter 32

A sympathetic friend had moved in with his parents to give us the use of his flat in Tetuan, and we spent the first few days revelling in the joy of being together without restraint. We then did what we had long dreamt of doing: hired a car to tour Morocco.

We went to Meknes to pick up the car, and from there, to Fez and Marrakesh. I was a little apprehensive about whether we would be accepted at hotels in a country where living together as man and wife when you are not married is against the law and punishable by a prison sentence. However, apart from refusals at two hotels, one in Meknes and one in Fez, we had no problems. This was low season and most hotels were practically empty - the laws of the land could obviously be adjusted to make way for the more pressing laws of economics.

Marrakesh seemed lovely at first, with its wide boulevards lined with orange trees and its lively market. But a closer inspection revealed large expanses of the most appalling slums I have seen anywhere, with lots of begging from children and adults, and with child slave labour running rife. It was a terrible sight, especially in contrast to one of King Hassan's many super-luxurious palaces just a stone's throw away. I pondered on whether His Majesty was aware of the abject misery of such a large percentage of his people, just round the corner.

The magnificent scenery surrounding Marrakesh provided a stark contrast to this squalor. The Atlas mountains loomed above us everywhere, with breathtaking views across the valleys.

One day when we were driving in the mountains, the road suddenly became a cart-track which, after a little while, we could not manage on four wheels. We stopped and hired two mules. The mule-owner and a guide accompanied us up the mountain-side. We went through the primitive little Berber villages and were followed every now and then by curious Berber children. The sun was hot even though it was January. Most of the mountain-side was deserted, a lot of it looking as if lifted from the Bible. There were large expanses of rock, very little habitation or vegetation, and now and then we would come across an old Berber shepherd, dressed in a long robe with a hood and with his combined long hair and beard practically covering his face. It was peaceful and there was a feeling of being in a bygone era, very close to nature.

We turned a corner, and suddenly the mule-owner pulled out a knife. I was paralysed for a minute. I thought, My God, he's going to kill us, then rob us. After all we had been through, for it to finish like this.

He made my mule stop and, just as I was preparing for an early death, to my distinct shame, he very gently picked up the mule's foreleg and, with the point of his knife, carefully removed a stone which was lodged there.

Once down from the mountain, we went to an eating-place which looked more like a farm and we sat outside with a *tagine*, the delicious Moroccan stew. Eating out along the route had become quite a ritual for us. We had noticed that the price of a meal tended to double if I were seen to be one of the consumers. So I would sit in the car while Jamal bargained the price in advance. Once the negotiations had been completed, I would then appear for dinner. It had never occurred to me to haggle over the price of a meal; to Jamal, it was quite natural.

We had planned to leave Marrakesh and go back to Meknes to deliver the car, but on the morning of our proposed departure, I said to Jamal: "Let's go south to Agadir instead of north!"

He wasn't difficult to persuade. He had been arrested at such an early age that he hadn't been even as far south as Marrakesh, and hadn't been to the sea, which he loved, for over 8 years.

So we went to Agadir. We spent the days bathing in the sea in the warm January sunshine, and the evenings strolling along the beach together singing, our arms around each other. Jamal was the ideal companion: cheerful, flexible and very knowledgeable about his country. It was all blissful, the honeymooners' dream: peace, tranquillity, freedom and love. I wanted it never to end.

On our way back, we stayed a night high up in the mountains at a place called Azrou, covered in snow. What a marked contrast! We walked and skipped through the snow, the first time ever for Jamal.

As we settled down for the night in Azrou, I pulled Jamal close to me and said something which had been on my mind for some time:

"Look, we don't know what may happen in the future. With the unpredictability of the Moroccan authorities, you could be arrested again on the slightest charge. I have to return to London in a few days. If anything should happen to you here, I feel I would be in a much stronger position to fight the authorities, if need be, if I am your wife. Let's get married here and now in Morocco!"

I reminded him of the time when I had been in trouble before and had been to the Ministry of Justice. I was not allowed access to the Minister as I was not married to Jamal.

The concept of marriage in itself meant nothing to me. I had always been sceptical of the idea that it was necessary to get a piece of paper from the Church or State to say that we loved each other. It was our business. However, we were not in a normal situation and I knew that, for our purposes, we would be more secure if we did have that paper. I had no doubts about my security vis-à-vis Jamal, but every doubt about the country he was still living in. It would really make sense to get married.

Jamal listened to me quietly, holding me close. Then he sat up in bed and looked at me intently.

"Joyce, darling, I love you dearly and want nothing else than to be with you. However, marriage here is different from marriage in your country. There is no such thing as a civil ceremony in Morocco. It has to be religious in accordance with the laws of Islam. I couldn't on principle enter into such an agreement as the one we would be forced to sign here."

I felt depressed at this. I fixed my eye on a Berber rug hanging on the far wall and said slowly:

"Jamal, far be it from me to force anyone into marrying me! But we have to think of our safety. Surely there can't be that much difference?"

"OK, let me give you a taste." Jamal grinned, obviously about to enjoy himself. "Under an Islamic marriage, I would have the right to prevent you from working, to keep you shut up in the house all day long, to have total control over you, and moreover, to have three other wives! How does that appeal to you?"

These were pretty convincing arguments (especially the last one). We decided, therefore, not to get married for the present. It was a decision which I lived to regret.

We left Azrou the next morning for Meknes, where we returned the car and then took the bus to Rabat. It was late at night and we took a taxi to a hotel, but it was full. We tried three other hotels, but in vain. This was unexpected, but we were told there was an international Islamic Head of State conference taking place in Rabat, which accounted for the unusual number of guests. We decided that I would wait with our luggage in the foyer of the hotel we were presently in, and that Jamal should go round the town to try and find us a room somewhere.

Then something amazing happened.

As Jamal was to tell me later, he turned up at a fairly central hotel where there was no room, but a friendly receptionist said he would ring around to other hotels. It appeared that the only other hotel with a room to spare was the Grand Hotel, but they refused to take us in unless we could produce a marriage certificate. Just as Jamal was discussing this with the receptionist, a tall man appeared in pyjamas, smoking a cigar. The receptionist looked at him with respect bordering on fear. The man asked what the problem was. Jamal told him of the predicament he and his 'wife' found themselves in and the man was sympathetic. He gave the receptionist the number of a hotel and ordered him to call them. As soon as there was a connection, the man took the receiver and said: "Good evening. This is Colonel Allaoui".

Jamal's jaw nearly hit the floor. This was a cousin of King Hassan - indeed, Allaoui is the name of the Royal family. The Colonel asked the person at the other end of the line if there was a room free at his hotel. The answer appeared to be negative. He then said: "I'm sending over two friends by taxi. By the time they arrive, I will expect you to have found them a room" - and he hung up.

He turned back to Jamal, who had just about managed to recover his equilibrium, and explained that his home was a house in the Palace grounds but that, owing to the Islamic conference, he had given it over to one of the delegations, while he himself had come to this hotel. He then gave Jamal the details of the hotel he had just called and wrote a note to the Director. By this time, we had been promoted to his 'dear friends' and we were to be given the best treatment. He gave the note to Jamal, told the receptionist to order him a taxi, and disappeared.

Jamal came back to where I was waiting and told me breathlessly what had happened. We got into a taxi which, after a few minutes, drew up in front of a hotel surrounded by palm-trees, stars above anything either of us could have dreamt of.

We approached the doorway and I went in tentatively while Jamal marched in as if he owned the place and 10 others like it.

"We've come from Colonel Allaoui."

Everyone jumped to attention at the magic words and Jamal produced the note with a flourish. The receptionist tremblingly told us that our rooms were being prepared. A phone rang from somewhere behind us and after a minute, someone came up to us and said: "Colonel Allaoui wishes to speak to you". Jamal took the receiver and said a hearty "Hello" as if the two of them were the best of friends and had gone fishing together as boys. Apparently, the Colonel asked if everything was all right.

"Well, it's not too bad," replied Jamal jovially, "no cause for complaint yet."

The Colonel urged Jamal to get in touch immediately if there was anything he needed or if he was displeased in any way. Then he hung up, after asking that Jamal's dear wife be given his compliments.

Jamal put the phone down and we looked around us. We were in a very large foyer with a sitting-room area. The decor was soft velvet furniture, marble surrounds and potted palms. Somewhere, we could hear an orchestra playing. It was the sort of hotel seen in early Hollywood films. Our gaze turned to the clientele. There were Heads of State in every corner, some of them with flowing robes and headgear. Then we saw that the whole place was packed with police, both in and out of uniform.

Our crime was threefold: firstly Jamal was not allowed to leave his home-town without special authorisation from the police (we had decided to ignore this requirement, as we didn't want the police breathing down our necks everywhere we went); secondly, Jamal was not allowed within a 10-mile radius of a town where any national or international conference was being held; and thirdly we were not, of course, married. However, Colonel Allaoui could not be wrong and so we were shown up to a luxurious suite.

As soon as the door closed behind us, I started to speak, but Jamal restrained me, mouthing the words that we should be careful, the place was certainly bugged. Using the same form of communication, I asked Jamal what we were going to do now. He replied, "We'll stay here for the night and then tomorrow morning, we'll get the hell out of here, as fast as possible!"

We went into the sumptuous bathroom and took a long and silent bath together. We felt tense. I didn't dare speak and I had a feeling that the police might come bursting through the door at any minute.

We finished the bath and threw ourselves on to the bed, exhausted. The room smelt of polish and disinfectant. It seemed ominously quiet around us. I lay down and tried to sleep but sleep just wouldn't come, I was much too much on my guard. Jamal couldn't sleep, either. I could feel his soft breath on my cheek as we lay there in silence, our arms around each other. It was progress from the prison days, but was it progress in the right direction? If ever I had contemplated living in Morocco with Jamal, then this was the time for facing the fact that it would be out of the question, at least during the survival of the present regime.

Suddenly, I sat bolt upright in bed. I could hear footsteps. Jamal tried to calm me. After all, he whispered, it was fairly obvious that there were going to be footsteps in a hotel full of people. The footsteps came nearer in measured pace and stopped, it seemed to me, right outside our door. I was almost too terrified to breathe. I looked desperately around for a window or a balcony. It was difficult to assess the escape potential beyond the long thick curtains on the other side of the room. After what seemed an age, we heard a key turn in the lock next door. We sank back into bed with relief.

A few minutes later, we tensed up again when the silence was broken once more by voices, soft voices. Another false alarm.

The whole night passed in this way. Sleep was out of the question, we were much too conscious of our situation. Cracks in the curtains showed us that night had turned into day, and bleary-eyed and exhausted, we got up and dressed slowly, our ears still straining for the slightest untoward noise, like a couple of cat-burglars.

We opened the door, took a swift look down the corridor, and then gingerly made our way downstairs. To our surprise, everything seemed normal. We didn't hang around in the reception area, or have breakfast at the hotel. We went instead to the medina in Rabat and breakfasted outside in the pale morning sunlight, amidst the familiar smells and sounds of the lovely old town. By this time, we were feeling much calmer about our situation and began to discuss its practicalities. We had planned to stay in Rabat until it was time for me to go back to London via Casablanca and, as we had seen, all the hotels were full. We decided to continue our extravagant life, therefore, at this particular hotel, but to be prepared to leave at the first hint of any trouble.

After a while, the receptionist managed to overcome his awe of us, and even dared to ask us if we were having a good time in Rabat. Jamal replied in the affirmative and, by this time really enjoying himself, added: "Of course, we spend our days at the Palace and then return here in the evening."

"Of course."

We spent three days in this luxurious hotel. We never caught sight of anything as vulgar as a bill - no doubt the Palace accountant is still scratching his head over that one.

It was now, sadly, the end of my stay. The usual trauma of parting was for me now accompanied by worry about what could happen in this unpredictable country. It had somehow seemed *safer* to have Jamal in prison.

We went straight from Rabat to Casablanca Airport. Jamal said that, as soon as we had parted, he was going to start the ball rolling to get his passport so that, with luck, our next meeting would take place in London. With this assurance, we said goodbye at the airport. But once again, the happiness we had experienced was soon to be overshadowed by the sinister events which followed.

Chapter 33

I returned to a wet and windy Heathrow Airport, feeling depressed at having left Jamal, but at the same time elated by the wonderful memories of the past couple of weeks and happy optimism for the future.

I had with me a bagful of photos to develop and print, and doing this caused me to relive the memories in a very powerful way. There were some excellent shots of Jamal at Marrakesh market with a snake around his neck, talking to some of the traders; photos of us on mules; a wonderful shot of an old Berber waving a stick among the rocks on the mountain-side; a picture of a camel - I remembered how Jamal had laughed when this camel, seemingly indignant at having his photo taken without consultation, chased me and bit me - and also shots of us in the sea together.

After I had been back for a while, there was a short four-line piece in *The Guardian* reporting riots in Morocco, although I hadn't noticed anything during my visit.

I then thought it strange that I had heard nothing from Jamal but it was another few days before the bombshell hit me. I woke up one morning to find an envelope in the post from Morocco. It was a very thin envelope and not in Jamal's handwriting or any handwriting I could recognise. I sat there for a while, staring at it. I had a premonition that I needed to brace myself for whatever I was going to find.

I tried to make out the postmark but it was obliterated. The handwriting also looked as if it had been written in a hurry. In fact, the only clear thing on the envelope was the hateful face of King Hassan, looking at me coldly from the stamp.

I ripped open the envelope. Inside was a tiny slip of paper which read: "Jamal has been re-arrested. Contact Lennart". That was all - it seemed that the writer had even been too terrified to sign. I stared at it long and hard. I felt quite numb. The words congealed before my eyes. I twisted the paper in all directions and held it up to the light, and turned the envelope inside out in the hope of finding some concealed message or any clue as to the identity of the author. There was none. It crossed my mind that it could be false or a joke but I was fairly certain it was true, it seemed so authentic. For a long while, I remained unable to move. Then I threw myself at the telephone. I tried to ring Morocco but couldn't get through. I rang Lennart in Sweden, I rang Amnesty, I rang Professor André Adam in Paris, who sounded distressed, saying he would try and contact the authorities to get Jamal released once again.

The days passed. I had given up my job and had been offered a new one, although there was some time to go before I started. At least that gave me some breathing space.

I certainly needed it. The anguish I went through was indescribable. After my initial bout of telephone-calls, I felt paralysed. With the paralysis came a sort of despair. I felt utterly hopeless and helpless, like a newborn baby who just has to wait for something to happen. At least with the baby, crying often produced reaction, but what about my cries? Who would listen to them? My inertia, coming at a time when I knew Jamal would be relying on me one hundred per cent, seemed particularly unforgivable.

Was this going to continue to be the pattern of my life? The blissful peaks, the devastating troughs! It was almost as if each moment of bliss had to be paid for, as if someone somewhere was marking up the pluses and minuses and as soon as the balance began to get tipped by the pluses, another set of minuses had to be created to achieve a new equilibrium. This time, it was really serious. I was frantic with worry about what could be happening to Jamal, where he was and whether he would ever be freed again. I also feared that he might become one of the many Moroccans to 'disappear'.

I renewed my efforts to get in touch with Morocco, but the lines were always down. How depressed and frustrated I felt. One day, I went into a shop to buy a birthday present for my father, and caught sight of a dressing-gown, identical to one I had bought Jamal at Christmas. I started to cry in the middle of the shop. A friendly assistant helped me to a seat and brought me a cup of tea. It was actually my birthday, and I compared this dismal birthday with the one I had spent so happily with Jamal, a year before.

Then one afternoon, I managed to get a telephone line through to Morocco. I had rung the Moroccan lawyer I knew. I asked him what was happening and he told me there had been a large wave of arrests and that all the detainees were going to be brought before the King's Counsel in a couple of weeks. I tried to press him for details, but he sounded frightened and unwilling to expand. I heard later that he had subsequently been arrested.

The British press kept up its dubious practice of maintaining almost total silence about the violations in Morocco. My only way of getting information was to go to a library stocking foreign newspapers and read *Le Monde* and the Spanish press. Bit by bit, I managed to piece together what had happened. Around Christmas-time, King Hassan had delivered a speech to the nation announcing his intention to withdraw subsidies for basic foodstuffs. People had taken to the streets to demonstrate against this decision - in a country where 40% of the population is living below poverty level, they no doubt felt they hadn't much to lose. There were also demonstrations by schoolchildren against rumours of a decision to levy a charge on all those wishing to take their 'A' level exams.

These peaceful demonstrations were met with astonishingly violent repression, not only by the police on the ground, but also by the army, who went up in helicopters and *machine-gunned down at the crowd*. The worst incidents had taken place in the North of Morocco, although there had been sporadic protests in other parts of the country, as well. Everyone with a political past had been arrested, as well as many people, including religious figures, whom the police had long been waiting for an excuse to detain. The King said it was a conspiracy from abroad which had instigated the riots, and most especially a collusion between the Zionists, the Iranians and - horror of horrors - *Ilal Amam*, the organisation which Jamal had belonged to.

I read the articles with growing concern and dismay. *Le Monde* reported the following on 24 January 1984: (my translation)

"... The King put the blame for the disorder on to the followers of Imam Khomeini, the Marxist-Leninist Communists and the 'Zionist Secret Services', to whom he sent a solemn warning. He forcefully confirmed: 'the last word will go to the authority and the law'.

"The riots broke out last Thursday in three Mediterranean villages in Morocco. After Nador, 14 kilometres away from the enclave of Melilla, and Al-Hoceima, it was the turn of Tetuan, about 40 kilometres from Ceuta, the second Spanish enclave.

"According to the Moroccan opposition, there were about 20 deaths, but the Spanish press estimated that there were between 150 and 200 of which, according to El Pais, *about 40 were in Nador and about 100 in Al-Hoceima. The underground opposition movement Ilal Amam estimated the number of deaths in Tetuan to be around 60. But it is obviously very difficult to verify the exactitude of these figures.*

"It is certain, however, that the confrontations were very serious, and according to the witnesses whom we have managed to contact by telephone, helicopters fired machineguns at the demonstrators in Nador - about ten thousand of them - and in Tetuan, while the army on the ground also opened fire.

In the beginning, the authorities tried to minimise the facts ..."

As I read the different articles, I noted the dates of the uprisings - they had taken place when Jamal and I had been on holiday together. This must surely show that he had had nothing to do with the demonstrations; moreover, I had the photos to prove it! Snapshots of Jamal and myself in the sea in winter would surely prove that we were in the South of the country, far away from any demonstrations. No-one could say that they were old photos, either, as Jamal had only been out of prison for two months, while he had had the perfect alibi for the past eight years!

I decided to return to Morocco armed with the photos, pick up a member or members of Jamal's family, and confront the authorities with our story and the pictures. I wasn't too hopeful; I realised I could be laughed at, disbelieved. Oh why hadn't we got married last month! Even if I was believed, I would have no hope of achieving anything in a country with a legal system as unjust as the one in Morocco and with a ruler as corrupt as Hassan 11. I wasn't sure of the reception I was going to get from Jamal's mother, either. Still, any action was better than no action, and I just couldn't sit there with my arms folded any longer.

I started to make plans for my trip. I had no means of letting Jamal's family know of my impending arrival, but that was probably just as well - in the obvious atmosphere of fear which pervaded the country, I wouldn't want it to look as if the family were in conspiracy with someone from abroad. Much better just to turn up.

With a heavy heart, I started packing my things. I had no idea where Jamal was, how he was, nor indeed if he still was. I compared my feelings with those of the previous times when I had been packing to go to Morocco. Once again, I reflected on the enormous differences in our lives. What had happened to Jamal was so far removed from anything in my experience, that it seemed as if we were living on different planets and 500 years apart. Where was he, what had happened since we kissed each other goodbye such a short time ago?

at.le 12. 1. 84

Très cher ami

je vous envoye ...
de mes meilleur
ami et je vous
prie de bien ... ...
une chambre, car
j'... trop ... ...
à la ... de
Tamanga et je ne
pourrai pas le
... logé. Merci

... ...
... Hadj ... P. R de
...

Chapter 34

I would find out afterwards. When Jamal had finished waving away the departing plane at Casablanca Airport, he went to see a friend, a European priest, who had introduced him to people who could perhaps be of help in the future if he had trouble with the police, or in getting a passport.

After a few days, Jamal took the bus back to his home in Tetuan. He slept on the bus and when he woke up in Tetuan, he was quite sure he was still asleep and dreaming. The place was under siege. The streets were empty of people, full of soldiers. Military vehicles and tanks lined the highway, with helicopters whirring overhead. All around were machine-guns carried by army officers looking as if they would unhesitatingly empty their contents into the guts of anyone whose face didn't fit.

The bus-station, usually crowded with vast numbers of homeless and beggars and thick with taxis vying for fares among descending passengers, was now completely deserted except for the heavy presence of the army. The bus stopped, and was immediately surrounded by the military, who yanked the astonished passengers off one by one and questioned them at gunpoint about their exact reasons for coming to Tetuan.

Jamal, totally unprepared for this sudden transformation of his home town, started to wonder if there had been a coup and if so, whether he should be feeling elated or depressed. To the accompaniment of machine-gun noise, he started walking down the street towards the new flat his family had just moved into, a distance of about half a mile. After about a hundred yards, he was required to stop by the point of a machine-gun, not the sort of request to be turned down. He was questioned and he pointed to his large suitcase as proof of his returning after an absence. He was then allowed to continue for about another 100 yards, when he was stopped by another patrol, and so on until he reached his

293

family home, where yet another reception committee was waiting for him. There was an anxious moment when he couldn't produce the key to the entrance, but in the end he found it and was allowed to enter. Once safely inside, his family related the events of the past few days.

It had started peacefully enough, with some high-school children marching through the streets to protest at the exorbitant charge which the authorities were going to levy on their 'A' level exams, which would have virtually excluded many of them from participation. All of a sudden, convoys of army and police had appeared and started beating the children up and then shooting.

In the surrounding cafés, which were filled as usual with large numbers of the unemployed and others, people stared in disbelief as school-children were mowed down by bullets in front of their very eyes. When they couldn't stand the sight any longer, they rushed out into the streets, taking half the contents of the cafés with them. Cups and saucers, pots and pans, chairs and tables were hurled at the antagonists with all the force of enraged indignation. Two men staggered out with a heavy iron railing and lobbed it over into the middle of a particularly aggressive army unit, while two other men in an adjoining café managed to dislodge the door, which was sent on a similar journey. Everything in sight became a weapon, and was put to immediate use. As more and more cafés emptied of people and contents, army reinforcements arrived from Meknes and war was now a harsh reality.

From this description of what had happened and from the tense fear which gripped the town, it soon became obvious to Jamal that it was only a matter of time before the police came for him. No-one dared venture out, homes were like prisons under siege. At one time Jamal's sister, overcome with curiosity, opened her window cautiously to peep out at what was happening in the street. Before she even got as far as looking in the direction of the town, however, two bullets whizzed past her nose. People tried to carry on with life as usual in their garrisoned homes, but the fear, the uncertainty, gripped them by the throat and paralysed them.

A few hours after Jamal's arrival at the bus-station in Tetuan, he was startled by a heavy banging on the door. The force and insistence behind the banging, left the family in no doubt who the visitors were and who they had come for. Indeed, four armed officers stood outside. They said to Jamal: "You will come with us."

"For what reason?"

"It's only for questioning."

For six hours, Jamal was made to sit in an office at the police-station watched by a solitary armed guard in a deathly silence broken every few minutes by the screams of someone being tortured. At around midnight, he was taken to another room full of people, some of whom he knew: teachers, students, engineers, each of them - like Jamal - marked in one way or another, which explained their presence. Some had taken part in a strike ten years earlier; others had been caught in the past handing out leaflets urging employees to demand better pay or conditions; still others had once said the wrong thing at the wrong moment to the wrong person etc.

One by one, these partners in crime were taken away for interrogation, and the room was soon infused with the grisly atmosphere of a dentist's waiting-room, all of the patients longing for and yet dreading their name being called next, and all of them envisaging the torture awaiting them in the adjoining room, their imaginations already fed by the screams of agony from other victims. The suspense was increased when faint sounds of the Moroccan national anthem on the radio floated into the room, heralding the start of an address to the nation by King Hassan. The King's voice could be heard, but tantalisingly, the sound was not sufficiently loud to enable the strained ears in the waiting-room to hear what was being said. This was almost the worst agony: to know that what was being said could determine your future, yet not quite to be able to hear it.

Soon, it was Jamal's turn for interrogation. He was led into a room where four policemen were sitting around a table. At a smaller table, sat a clerk, making out a *procès-verbal* on his typewriter. The line of questioning centred on *Ilal Amam*. Jamal was told of the King's contention that this organisation, along with the Zionists and Khomeinists, was the one responsible for the rioting. As it was well-known that Jamal, before his arrest, had been the *Ilal Amam* representative in Tetuan, would he be kind enough to give the police the exact details of how these present riots had been planned, where the meetings took place, what was discussed there, who took part etc.

Jamal replied: "I am not in any way responsible for these uprisings, but I do happen to know the instigators and, if you like, I'll give you the details."

Four mouths dropped open and four necks craned forward at this unexpected statement. The typist stopped typing and turned around in his chair to stare at the person who was about to divulge everything the nation was longing to know.

In the dead silence that followed, Jamal looked at each one of his interrogators long and hard before saying:

"Behind what has happened are the following: extreme poverty, abject misery, total corruption and massive abuse of power."

He was immediately taken outside by two of his captors and down a long flight of stone stairs, leading to a damp and smelly dungeon. He was then pushed into a cell the size of an average living-room, which was filled to bursting point with about 45 other people. It was so packed that there didn't appear to be any floor space left for anyone else. This situation was remedied by the police giving one enormous shove to those people unfortunate enough to be right by the door, cramming Jamal in and then banging the door behind him.

Those in the immediate vicinity of the door glared at this latest arrival with ill-concealed resentment at what was obviously yet one more of the many assaults on their tiny piece of space.

There was no room for anyone to sit down, they were all packed together in this tiny cage like matchsticks in an overfilled matchbox. Some of them were in a lamentable state. Deep wounds were patently visible on arms and legs, faces were disfigured and there was blood everywhere. People who were dying were completely ignored and left to die without even being taken away. It was in the face of this carnage that Jamal took a decision: if ever he managed to get out of here alive, he would leave Morocco for good. He just didn't want to go on living in a country where innocent people were being slaughtered for trying to register peaceful protests. He also saw that in the event of any future uprising, he would be among the first to be arrested even if, as this time, he was hundreds of miles away from the scene. The police must have their scapegoats and what they don't find, they invent.

Jamal had to face up to the sobering reality: *he didn't want to be part of his own country any more*. This was where he had his roots, this was the country of all his memories, his joys, his sorrows, his childhood, his first love, his adolescence, the beginnings of his political awareness, his struggles for justice, equality and independence. Yet what hope was there for any worthwhile future with this corrupt regime? How could he ever wish to play any part in it when any concrete input would only serve to strengthen it?

He began to talk with the others in the cell. A clear picture of the objectives of the authorities began to emerge. He could identify three different types of prisoners. First of all, the police had rounded up all the people in the town with a criminal record, even those whose criminal activities were long since past and who had been miles away from the rioting. *Objective*: to show that the demonstrations were criminal in nature.

Secondly, there had been wide-sweeping arrests of young intellectuals, often those with radical views whom the police had been longing to arrest for a considerable time. *Objective*: to lump the intellectuals along with the criminals. The intellectuals had plotted and planned the demonstrations and the criminals had then put the plans into action.

Thirdly, there were the passers-by, people whose sole crime had been to witness the abominations taking place. *Objective*: to inspire fear among ordinary people. Basically, the police wanted to terrorise the whole town, to get their revenge and also to prevent anything like that from happening again.

Some of the detainees, many of whom had nothing to do with the demonstrations and had even been out of town at the time, were subsequently given extraordinarily heavy jail sentences. One such was a trainee teacher whom Jamal knew, named Bakhali, who was taken from his classroom during the riots while he was teaching, and suddenly found himself being tortured at the police station for information he didn't possess. He was in no way involved in the rioting but he had been a bit of an activist when he was a student. He was later given a 20-year jail sentence.

Jamal spent two weeks in this crowded cell, just existing, listening to the misery of his cell-mates. Now and then one or the other of them was taken away for questioning, usually to reappear hours later shocked, bruised and swollen. For some reason, Jamal was not questioned again, he was left alone by the authorities. Then one day, a policeman came along, opened the cell door and told him he was free to go. He felt pangs at leaving the others behind in a place where sleeping was out of the question, where the diet was a crust of bread and some water each day, and where people were herded together, sick and dying. However, it was not the sort of order to turn down and what possible use could he serve being buried in this living grave? We will never know why Jamal was freed this time - perhaps it was a call from André Adam which did the trick. Next time, he might not be so lucky.

He spent the next few weeks organising medical help for the wounded in town. Many people, a fair proportion of whom were innocent bystanders, had suffered severe injuries from the indiscriminate brutality of the army, but were too terrified to seek medical attention in case their injuries would be taken as proof

298

they had been actively involved in the demonstration. So Jamal organised a team of sympathetic doctors and nurses who were willing - often at great risk to themselves - to tend the sick in secret.

He had, of course, rung me the moment he had been released, just as I was in the middle of packing to leave. My relief was indescribable. My only thought was to get to him, to be with him. I rang my prospective boss to see if I could start my new work later than we had arranged, which would give me several weeks to spend with Jamal in Morocco. There was no problem. Soon I found myself once again on the plane to Tangiers, where I arrived late one Saturday afternoon.

Chapter 35

I went through immigration with my hand-luggage, straight into Jamal's welcoming arms. We hugged and kissed and started chatting while I waited for my other luggage to come off the plane. It was an unbelievable luxury to snuggle up to Jamal even in the middle of the crowded airport and feel his calm reassuring presence, especially after the anguish of the past weeks.

Tangiers Airport had the familiar smell of stale cigarette smoke mixed with sweaty bodies and dust. It was a tiny old-fashioned airport, a bit dark and depressing. In fact, it didn't seem like an airport at all but more like a provincial bus-station. Jamal's presence transformed it into a palace and I sighed with joy and relief as I hugged and hugged him, inhaling strength from his warm body.

My joy, however, was short-lived. Two men suddenly approached me and asked to look at my passport. I showed it to them, somewhat surprised, as I had already been through passport control. They scratched their heads.

"There is an irregularity. Please will you follow us." There was nothing to do but obey.

It was with a sinking feeling that I followed the men into the interior of the airport. I didn't dare look back at Jamal, mirroring my feelings, hoping for the best but anticipating the worst. I wondered miserably if my Amnesty record had at last caught up with me.

Once behind the immigration desk, one of the men said: "Your passport shows that you came to Morocco on December 25th last year. But there was no plane from London which arrived in Tangiers on Christmas Day."

"Oh, is that all!" I nearly hugged him with relief. "Well, there's a simple explanation. You see, the plane was 6 hours late, so instead of arriving at 7p.m. on December 24 as scheduled, it arrived at

1 a.m. on the 25th."

I stretched out my hand for my passport, but the men shook their heads. "No, there is something we will have to check." They disappeared out of sight with the passport.

I stared after them in disappointment and dismay. Time passed. Minutes turned into hours and still no sign of my passport. I demanded several times to know what was going on, but all I was told was that they were awaiting orders from higher up. It was an argument I had become familiar with.

I spent the night sitting on the floor of the immigration area - sleep was out of the question. The higher-up orders did not appear to be materialising.

Saturday night turned into Sunday morning and still no action. My heart ached for Jamal and I wondered miserably what he was doing, how he was feeling and what action was open to him in the face of this unexpected curtailment of our longed-for reunion. I knew that he would do everything in his power to get me out. It struck me that our situations had been reversed: I was now imprisoned by the Moroccan authorities and the need for action lay with Jamal. Like him in the past, all I could do was wait.

I learned later that Jamal had waited a long time on the other side of the immigration desk when he suddenly caught sight of 2 policemen from Tangiers who had interrogated him when he was arrested for the first time. The idea he had toyed with of creating a fuss at the airport vanished. He had no wish to attract attention, especially now when he was going to try and set the wheels in motion to get his passport to leave Morocco for good. So he went to a hotel and, like me, spent a sleepless night.

Early the next morning - Sunday - he rang the British Embassy in Rabat and spoke to the woman who had helped me so much in the past. She advised him to contact the British Consulate in Tangiers, so he went there and was told that the Consul was probably at the Catholic Church. He wasn't, but instead Jamal found the British Ambassador to Spain, who was friendly and helpful. He suggested that they go to the Anglican Church, as the British Ambassador to Morocco was in Tangiers for the weekend and was most likely to be found there. Apparently, I had picked a good weekend to get into trouble, as there was a British Embassy conference here, and British Ambassadors were flooding into the town thick and fast.

Jamal arrived at his destination with his unpredicted companion. It was his first appearance at the Christian church. He sat down gingerly on a pew at the back of the church with the Ambassador to Spain, feeling vastly out of place as he surveyed what were probably armies of British Ambassadors all praying in silence. The Ambassador to Spain pointed out the Ambassador to Morocco, and when the praying stopped Jamal began to get up, but was restrained by his companion. With Jamal feeling that every minute was precious, he was then forced to sit through a long sermon delivered in English. As his impatience grew, he found consolation in telling himself that this was perhaps not such a bad moment to ask a Christian soul to save another one in distress.

At last the vicar seemed to have run out of material and Jamal breathed a sigh of relief and jumped up again, only to find that further prayers were being said. When the British Ambassador to Morocco had finally finished purging his soul, Jamal practically leapt on him and told him what had happened. However, he was disappointed. Any orders which *this* official had received from (much) higher up during the past 30 minutes or so, appeared not to be too heavily weighted in my favour as he showed himself to be un-Christianly loathe to take any action.

At this moment, the vicar suddenly appeared, beaming. Addressing Jamal, he said: "How delightful to see a *Moroccan* in my church. Have you come here to pray?"

"Well, not exactly, I ..."

"No, you needn't be modest. We all worship the same God."

"Well, I'm here because ..."

"No, don't tell me. I can guess. You came to listen to my sermon. Well, I do hope you enjoyed it and that it has given you courage to face the future. I also hope that we'll see you again here, often. Do feel free to drop in whenever you like."

The Ambassador to Morocco started shuffling his feet and the vicar went to look for another soul to convert. As soon as he had gone, both Jamal and the Ambassador to Spain started putting pressure on the other Ambassador to do something, and in the end got him to agree to phone the airport and give Jamal a rendezvous to meet him there. However, when Jamal arrived at the appointed time he found no sign of any Ambassador, just a note saying there was nothing he could do.

Jamal then rang our contact at the British Embassy in Rabat. She told him that the Consul had gone to the airport and had insisted on seeing me, but was refused permission to do so. The only information they could glean was that my name was on a black list of people not allowed entry into Morocco.

Back at the airport, nothing happened until about 5 o'clock in the afternoon when things began to liven up a bit. I had my passport returned to me with the original entry stamp cancelled, and I was told there was a plane to Gibraltar leaving in 15 minutes, which I was to board. I was also told that I was *persona non grata* in Morocco, and that if I ever needed to visit the kingdom again, I would need special authorisation - it was amazing how they all used the same language.

I boarded the plane feeling devastated. Of all my past experiences with the Moroccan authorities, this one definitely felt the worst. The knowledge that I would probably never be allowed back into Morocco again, and that there was no guarantee that Jamal would ever be able to leave, left me feeling crushed. Once again, it was the violent contrasts in the situation which affected me strongly: the bliss of seeing Jamal again followed by the misery of being torn apart and the harrowing uncertainty of the future.

Gibraltar seemed an attractive place but I was in no mood to appreciate the scenery. I spent a miserable night in a hotel, and next morning, took the first available flight to London.

304

What a depressing experience it was, to arrive back in London, my mission so totally unachieved. I had only been indoors for about half-an-hour when the phone rang. It was Jamal. He didn't know whether it was good news or bad to hear my voice on the phone: good news because it meant I was safe, bad news because it underlined the vast distance between us, with not much hope now of lessening it.

About one week after my abortive attempt to enter Morocco, Jamal had a visit from the secret police. They asked him lots of questions about me: who I was, what I did, how Jamal had got to know me, what our relationship was etc. Jamal gave as few details as possible. His sole object was now to concentrate on attracting the minimum amount of attention, in order to facilitate his getting a passport.

Getting a passport in Morocco is a daunting experience and an ordeal survived by only the strongest.

First, you have to get three copies of your birth-certificate. In order to get these, you have to go in person to the town where you were born. This part of the process can take a long time, as you have to appear daily at the appropriate office and keep badgering the staff there and battling through their excuses that they have never received your application, they've never heard of you, this is the wrong town, they gave it to you yesterday etc. Sooner or later, it dawns on you what the missing part of your application is, and you hand the official that extra little 'stamp duty' required to save your birth-certificate from extinction. The speed with which s/he then manages to locate it is usually dependent on the size of the stamp duty you can produce.

Secondly, you must collect two certificates of residence, i.e. proof that you live at the address where you say you live. One of the certificates is to be obtained from the police, the other from the Ministry of the Interior. This done, you must next get a work-certificate specifying your income or - for a student - proof of grant. Then you must get a police record certificate and six photos.

If you are a woman, you can forget the whole idea unless you are the King's wife or blessed with a liberal husband or broad-minded father, as women also have to get a certificate of approval from their menfolk.

If you have managed to survive this amassing of documents with your job, finances and sanity relatively intact, you are then faced with the process of shipping them around the various offices. Your application makes the following journey:

1. To the Ministry of the Interior.
2. To the police.
3. Back to the Ministry of the Interior.
4. Forward to the local Council.
5. Sideways to the office of the Governor of the town.
6. Onwards to a sort of Intelligence Service.
7. To the passport office for a recommendation.
8. Back to the Governor for a final decision.
9. Finally back to the passport office.

Your application can wait for periods of a month or more at each and every one of the above offices.

The unwritten rule for exclusion from getting a passport altogether is valid for the following groups:

- the working class and all others with insufficiently high income;
- the unemployed;
- all those with any sort of criminal or political record;
- women failing to get authorisation from their menfolk;
- divorced women;
- students with little or no grant.

It was thought to be only in the Soviet Union or in the Eastern block where people were in the past refused passports. However, as can be seen from the above exclusion groups, the majority of the Moroccan people are denied passports, and this in a country where the Constitution declares that all nationals shall have freedom of movement!

Furthermore, according to Moroccan civil aviation law,

306

Moroccan citizens are not allowed to avail themselves of charter flights, either into or out of the country. This discriminatory law, especially as it is the Moroccan authorities discriminating against their own people, makes it all the more difficult for a Moroccan to leave the country.

(A Moroccan friend living in London, finding that he was unable to take a cheap flight to visit Morocco, appealed to The Commission for Racial Equality in London, on the grounds that it was racial discrimination to refuse to sell him a cheap ticket available to everyone else, solely on account of his Moroccan nationality. The CRE looked into the case and, finding that it was indeed discriminatory to do this, approached the Royal Moroccan Airlines about it. The RAM replied that, OK, they would comply with English law by selling the APEX ticket to anyone, regardless of race or nationality, but the minute any Moroccan carrying such a ticket set foot in Morocco, they would levy a surcharge on him or her for the difference.)

The Moroccan authorities thus wished to exercise enormous control over their citizens, particularly those engaged in any political activity. There are two main trains of thought concerning activists living under repressive regimes: some countries are pleased to get rid of them on the grounds that the troublesome element is removed and there is less danger of them inciting others; other countries keep a tight hold on their activists, on the grounds that they can be controlled by force as long as they remain within jurisdiction. Morocco belonged very firmly to the latter category.

If it is as difficult as this even for the ordinary citizen to get a passport, however did Jamal - with his prison record - imagine that he would ever get one?

Jamal kept me advised of the situation by letter and phone.

His main strength was that he had a good and acceptable reason for wishing to leave. He was studying for a doctorate at the Sorbonne in Paris and under a professor of such high standing with the King as be to instrumental in securing Jamal's release. Moreover,

307

Jamal had been elected member of the Third World Institute attached to the University of Paris, and had also, along with all the necessary documents, a letter from the University, requiring him to be in Paris on a certain date to undertake some paid research work at the Institute.

A good omen was when Jamal got his police record certificate and it showed a clean slate! No-one will know how this mistake was made but he was not going to complain about it.

His tactics were then to try and bypass all the first seven stages of the passport procedure by playing on the time factor. He accordingly got an interview with the Governor of the town on the pretence that he was sent by a Minister. He went along armed with letters from the University of Paris which stated that he was urgently required to present himself there by a certain date. Jamal explained that he had to go immediately, which was why he was approaching the Governor for a direct decision on his passport.

Unfortunately, it didn't work, and the Governor, smelling a rat, sent Jamal's entire file to the police. They kept it there for 6 weeks, after which he was told that he would, believe it or not, need special authorisation from the Ministry of the Interior in Rabat. Jamal moved - along with his file - to Rabat.

After some time and a lot of patience, he managed to secure an interview with Mr. Ben Hachem, Head of Security Services and Number 2 at the Interior Ministry. Ben Hachem had received a letter from André Adam, but he said that, before making a decision, he would first have to get a report on Jamal from the secret police. Jamal learnt later that three different Secret police units had been put on to his case: the DST (Direction de la Surveillance du Territoire); the RG (Renseignements Généraux) and the DJET, responsible for espionage and counter-espionage.

For two months, Jamal went to the Ministry of the Interior every single day, to try and see Ben Hachem. He was put off every day with a variety of excuses: he was out, he was away, he was at a meeting, he didn't work there, he was sick, busy and so on.

Eventually, he managed to get an appointment only to be told that he hadn't yet received the report of the secret police investigation.

My failed trip to Morocco had been in February. It was now June. For the whole of the summer, Jamal persisted in attempting to obtain this basic civil right: freedom of movement. He had left the relatively small prison of Kenitra to enter the bigger prison of Morocco: his own country.

The authorities employed their usual time-wasting tactics. "There's no problem but just now it's Ramadan, people are not working properly. Come back afterwards." After Ramadan, it was: "Well, it's the holiday season. Come back when people have returned to work." When people were then apparently back at work eager and raring to go and dying to get Jamal his passport, it was then the marriage of the King's daughter which paralysed the working force.

In the meantime, back in London, I had received a curious letter from Ceuta in Spain, purporting to be from a Moroccan called Abselan Hamadi Hamed. In faultless Spanish, the writer of the letter informed me that he had been given my name and address by a North American priest called Marcos. He had apparently heard of my concern about human rights issues, and he was seeking my help in exposing the atrocities committed against the Muslim population in Ceuta, by both the Spanish and the Moroccan authorities. He further wished for some information about the address of Amnesty in London and also the United Nations Human Rights Committee. I understood later that this letter was in fact written by DJET, the secret police, in an attempt to start a dialogue with me about my human rights activities.

In October, judgement was finally declared on Jamal: "passport refused for security reasons."

Chapter 36

Jamal now had one more card to play: to change address. So he went to stay with a friend in Meknes, with the aim of starting the whole process again where he was unknown, and playing on the time factor once more.

He had to apply for a new identity card in his newly-adopted town. Then he had to go through the whole process of collecting all the documents again, as documents for such a purpose were not allowed to be more than 3 months old. He applied for a police-certificate and this finally put an end to all his hopes: the computer had by now realised its previous mistake and, dedicated to the last, wished to put matters straight. The whole of Jamal's past political activity, his arrest, imprisonment, re-arrest, the whole works were there for all and sundry to see. No Governor in his right mind would dare to issue a passport on the spot to such a character.

Having now spent almost a year exhausting all the legal means of getting a passport, Jamal began to spend his time looking at other possibilities. At least he didn't have any acute financial problems as he had saved some money before his arrest when he was working as barman, and also I sent him some whenever I could.

First, he entered into discussions with a European priest. This priest had contacts with many Embassies and he promised to find someone who would give Jamal a foreign passport. However, this did not lead to anything.

Then an acquaintance introduced him to a European Ambassador with whom he became friendly. The Ambassador was very sympathetic and did for a while actually consider issuing Jamal with a passport. In the end, however, he backed down.

Jamal was then brought into contact with a very shady character called Georges - a wealthy retired Mafia boss. His latest talents were directed towards currency smuggling, and he

311

specialised in smuggling out large sums of money for Ministers and other high-ranking officials. He promised to use his money and dubious contacts to get Jamal a forged passport, but he too failed to deliver the goods.

There now remained only one possibility: escape without a passport.

Letters between us were not very frequent now, as I didn't have anywhere to send the letters since Jamal was moving about quite a lot; and Jamal had been putting all his energy into trying to leave the country. This was Jamal's last letter to me:

"Rabat, 24 December 1984

My darling, how I would love to be with you during the Christmas holidays, but alas! this hasn't been possible. You cannot know how much I've suffered and am still suffering through this long separation imposed on us. But deep down inside me, I have a great hope that I will be meeting you VERY SOON. I can tell you it certainly will be soon.

My life here has no sense. I feel deep down an emptiness, a great emptiness which obsesses me, torments me and harasses me wherever I am and whatever I do. I can't escape from this terrible feeling of being a bird without wings. But the day will come when this miserable bird, through its irrepressible will and profound yearning for happiness and liberty, will see its wings grow, fly and cross the sea and oceans.

I am this bird, battered with humiliation, wounded with sufferings, this bird strong in its soul, fierce with hope, which is asking for shelter in the warmth and tenderness of your great love, this bird who, with this raison d'etre, *doesn't accept living tamely in a cage, even a very large golden cage.*

I must tell you that I've tried to look for all sorts of compensation to deaden the horror of the life I am leading. But I've always remained the man alone and who, without you, can only survive on the periphery.

Oh, my darling, you can never know how much I feel a great great need for you.

I love you.

Jamal, your great love for ever. Happy New Year 1985, the year of our UNION."

Jamal, thinking of escape, spent several sleepless nights eliminating the possibilities one by one. Morocco's Eastern border was with Algeria, but the deep conflicts between these two countries meant that the borders were heavily guarded by the Army. In the South of Morocco, there was the war with the Sahara. The West and North were both coastlines. In the North mainland there were also two Spanish enclaves: Ceuta in the West and Melilla in the East. However, a mountain range separated each of these enclaves from Moroccan territory and again, the borders were heavily guarded, army patrols having been given orders to shoot anything that moved. It was far too risky. That left the sea. But where was the boat?

The next few days Jamal spent looking into the boat option. The Mediterranean coast was out of the question as he was too well-known in that part of Morocco, so he was down to the last possibility: the Atlantic coast. He began his search. It was a mammoth task. One day, Jamal got his lucky break. He had been looking around in a small port on the Atlantic coast and had made friends with some of the fishermen there when he discovered that one of them - we'll call him Majid - managed a small fleet of fishing vessels. More importantly, he was a member of the same tribe as Jamal's late father. Tribal solidarity is still strong in Morocco, and can supersede all other concerns. Jamal asked Majid if he could give him a job, and as the two men got friendly, he mentioned casually that he would like to go to Spain to try his luck there, but didn't have a passport. It so happened that Majid had some relatives in Southern Spain whom he wanted to see, so it was agreed that they should go to Spain together.

313

The man who operated the engine of the boat, Ali, would also have to be included. Ali was a small wiry man in his 30s with prematurely thinning hair and an expression of permanent discontent on his face. Life hadn't been very favourable to Ali and so he was wont to treat others with a mixture of suspicion, resentment and ill-grace. Jamal and Majid did not know if they could trust Ali, so for safety reasons it was decided not to tell him that the object of the trip was to go to Spain. He was therefore told that the boat was to go to Tangiers to pick up some fishing equipment needed for some other boats. With hindsight, this was a fatal mistake.

Jamal spent some time mingling with the fishermen so that people would become accustomed to his presence and would accept him as one of them. He did some research on fish, hung around with the fishermen in cafés, took great interest in their hauls, and tried to chat with them in a knowledgeable way about different varieties of fish and fishing equipment. At last, it was time to leave. Jamal got on Majid's boat as usual and busied himself with a few routine tasks, all to preserve a state of normality and to disguise the turbulence in his mind. He wondered whether there could be police checks, wondered if he could have been recognised by anyone, wondered if, indeed, he would manage to pull it off or if there were yet another nasty shock just around the corner.

Just as the boat was about to leave, the men suddenly became aware of a stir of excitement and lots of people gathering in the port. Jamal's heart sank, as any deviation from normality posed a threat. Soon, however, it became apparent that they were in luck. A wreck had been discovered just by the port and was being lifted up that very day. Everyone - citizens, coastguard officials, fishermen, police - had all eyes riveted on the spectacle of the raising of the wreck, while Jamal and company managed to slip away on the boat completely unnoticed. What a good start to the escape!

The sun was shining and the sea was calm. Jamal's feelings, however, were anything but calm. His mind was in turmoil. He felt a panicky need to get further and further away from Morocco so that chances of discovery would diminish. There was also a great sense of relief that this moment, so anxiously and nervously anticipated, had at last arrived, mixed with a strong feeling of bitterness at being forced out of his own country in this way - it felt like betrayal. Then Jamal dwelt on what he would miss in Morocco - the simplicity of the ordinary people, the mint tea in cafés, the beaches he had frequented as a boy, all the memories. It was an irrevocable step he was taking - this was no charter trip to the Costa del Sol. At the same time, there was a sense of excitement at the thought of venturing into the unknown, starting a completely new chapter in his life.

The boat started to approach the Bay of Tangiers. Then as had been arranged with Majid the boat started to steer away from Morocco and towards Spain. Ali, down in the engine room, began to protest vociferously and Majid told him:

"I am the Captain of this boat - you do as I say."

They had got about half-way between Tangiers and Algeciras in Spain when disaster struck. The boat hit a rock and became grounded. They managed to pull it off the rock but it had become damaged and was certainly in no fit state to continue the journey to Spain. As Majid and Jamal, worried and distressed, tried to think of a solution, Ali took a spiteful pleasure in reminding them that this would never have happened if they had gone to Tangiers as previously arranged. This was God's way of punishing them.

At that moment, a large Spanish fishing vessel pulled up beside them and asked if they could be of any help. They informed the luckless Moroccans that they were on their way to Ceuta, the Spanish enclave on the Mediterranean coast, and that they could tow the boat there for them if they wished. Ceuta was in the wrong direction, but it was better than being marooned in the ocean, and at least it was Spanish territory, so it wasn't quite so humiliating or dangerous as to have to return to Morocco.

Majid, accepting their offer, said to the others: "We will get the boat mended in Ceuta and from there, go to the Spanish mainland." Jamal looked relieved; Ali glowered but said nothing. He was saving up his revenge for later.

They arrived in Ceuta with no further mishaps, and Jamal telephoned me to tell me the wonderful news. He said: "I hope to be in Madrid tomorrow. I'll ring you from there."

I began to prepare for Jamal's coming, with a song in my heart mixed with a slight premonition of doom in view of all our previous experiences. I had got to the stage where I could never properly enjoy a potentially favourable situation any more because of the lurking fear of the devil in the background, waiting to pounce the moment things looked too good. This apprehension clouded my joy. There could still be many dangers ahead. Jamal was out of Morocco, but only just. I didn't dare tell anyone, even though I was bursting to shout it from the roof-tops. So I cleaned the house, paid off a few outstanding bills and washed and ironed all my clothes in case I might have to leave at a moment's notice. I wasn't sure whether I would be going to Madrid to meet him or not. It would probably be the sensible thing to do in view of his lack of papers and I would also want to make quite sure that nothing went wrong - I'd feel more in control of the situation if I were there with him. Thus I waited in joyful and yet unbelieving anticipation for Jamal to ring me from Madrid the next day.

The boat, however, took longer to be repaired than Jamal had imagined, and on each of the next two days when he rang me, he was still in Ceuta.

At last it was ready. As they prepared to leave, the problems started with Ali. He raged and stormed at the other two and said he refused to move unless his share of the cake was specified in advance. In vain, Jamal and Majid tried to convince him that the only object of the trip was to have a bit of fun in Spain. Ali repeated his belief that they were up to something shady and if he were to be included, he should at least share in some of the profits. In the end, Majid had to use his authority as Captain once more and order Ali to accompany them.

316

Majid then went off to buy some food for the journey, Ali went off in a sulk, and Jamal was left alone in the boat, bobbing up and down on the water. He stretched out on the deck in the strong sunlight, feeling warm, happy and free, and drifted into sleep.

He came to, aware of a voice shouting at him from the beach. The voice seemed to belong to an enormous stomach in silhouette against the sun. The voice was shouting: "Get off my boat! Out! Out!"

There was nothing to do but obey before the entire population of Ceuta had its attention attracted to the situation. As Jamal, humiliated, depressed, rowed to the beach, he could see Majid arriving on the scene. They soon discovered exactly what had transpired. Ali had telephoned the owner of the boat who had rushed to Ceuta to prevent it from leaving. Jamal was now well and truly stuck in Ceuta.

When this realisation dawned on me, I saw that I would have to stage some sort of rescue operation in Ceuta. My knowledge of this Spanish enclave was not so great. I imagined it to be some sort of rock, wedged in as it was between Morocco and the sea, with a handful of fisherman's cottages and a few bars.

I rang Lennart in Sweden to tell him what was going on. He was calm but concerned and interested and promised he would get back to me with some information.

I spent the next few days collecting documents and promises. Fortunately, the British authorities were already aware of the situation, since when it had become apparent that I was prevented from entering Morocco and Jamal prevented from leaving it, I had written to my Labour Member of Parliament, Norman Atkinson, to see if there were any pressures which Britain could apply. He had contacted the Foreign Office and sent me a copy of their reply, stating that there was nothing they could do, as they had no jurisdiction over a Moroccan national, and they had no power to force another country to open its doors to a foreign citizen.

It was, of course, what I had expected, so I had no reason to feel let down, especially as the tone of the letter was friendly and even spoke sympathetically of my plight. The most encouraging part, however, was an accompanying letter from Norman Atkinson. A typewritten couple of sentences expressed his regret at not being able to help, while underneath, he had written in his own handwriting: "Let's hope that Jamal will 'turn up' somewhere outside Morocco". I had understood this to mean that if Jamal did 'turn up' he could expect the British authorities to give him full support.

I went to the House of Commons to see Norman Atkinson. I brought him up to date with developments and he was most friendly and eager to help. I wrote down all the details for him.

I then paid a visit to the Foreign Office, with whom I had been in close contact on the phone the previous day. They were supportive and promised to do all they could to assist. They said they were sending a "coded telegram" to the British Embassy in Madrid and they offered to "smooth things over" for me with the Home Office. I was overwhelmed by their concern and compassion.

Lennart rang me. He had found out that Ceuta was a sizeable place in its own right, with many hotels and a flourishing tourist trade. He had even managed to dig up a Swedish Consul there! He offered me assistance in any possible way, including sending me money, he was really thoughtful.

Next, I went to Amnesty's office where I was given a letter in English outlining the background of Jamal's case. Amnesty had played such an important role for Jamal. Although he had been freed on the strength of his professor's letter to the King, without all the previous build-up his case would never have been brought to public attention and he could well have become one of the many forgotten prisoners stowed away somewhere in indefinite secret detention. The knowledge that people on the outside were working on his behalf also gave him - as it had so many others - the morale to fight the injustice, continue his studies and not to despair. It broke the sense of isolation and abandonment generally felt by prisoners.

My final port of call was the United Nations High Commission for Refugees (UNHCR). I gave them the details and told them I was going to Spain, so they gave me the name and number of a lawyer operating from their Spanish offices.

Everything was ready now and I rang Heathrow Airport to enquire about the first plane leaving for Madrid in the morning. Fortunately, it was January, so there was no difficulty booking on a plane leaving at 9.30.a.m. My plan was to go to the UNHCR in Madrid to put my story to them and see if they could help in any way.

Sitting on the plane, I felt elated. After months and months of passivity, here I was at last in action. Whatever happened, at least I would be involved.

The plane arrived at Barajas, Madrid's International Airport. It was nearer to Morocco than London was but it felt so safe to be in Spain! I took a taxi to the UNHCR office.

There they gave me some information about Ceuta and told me to look up the Red Cross there. It did not seem very useful, but at least I had made the contact. I took the night train to Málaga and the day-boat to Ceuta.

It was a short trip. As the boat approached the harbour, I thought I could just make out the wonderfully familiar figure of Jamal. He was indeed there, waiting for me with Majid.

It was a rapturous reunion. We got into a taxi smothering each other with kisses. I asked Jamal about his lodgings as I had wondered wherever he could be staying when he had no identification papers. He told me that, upon arrival in Ceuta, they had had to sleep on the boat. Then, in the course of looking for a boat to take them to Spain, they had come across a wealthy boat-owner who knew Majid. However, he was wary of Jamal, whom he didn't know, and would not therefore help them across the sea. But what he did do was to take them to a small *pensión* run by a Spanish woman, Señora López, who 'never bothered about papers'. It was there that Jamal and Majid were staying, and where

319

I went as well. To get there, we had to climb many stairs until we came to a flat at the top. There was nothing to say that this was a pensión . It was small and fairly primitive, but it was safe and it was with Jamal!

Señora López, a smallish woman with an enormous disfiguring boil on one side of her cheek, greeted me kindly and I was introduced into this strange household with its air of secrets. There were two other inhabitants. One was a man whom Jamal and I never saw, whose door always seemed to close just as ours opened and to open just as ours closed. The other was a Moroccan in his sixties. Jamal told me about this man, who lived in Spain but stayed in Ceuta for two months at a time. Ceuta is a transit place, not somewhere where people come for lengthy holidays. It had transpired that this man came from the same tribe as Jamal's family, which made him receptive to Jamal's friendly approach. He was unable to return to Morocco, as he had been involved in the Rif uprising in 1958 when he had had to leave. He had moved to Spain where he had married a Spanish woman and lived in Sevilla. She had subsequently died so now he was quite on his own, the nearest contact with his roots being to come to Ceuta whenever he could and stare wistfully across the sea to Morocco.

Jamal was depressed by this. It had happened nearly 30 years earlier and there was no change in the regime. He became haunted by the thought that in 30 years time, he would be approaching his sixties and would perhaps become like this figure: lonely, rootless and full of longing, and with the corrupt regime still as strong as ever. King Hassan probably wouldn't still be around, but he had sons who would have sons.

No-one knew Jamal's story and no one asked (although Jamal sensed that the Moroccan understood). He had been passed off as a fisherman and that was how he had to behave.

The elderly Moroccan would spend his evenings playing cards with Señora López, the television on full volume. All around, there were cheap tasteless ornaments and on the mantelpiece, a portrait of Franco in a silver frame, bedecked with flowers. Señora López might be discreet about the state of morals of her guests, but she certainly had something to say about the state of morals of her country and lost no opportunity to do so, competing with the television for volume. Her main themes, with astonishingly little variation, centred around the fall in moral standards, the diminishing influence of the church and all the sin which that brought with it, the lack of respect for authority and the Reds taking over. One day, she was talking to Jamal about the Civil War, when Jamal, who had tried up to then to retain his fisherman's image, without thinking corrected her on a detail, proving his knowledge of history. She looked at him long and hard and then remarked: "You know, you don't have the head of a fisherman." It was the nearest she ever got to expressing open curiosity about her young Moroccan guest.

12 November 1984

Joyce Edling
37 Keston Road
London N 17 6PJ

Dear Joyce Edling

Further to my letter of 8 October
I have now received a reply to the
letter I sent to the Minister of
State at the Foreign Office and I
enclose a copy.   There seems nothing
more that I can do at this stage.

Yours sincerely

Norman Atkinson MP

Perhaps we can hope that Jamal will "turn up" outside Morocco?

Letter from Norman Atkinson, MP 12/11/84

Chapter 37

Once we had overcome the euphoria of being together, we started serious talks about how we were going to get out of Ceuta and across the sea to the Spanish mainland.

There was the boat I had arrived on, going between Algeciras and Ceuta. However, even though both places belonged to Spain, there were still passport and identity checks. We discussed going to the police but Jamal said: "The Spanish police could be in collusion with the Moroccan police. They could hand me straight over." It was too risky to be contemplated.

There were other possibilities: smugglers and drug smugglers. Jamal had spent days getting to know all sorts of people, getting up at 5 o'clock in the morning, hanging around bars, spending a whole day with someone he thought could help only to find it was no good and another precious day was wasted. There was also the fear that the police would appear while he was in the company of some shady characters. Crime was rife in Ceuta and the police were everywhere.

Among the drug smugglers there was a woman courier who actually did business with the police in return for them turning a blind eye on her activities. There were also four Englishmen on a yacht who, when they weren't living it up on board or ashore, were earning the means to do so by lucrative trips between Ceuta and the Spanish mainland. A currency smuggler who had changed money for Jamal understood that Jamal needed some help, and said to him: "I do other jobs, too". Jamal said that he wanted to get to Spain but had no papers, whereupon the other man replied: "The size of the problem will determine the price". He said he knew a policeman he did 'business' with whom he would approach.

Then there was a European diplomat whom Jamal knew in Morocco who had promised to smuggle us out in the boot of his car which, having diplomatic protection, would not be searched.

These were the possibilities. However, the smugglers were too unreliable to be trusted; the drug smugglers wanted us to carry drugs for them which was out of the question; the corrupt policeman pledged his support, but the size of Jamal's problem must have rated pretty high on the dilemma hierarchy as he wanted £300. This was expensive and there was no guarantee of his trustworthiness - he might be upstaged by the Moroccan authorities who could rate the problem even higher and might well offer to rid the Spaniards of it altogether. That left the diplomatic car but, although the diplomat was more than willing to help us, his duties prevented him from getting to Ceuta for another two weeks. We felt we couldn't afford the delay: Morocco was only a couple of miles down the road and there was a sense of panic when Jamal one day saw two Moroccan policemen on the street, one of whom had tortured him in the past. It was an unreal situation - here we were, as guilty as if we were criminals, in hiding from the police who were supposed to be there to protect us. I didn't dare let Jamal out of my sight and the sense of claustrophobia was overwhelming.

One day, when we were out walking in the street, we saw a sign saying 'The Red Cross'. Remembering the advice given by the United Nations High Commission for Refugees, I thought it worth a try.

We entered, to find a young woman sitting at a desk. We gave her brief details of our predicament. She rang up someone who came and translated the Amnesty letter into Spanish, which she then stamped with the Red Cross insignia. She gave us free use of her telephone to ring London or wherever for instructions. She then took us to another building to meet her senior, a kindly compassionate man in his sixties. He said: "You'll have to go to the police," and without even stopping to ask our permission, he rang them and got an appointment for a few hours hence. He noticed our anxiety and said: "Don't worry, you are under our protection now. Go back to the office of my colleague here and when the time comes, we will go with you as a guarantee."

As we went back and waited and made phone-calls, there was suddenly a knock at the door. A waiter from the café downstairs stood there with two enormous fruit sundaes piled high on a dish and covered with fresh strawberries - it was an offering from the senior Red Cross official.

Four o'clock came and we all went to the police station. The policeman who questioned Jamal was a senior official, hostile and suspicious. One of his main concerns was to find out how Jamal had managed to enter Ceuta undetected. It was the only part of his story that Jamal was not willing to be truthful about, for fear of incriminating others, so he made up a story about having been picked up by some people in a speedboat who were out for a lark.

If anyone is used to handling the police it is Jamal and, using his impeccable Spanish, he broke down the barriers bit by bit. He had some impressive documentation to support his story, including not only the Amnesty letter but also the police record certificate to show that he had indeed served time - at last this certificate had come in useful! My presence with my *bona fide* British passport also helped the situation as we explained that we weren't at all interested in staying in Spain - still less did we want to end our days in Ceuta. All we wanted was a *laissez-passer* over the Straits of Gibraltar to enable us to reach Madrid and the British Embassy and then hopefully to leave Spanish soil altogether.

The police, by this time mollified, said they would have to check a few details and we were to return there the next morning. In the meantime, they gave us a paper which we could use if we wanted to go to a hotel. The senior Red Cross official told us that he had been to see the Governor of Ceuta about our case and he had been sympathetic and co-operative.

The next day, we went to the police station. Our police officer, by now friendly and smiling, told us that everything was in order and would we like a passage on the afternoon boat? That was the only time in my life when I have felt like hugging a policeman.

We rushed back to the pensión, packed our things and went straight to the dock. The passport control was an informal check outside, just at the entrance to the boat. Then, after all this fuss, we were neither stopped nor even challenged! We felt almost indignant, we were so proud of the *laissez-passer* so dearly obtained, and no-one even wanted to see it.

We boarded the boat, looked down at the passport control and noted the sort of people being stopped: poor or working-class people, people with large families. Jamal and myself, as a couple in reasonably smart European dress, did not come into question as undesirables on Spanish territory. It was the all too familiar pattern of discrimination. However, we couldn't worry about that now. Our overall feeling was such joy and relief after all the terrible things that had happened which we were thankfully leaving behind.

As the boat pulled out of Ceuta harbour, Jamal and I stood on deck hugging each other. As the continent of Africa grew smaller and smaller, we sang and danced on deck, to the surprise of the other passengers, Jamal singing some Spanish republican songs. We were euphoric.

We took the night train to Madrid, although we were far too excited to sleep, and we arrived there on a Sunday morning. We found a comfortable hotel centrally located and went out to look at the town, the first capital city Jamal had seen apart from Rabat. I wanted to explore the interesting-looking little side-streets while Jamal just wanted to stroll along the main boulevards with the crowds. He won, as he explained how good it felt to mingle with the crowds in welcoming, lighted streets, after being confined to - at best - a prison cell for eight years!

We went to the British Embassy the following morning. They were expecting us. We were told that it would take about a week for them to issue Jamal with a declaration of identity and an entry clearance. We left the Embassy and I rang a delightful Spanish family I knew in Barcelona, Ramón Franquesa and his family. I had put them in the picture before leaving London and they said that we would be welcome to spend that week in Barcelona. So we stayed there, looking around the town, wining and dining with Ramón and his family and generally feeling safe and happy.

We rang the Embassy some days later to find that the papers were ready. The day we left Barcelona, however, we had a minor setback. We stopped in Ramón's car to look at a famous building for about 15 minutes and when we emerged, we found that the car had been broken into and our suitcases stolen. Ramón felt distressed on our account and also a bit responsible, but later said philosophically that if Jamal were to start from scratch, then why not completely from scratch.

We picked up the precious documents in Madrid, secured an exit visa for Jamal to leave Spain, and then took the plane to Gatwick Airport.

So it was that Jamal arrived in his new country one February evening to a temperature of minus 10 degrees, with nothing more than the clothes he stood up in, but with his main capital intact: his indomitable spirit.

Two weeks later, we were married.

*André Adam, Professeur Emérite à l'Univerité **René-Descartes** (Paris V), à La Majesté Hassan II, Roi **du Maroc**.*

Sire,

    Dans ma carrière de professeur, que j'ai commencé au Maroc en 1937, j'ai servi votre noble pays pendant près d'un quart de siècle. Je l'ai achevée comme directeur de l'Ecole Marocaine d'Administration, et c'est votre Auguste Personne qui m'a fait l'immense honneur de me remercier des services que j'avais pu rendre quand j'ai quitté mes fonctions en 1960.

    Depuis que j'ai enseigné dans les Universités francaises, notamment à la Sorbonne, j'ai eu le plaisir de diriger dans leurs travaux de nombreux chercheurs marocains en vue de leur doctorat de 3ème Cycle ou de leur doctorat d'Etat.

    Parmi les candidats au Doctorat de 3ème Cycle que je dirige actuellement, l'un d'entre eux présente la particularité d'être en prison, à Kénitra. Il se nomme Jamal Eddine BENOMAR. Il purge une longue peine puisqu'elle dure depuis près de huit ans et qu'il lui en reste plus de deux à subir.

    C'est un garcon d'un grand mérite. Quand il fut arrêté, il n'avait fait que des études élementaires. Tous les titres universitaires dont il dispose: licence, maîtrise, Diplôme d'Etudes Approfondies (passé en 1:e année de 3:e cycle), il les a conquis et mérités par son travail en prison. Je ne le connaissais pas quand il s'est adressé à moi pour me demander de diriger sa thèse. Et je ne le connais toujours que par ses lettres et ses travaux. Il a fourni un travail intense, au mépris même parfois de sa santé.

    Je ne connais pas exactement les faits qui lui ont valu sa lourde peine. Je sais que la plupart des jeunes qui avaient èté condamnés dans les mêmes circonstances ont bénéficié, depuis plus ou moins longtemps, de la clémence de Votre Majesté. S'il n'a pas merité la même faveur, je crois savoir que c'est en raison de la position qu'il avait prise sur le retour des provinces sahariennes au sein de sa patrie: il aurait dit publiquement que cette question devait être soumise à un référendum. Dans l'atmosphère patriotique qui animait alors, sous l'impulsion de Votre Majesté, la quasi-totalité du peuple marocain et, sur le plan politique, l'opposition tout autant que la majorité, on comprend que son attitude ait indigné et que les juges aient été sévères.

Mais le temps a passé. Les circonstances sont bien différentes, grâce à la ferme et habile politique de Votre Majesté, l'espoir se confirme chaque jour un peu plus que cette rude épreuve touche à sa fin et que la déclaration publique et solennelle, par les populations sahariennes, de leur appartenance à la Patrie Marocaine mette un terme définitif aux manoevres internationales qui avaient embrouillé et aggravé cette question.

C'est pourquoi je me permets de faire appel à la profonde bonté de Votre Majesté pour que ce jeune Marocain retrouve bientôt sa liberté qui lui permettra de mettre au service de sa Patrie ses grandes qualités intellectuelles et son exceptionelle puissance de travail.

Je vous prie, Sire, de daigner agréer l'expression des sentiments de mon profond respect et celle de ma fidelité à votre beau et cher pays.

André Adam.

Author's translation

Your Majesty,

During my teaching career, which I began in Morocco in 1937, I served your noble country for nearly a quarter of a century. At the close, I was Director of the Moroccan School of Administration, and it was your august person who gave me the great honour of thanking me for the services I had been able to contribute by the time I left office in 1960.

Since I have been teaching in French Universities, most notably at the Sorbonne, I have had the pleasure of supervising the work of many Moroccan researchers pursuing their doctorate.

Among the doctorate candidates I am involved with at the moment, there is one who is in the special situation of being in prison, in Kenitra. His name is Jamal Eddine BENOMAR. He is serving a long sentence which has already lasted 8 years and he still has two years left.

He is a youth of great merit. When he was arrested, he had only completed elementary education. All his subsequent University titles - basic degree, master's degree, M.Phil - have been achieved while in prison. I did not know him when he wrote to me and asked me to supervise his doctorate, and I still only know him through his letters and through his work. He has worked long and hard, sometimes even at the cost of his health.

I do not know the exact details which caused him to be given such a heavy sentence. I do know that most of the young people who were sentenced under the same circumstances have been pardoned by Your Majesty. If he himself has not benefited from this, I believe it may be because of the position he took on the return of the Saharan provinces to the nation; it seems that he stated publicly that the question should be put to a referendum. In the patriotic atmosphere of the time, given impetus by Your Majesty and nearly all the Moroccan people including the opposition, it is easy to understand that his attitude met with indignation and that the judges were severe.

But time has passed. The situation is quite different now, and thanks to the firm and skilful hand of Your Majesty, more and more hope is manifest each day that this difficult period of trial is drawing to a close and that the serious public statement by the Saharan populations concerning their belonging to the Moroccan nation will put a definite end to the international manoevres confusing and aggravating this question.

It is for this reason that I am taking the liberty to appeal to the profound benevolence of Your Majesty for this young Moroccan to be set free soon, in order for him to put his great intellectual qualities and his exceptional capacity for work, to the service of the nation.

I ask you, Your Majesty, to deign to receive my feelings of profound respect along with those of my fidelity towards your beautiful and dear country.

André Adam.

Appendix II

Extracts from letters of the 58 officers dumped at Tazmamart Prison in 1973 (see page 177) All letters have been translated from French by the author.

From 1979:

"With total isolation, half rations, the cold, the disease, no control, no contact with anyone in charge, the toll is already heavy; more than 10 of our colleagues are no longer with us, 2 from our building and 8 from the other. All you hear are the agonies of death for 1 or 2 days until gradual extinction. When they come for the dead, they cover them in a blanket with more than seven years accumulated dirt on it. You hear the sound of shovels and pick-axes from outside and the operation is over ...

I often ask myself who is next, for death is watching us at every minute: a bite from a mosquito or a scorpion in the summer (summer 4 months; winter 8) is fatal. The permanent lack of sun, the shadows and darkness, the lack of hygiene ... the noise, all these as well as the other greater problems which are deadly.

Three-quarters of the prisoners walk on all fours along the walls of the cell ... If no-one acts soon, there will only be forgotten tombs at Tazmamart."

Another letter from December 1979 included the following:

"I don't know if you have any idea of the hell here at Tazmamart: the continued isolation, the half-ration of a soldier, the boredom, cold, hunger, darkness and loneliness, various illnesses with no recourse to medical care or medicine. The toll is heavy, already eight colleagues have ceased to exist. My health is precarious. I've lost my teeth, my stomach is weak, I

urinate 12 times a day and eczema is eating away my entire body. Rest assured that I do not fear death at all, the only thing I ask is that it comes softly and in accordance with Islamic norms."

From 12th July 1980:

"Dearest mother, dear father, beloved brothers and sisters, my family, I can find neither the words nor any expression able to describe the situation for a few of us poor suffering human beings here. Because since the arrival of Adam on Earth, you have seldom seen anything like it. A horrible death which we are absorbing drop by drop. Since our arrival at this black hole, we haven't been out of the sun for a single day ... the hunger ... the darkness ... the filth ... the loneliness ... the disease ... The lack of care, the monotony, the lack of ventilation, the despair. Result: nearly a quarter of our colleagues have died in the most awful conditions.

A prisoner moaning in solitude, then faded away bit by bit without finding anyone to bring him a glass of water, in a pile of rubbish. He was wrapped up in a dirty blanket and buried in the prison yard, a few feet away from the cells, in a stealthy manner. This is how the walls of Tazmamart hide the most horrible secret known to humanity. As for those of us who are left, some just lie down the whole time, others get around on all fours ... Disintegrating bones, dried-up skins.

Oh, if only you knew! Come to our aid if the memory of us is still present in your hearts, rescue us before it is too late; speak about us, don't keep silence about this massacre, get together, ask for our freedom. There is a Parliament, a palace, there are lawyers and there is the press. It is unbelievable that no-one has spoken about us for seven years.

I will keep contact with you by different means. Finally, I send you my love and ask you not to forget me."

The trials of the Tazmamart detainees took place in 1972. A large number of the convicted received sentences of five years or less. This was thought at the time to be excessively lenient, for a coup against King Hassan. The revenge came later, as these letters testify. The real sentence was perpetual incarceration in conditions guaranteed to result in a slow and painful death.

It emerged later that there were two blocks in Tazmamart: Building 1 and Building 2. Building 2 had the harsher regime of the two. Prisoners in both buildings were kept locked up twenty four hours out of twenty four and in total isolation. Now and then they would be able to communicate with the other prisoners by shouting to each other through the walls. On rare occasions, the occupants managed to procure writing materials and smuggle out these letters, with the help of a sympathetic guard or two.

The following letter, written in August 1980, gives a heart-rending account of the daily life for the Tazmamart prisoners:

"Tazmamart, 5th August 1980
In this letter, I am trying to go through everything which happened since our transfer from Kenitra Prison to the wretched prison of Tazmamart.
The memorable night of 7 August 1973 changed our lives. We were woken up brutally and without warning, bound securely, blindfolded, and finally thrown like sacks on to a military lorry which drove us to an airbase. Two military planes transported us like canvas bags to Ksar Ksouk where some other military lorries convoyed us in the same way to Tazmamart, the terrible Bastille. We were stripped and led double-quick to our concrete dungeons; we were locked up individually, never to emerge.
The cells are 4 metres square with no light or ventilation; they are nauseating: the badly-made toilets with no flushing are in a corner. There is no window. A pale light appears from

a hole in the ceiling; making a poor reflection, there is a double ceiling in corrugated iron which helps us distinguish night from day in this continual gloom. Veritable furnaces in the Summer, they transform into cold storage in Winter (8 Months). The furnishings are reduced to a pitcher, a plate and a misshapen plastic jar. Two blankets, eaten away by moths, and spread out on an 'interior-sprung' base of stone constitute the bedding of the prisoner, shared with bugs and cockroaches, the uncontested masters of the premises. Scorpions proliferate. Snakes appear sometimes to chase the rats in the corridor, to the great mirth of the jailers armed with sticks, 'wretched guards of hell' who revel in these macabre sights. The croaking of the crows and the screeching of owls set a tone of abandon in this sinister prison.

The Prisoner Director 'a good businessman', has managed to get the best out of his cushy job by transforming the prison yard, intended for exercise, into a sheep-fold. Thirsty sheep and goats come and wake us with a start in the middle of the night, by bashing their horns against the prison gate. We know when it is dawn by the familiar braying of a village donkey nearby, a sympathetic creature reminds us of another brighter world. Our only friend seems to be an old toad which comes regularly to laugh at the grotesqueness and the insignificance of man ...

We viewed the change in our prison conditions at first with surprise and then with concern. The unshakable and sceptical guards open the cells one after the other and just long enough to hand over the alimentation (3 times a day), such a big word for so little substance. The meals invariably consist of a glass of black coffee, cold and tasteless, and a crust of bread, often stale if not mouldy, (the daily ration) for breakfast. Under the guise of lunch, they distribute hapazardly and quickly (for the smell irritates them) some washing-up water they call soup and in which there is some leguminous plant swimming. The same ceremony is performed in the evening, a bowl of noodles mixed with the remains of the midday meal. When they give us a piece of meat, a few grams, often just a bone, once a fortnight, it is like a real godsend. The distribution of two sardines and a hard-boiled egg after many years of deprivation was for us a major event and formed the basis of our (shouted) communication with each other for several weeks. The water is insufficient and rationed daily in a five litre pitcher.

The life of the prisoner is a constant battle. There is a battle against the cold: the winter is icy, it snows in Tazmamart. The prisoner awakened in the middle of the night, numb and shaking with cold, indulges in a mad dance. The creaking of the iron ceiling lends a Satanic character to this wake. If a small piece of rusty iron is found by chance in the cell, it is promptly transformed into a needle, a precious instrument in prison, given the condition of the blankets. In the summer, there is a torrid heat, you nearly suffocate in the dungeons and the prisoner is forced to glue his nose on to the judas-hole in the door in order to draw in some air; and when, exhausted, his chest on fire, he goes to rest on his stone bed, he is attacked relentlessly all over his body by every sort of parasite: bugs, fleas, mosquitoes, cockroaches, spiders, etc ... The scorpions worm their way stealthily into the blankets; the spectre of this hideous animal stops us from making any rash movement; several prisoners have been stung.

Boredom weighs heavily on both the morale and the physique of the prisoner. In order to break this deathly routine, he is obliged to feel his way around but there is very reduced space.

Any normal conversation (with the prisoners in other cells) is practically impossible, the arrangement of the dungeons forbids it and the hubbub of other voices transforms the building into quite a circus. The only refuge left to him is

337

prayer and prostration. The Koran has been a great support to us during our time here (several of us have learnt it by heart, obviously orally).

The prisoner, dressed in rags, barefoot and with hair and beard which have not seen a barber for many years, gives the unreassuring appearance of an authentic tramp. The rains of Autumn transform most of the cells at first into a pond and then into a swamp.

The days follow on, one after another. Those in charge do not seem to want to grant us our rights. We make demands and the reply comes swiftly and categorically. It came from the mouth of a jailer, a little more dutiful than the others, who breathed: 'Don't waste your saliva. You have only one right here, that is to keep quiet.'

We tried our first hunger-strike for a week. There was total indifference from those in charge and actually it suited the jailers very well to have to come only once a day to discharge themselves of a duty already too heavy. In effect, the only result was the reduction in food, already at an insufficient level. The jailers became much stricter and much more spiteful. It became more and more painful for us, the heat became more intense and with the complete lack of hygiene the first diseases set in. If a colleague fell ill 'let him die if that's what he wants.' We protested: 'His Majesty the King, glorified by God, would never condone atrocities like these.' We were then punished for four days without food, punishment which was to be repeated several times.

In July 1974 two colleagues had served their time and, since they were not freed as expected, one of them complained. 'How long were you given?' the jailer asked him. 'Three years.' 'You shouldn't say three years, but forever ...' Illnesses followed on from each other. The jailers became more and more cruel and punishment rained down on us: the merest hesitation, the slightest badly-interpreted gesture met with severe sanctions.

The punishments varied according to seriousness, between five and ten days and beware of doing the same thing again.

The corridor had become an absolute tip: in the end the jailers, unable to stand the smell any longer, came to wash it. A colleague who had previously enjoyed excellent health told us that he had had a copious nose-bleed; later on, he told us that his legs would no longer support him. On his own, he could no longer come to the door to get his food and he began to fulfil his toilet needs in his rags. The jailers merely came to open up and close, it did not matter to them whether he ate or not. This colleague was a brave man and he gave us a daily run-down on his health. His morale was good. Then a partial paralysis set in and spread itself to the whole of his body. Later, his delirium made us share in his nightmarish nights. When he stopped speaking, they came to cover him in blankets and take him away. A few minutes later, they brought him back and stuck him down any old how on the icy floor of the jail. 'We've given him an injection,' they said hypocritically. The next day, the colleague breathed his last. They came wearing masks (because of the smell) and took him out in his rags and buried him in the yard without any sort of religious ceremony.

We found out later that this was on the 25th October 1977. An unexpected transfer of a few colleagues to another building taught us that, by this date, there were already six deaths. We learned from other sources that there was an enormous pit in the middle of the yard. This was without doubt a communal grave, destined to receive the bodies of the deceased. This unhappy knowledge changed our way of acting. Every time there was a national holiday, we asked to write to His Majesty that God protects. The response was negative. Things picked up in momentum, we became weaker and weaker and the food became worse and worse. On 2nd January 1980, a second colleague finally succumbed after anal haemorrhage. There was the same ritual as with the first one.

A third of us are dying. Three others are seriously afflicted and are half-paralysed, the remainder have at least three ailments: digestive problems, various bleedings, problems with eye-sight, psychotic disorders, scurvy, etc ...

Such is our present situation and the spectre of death haunts us day and night. An equivocal silence hovers over the building and at times, one of us revolts. He is immediately set upon with fists and sticks. Those of us who are left are bordering on madness. The Director and his henchmen are keeping watch. This letter constitutes an exact testimony of our situation. "

What happened to the Tazmamart prisoners?

This extract from a letter written in 1989 (nine years after the one above) shows the situation as it was then:

"Open the first cell: it's empty, except for a stretcher to carry the dead, and a big electric torch. The second cell is empty, too. Open the third and your blood freezes at the sight of the human corpse lying on a cement shelf: a skeleton with a long thick beard hanging down over his chest, long dirty hair like primitive stone age man; long nails looking like serpent's claws; a strong smell makes you want to vomit, the stench of human waste mixed with the smell of sweat, fear and death. An attempt to call out shows that the wretch is still alive, but in agony."

By 1991, half the prisoners at Tazmamart had died. One of them - Mimoun Fagouri - who should have been released in 1975, hanged himself in June 1990. Another died from a scorpion bite. Others died delirious and in fever. One woke up one day paralysed, his knees bent up to his chin. He remained like that until his death, four years later. Still others went out of their minds and died of neglect. Most of them died years after the expiry of their sentences.

On 15th September 1991, the thirty surviving prisoners were moved from Tazmamart to an unknown location were they were given proper food and medicine to make them look presentable before their release. One to three months later.

Three brothers, Bayazid, Midhat and Ali Bourequat - whose sole crime had been to report to the king that they had evidence (it turned out to be well founded) of a coup being plotted against him, were arrested on 8th July 1973 and released on 30th December 1991, a little later than the others, owing to their severe medical condition. The first two brothers had been unable to move from an upright sitting position for over four years. The brothers, in a later interview, said "They brought all three of us before the Military Prosecutor General at Rabat. They told us that the Prime Minister did not have a sufficient charge to bring against us and that we were free. It was 30th December 1991 ... But we said: 'but where shall we go? We don't know if we've still got a family, we've no money or papers.' So they contacted our old address and phoned our brother-in-law ..."

The eighteen long years spent isolated, and in such appalling conditions, left the surviving prisoners in such a state that, according to Amnesty International, "A return to normal life is impossible. Most are now between ten and twenty centimetres shorter in height than when they were sent to Tazmamart ... and they continue to, live under threat of reprisals on themselves and their families if they speak about their experiences in Tazmamart. They were told upon release to forget that Tazmamart ever existed."

Amnesty representations.
Amnesty International first expressed concern during a visit to Morocco in 1981. Their concerns included the secret detention of the prisoners and why 15 of them were still incarcerated when they had served their sentences. There was no answer to this enquiry or subsequent requests for clarification.

In 1988, another delegation was told by the Justice and Interior Ministry officials that the information they sought came under the auspices of the Ministry of Defence. Amnesty were not, however, given access to any official from this ministry.

King Hassan and Tazmamart.

In 1990, another delegation from Amnesty International had a meeting with the King himself. He denied the existence of Tazmamart and told Amnesty that "The prisoners were being held under house arrest for their own protection."

In July 1991, a public statement by King Hassan proclaims that: "Tazmamart existed only in the minds and imaginations of ill-intentioned people."

In July 1992, during an interview with a French newspaper, *Liberation*, the king said that Tazmamart "... was a place used to keep persons administratively assigned there ... it has no further reason to exist. The chapter is closed. It existed. It no longer does. That's all."

In September 1992 King Hassan, speaking on French television, said: "there have been excesses, but I must say this was out of negligence or forgetfulness rather than out of a desire to do harm."

Index of Amnesty International addresses (as of Autumn 1996)

There were 4354 local Amnesty International groups registered with the International Secretariat at the start of 1996, plus several thousand school, university, professional and other groups, in 92 countries around the world. In 54 countries these groups are co-ordinated by sections, whose addresses are given below. In addition, there are individual members, supporters and recipients of Amnesty International information (such as the monthly *Amnesty International News*) in over 150 countries and territories.

SECTION ADDRESSES

Algeria:
Amnesty International
Section Algérienne
BP377 Alger
RP 16004

Argentina:
Amnistia Internacional
Sección Argentina
25 de Mayo 67, 4º Piso
1002 Capital Federal
Buenos Aires

Australia:
Amnesty International
Australian Section
Private Bag 23, Broadway
New South Wales 2007

Austria:
Amnesty International
Austrian Section
Apostlegasse 25-27
A-1030 Wien

Bangladesh:
Amnesty International
Bangladesh Section
100 Kalabagan
1st Floor, 2nd Lane
Dhaka-1205

Belgium:
Amnesty International
Belgian Section
(*Flemish Branch*)
Kerkstraat 156
2060 Antwerpen

Benin:
Amnesty International
BP 01 3536
Cotonou

Bermuda:
Amnesty International
Bermuda Section
PO. Box HM 2136
Hamilton HM JX

Brazil:
Anistia International
Rua dos Andredas 1560
Sala 2525 900020-010
Porto Alegre, RS
CEP 04619-032
Sao Paulo, SP

Amnesty International
Section belge francophone
Rue Berckmans 9,
1060 Bruxelles

Côte d'Ivoire:
Amnesty International
Section Ivoirienne
04 BP 895
Abidjan 04

Canada:
Amnesty International
Canadian Section
(English-speaking branch)
214 Montreal Road
4th Floor, Vanier
Ontario K1L 8L8
Amnistie Internationale
Section canadienne francophone
6250 boulevard Monk
Montréal
Québec H4E 3H7

Chile:
Amnistia Internacional
Sección Chilena
Casilla 4062
Santiago

Colombia:
Señores,
Apartado Aéreo 76350
Bogotá

Hong Kong:
Amnesty International
Hong Kong Section
Unit C 3/F, Best-O-Best Building
32-36 Ferry Street
Kowloon

Denmark:
Amnesty International
Danish Section
Dyrkoeb 3,
1166 Copenhagen K

Ecuador:
Amnistía Internacional
Sección Ecuatoriana
Casilla 17-15-240-C
Quito

Faroe Islands:
Amnesty International
Faroe Islands Section
PO.Box 1075, FR-110
Tórshavn

Finland:
Amnesty International
Finnish Section
Ruoholahdenkatu 24 D
00180 Helsinki

France:
Amnesty International
Section francaise
4 rue de la Pierre Levée
75553 Paris,Cedex 11

Iceland:
Amnesty International
Icelandic Section
PO.Box 618
121 Reykjavik

India:
Amnesty International
Indian Section
13 Indra Prastha Building
E-109 Pandav Nagar
N.Delhi-110092

Ireland:
Amnesty International
Irish Section
48 Fleet Street
Dublin 2

Israel:
Amnesty International
Israel Section
98 Allenby Street
PO.Box 14179
Tel Aviv 61141

Italy:
Amnesty International
Italian Section
Viale Mazzini 146
00195 Rome

Germany:
Amnesty International
German Section
Heerstrasse 178
D-53108 Bonn

Japan:
Amnesty International
Japanese Section
Sky Esta 2f.
2-18-23 Nishi Waseda
Shinjuku-ku
Tokyo 165

Ghana:
Amnesty International
Ghanaian Section
PO.Box 1173
Koforidua E.R.

Korea (Republic of):
Amnesty International
Kyeong Buk RCO Box 36,
706 600 Daegu

Greece:
Amnesty International
Greek Section
30 Sina Street
106 72 Athens

Luxembourg:
Amnesty International
Luxembourg Section
Boite Postale 1914
1019 Luxembourg

Guyana:
Amnesty International
Guyana Section
c/o PO.Box 10720
Palm Court Building
35 Main Street
Georgetown

Mauritius:
Amnesty International
Mauritius Section
BP 69 Rose-Hill

Mexico:
Sección Mexicana
de Amnistía Internacional
Calle Aniceto Ortega 624,
(paralela a Gabriel Mancera
esq. Angel Urraza-eje 6 Sur)
Col de Valle
Mexico DF

Nepal:
Amnesty International
Nepalese Section
PO.Box 135, Bagbazar
Kathmandu

Netherlands:
Amnesty International
Dutch Section
Keizersgracht 620,
1017 ER Netherlands

Nigeria:
Amnesty International
Nigerian Section
PMB 3061. Suru-Lere
Lagos

Peru:
Señores
Casilla 659
Lima 18

Portugal:
Amnistía Internacional
Seccão B Portuguesa
Rua Fialho de Almeida
Nº 13, 1º,
1070 Lisboa

Senegal:
Amnesty International
Senegalese Section
c/o Isma Daddis Sagna
Cabinet M'baye Jacques DIOP
13 rue de Thiong
Dakar

New Zealand:
Amnesty International
New Zealand Section
PO.Box 793
Wellington 1

Norway:
Amnesty International
Norwegian Section
PO. Box 702 Sentrum
0106 Oslo

Philippines:
Amnesty International
Philippines Section
PO.Box 286
Sta Mesa Post Office
1008 Sta Mesa
Manila

Puerto Rico:
Amnistía Internacional
Sección de Puerto Rico
Calle Robles No54-Altos
Oficina 11, Rio Piedras
Puerto Rico 00925

Sierra Leone:
Amnesty International
Sierra Leone Section
PMB 1021, Freetown

Slovenia:
Amnesty International
Komenskega 7,
61000 Ljubljana

Spain:
Amnesty International
Sección Española
Calle Barquillo 17 6º B,
29004 Madrid

Sweden:
Amnesty International
Swedish Section
PO.Box 23400
S-104 35 Stockholm

Switzerland:
Amnesty International
Swiss Section
PO. Box
CH-3001 Bern

Tanzania:
Amnesty International
Tanzanian Section
PO.Box 4331
Dar es Salaam

Tunisia:
Amnesty International
Section Tunisienne
48 Avenue Farhat Hached
3ème étage
1001 Tunis

United Kingdom:
Amnesty International
British Section
99-119 Rosebury Avenue
London EC1R 4RE

United States of America:
Amnesty International of the USA
(AIUSA)
322 8th Avenue
New York
NY 10001

Uruguay:
Amnistía Internacional
Sección Uruguaya
Trist Narvaja 1642, Apto 2
CP 11200 Montivideo

Venezuela:
Amnistía Internacional
Sección Venezolana
Apartado Postal 5110
Carmelitas 1010-A
Caracas

COUNTRIES AND TERRITORIES WITHOUT SECTIONS BUT WHERE LOCAL
AMNESTY INTERNATIONAL GROUPS EXIST OR ARE BEING FORMED:

Albania	Egypt	Pakistan
Aruba	Gambia	Paraguay
Azerbaijan	Gaza Strip & West Bank	Poland
Bahamas	Georgia	Romania
Barbados	Grenada	Russia
Bolivia	Hungary	Slovakia
Botswana	Jamaica	South Africa
Bulgaria	Jordan	Taiwan
Cameroon	Kuwait	Thailand
Central African Rep.	Lithuania	Togo
Chad	Macao	Turkey
Costa Rica	Malaysia	Uganda
Croatia	Mali	Ukraine
Curacao	Malta	Yemen
Cyprus	Moldova	Zambia
Czech Republic	Mongolia	Zimbabwe
Dominican Rep.	Morocco	